Health and Physical Education for Elementary Classroom Teachers

An Integrated Approach

Retta R. Evans, PhD, MCHES

University of Alabama at Birmingham

Sandra K. Sims, PhD

University of Alabama at Birmingham

SHAPE America SOCIETY OF HEALTH AND PHYSICAL EDUCATORS®

health. moves. minds.

Human Kinetics

Library of Congress Cataloging-in-Publication Data

Names: Evans, Retta R. author. | Sims, Sandra K., 1961- author.
Title: Health and physical education for elementary classroom teachers : an
  integrated approach / Retta R. Evans, PhD, Sandra K. Sims, PhD.
Description: Champaign : Human Kinetics, Inc., [2016] | Includes
  bibliographical references and index.
Identifiers: LCCN 2015033961 | ISBN 9781450459914 (print)
Subjects: LCSH: Health education (Elementary)--United States. | Physical
  education and training--Study and teaching (Elementary)--United States. |
  Health education--Standards--United States. | Physical education and
  training--Standards--United States.
Classification: LCC LB1588.U6 E83 2016 | DDC 372.370973--dc23 LC record available at http://lccn.loc.gov/2015033961

ISBN: 978-1-4504-5991-4 (print)

The web addresses cited in this text were current as of November 2015, unless otherwise noted.

Acquisitions Editor: Ray Vallese; **SHAPE America Editor:** Joe McGavin; **Developmental Editor:** Jacqueline Eaton Blakley; **Managing Editor:** Derek Campbell; **Copyeditor:** Joanna Hatzopoulos Portman; **Indexer:** Dan Connolly; **Permissions Manager:** Dalene Reeder; **Graphic Designer:** Angela K. Snyder; **Cover Designer:** Keith Blomberg; **Photograph (cover):** iStock.com/mediaphotos; **Photographs (interior):** © Human Kinetics, unless otherwise noted; Christopher Futcher/iStock.com (pp. 3, 51, and 84), CDC/Reuel Waldrop (p. 8), Steve Debenport/iStock.com (pp. 19 and 113), MichaelDeLeon/iStock.com (p. 33), SolStock/iStock.com (p. 67), xefstock/iStock.com (p. 77), michaeljung/iStock.com (p. 79), Photodisc (p. 86), svetikd/iStock.com (p. 97), vgajic/iStock.com (p. 143), bonnie jacobs/iStock.com (p. 163); **Photo Asset Manager:** Laura Fitch; **Visual Production Assistant:** Joyce Brumfield; **Photo Production Manager:** Jason Allen; **Senior Art Manager:** Kelly Hendren; **Associate Art Manager:** Alan L. Wilborn; **Illustrations:** © Human Kinetics, unless otherwise noted; **Printer:** United Graphics

SHAPE America – Society of Health and Physical Educators
1900 Association Drive
Reston, VA 20191
800-213-7193
www.shapeamerica.org

Printed in the United States of America

10   9   8   7   6   5   4   3   2   1

The paper in this book is certified under a sustainable forestry program.

Human Kinetics
Website: www.HumanKinetics.com

United States: Human Kinetics
P.O. Box 5076
Champaign, IL 61825-5076
800-747-4457
e-mail: info@hkusa.com

Canada: Human Kinetics
475 Devonshire Road Unit 100
Windsor, ON N8Y 2L5
800-465-7301 (in Canada only)
e-mail: info@hkcanada.com

Europe: Human Kinetics
107 Bradford Road
Stanningley
Leeds LS28 6AT, United Kingdom
+44 (0) 113 255 5665
e-mail: hk@hkeurope.com

Australia: Human Kinetics
57A Price Avenue
Lower Mitcham, South Australia 5062
08 8372 0999
e-mail: info@hkaustralia.com

New Zealand: Human Kinetics
P.O. Box 80
Mitcham Shopping Centre, South Australia 5062
0800 222 062
e-mail: info@hknewzealand.com

E6007

Contents

A Note From SHAPE America   vii

Preface   ix

Acknowledgments   xi

Accessing the Web Resource   xiii

Part I   Role of Health and Physical Education in the Classroom   1

Chapter 1   Healthy Bodies, Healthy Minds   3

Defining Health in the 21st Century   4

History of Health in Culture   6

History of Health in the United States   7

Health Today in the United States   10

Individual Behaviors and Health   13

Responsibility of Classroom Teachers   14

Summary   17

Review Questions   18

Chapter 2   Coordinated School Health: A Team Approach   19

National School Policies Focusing on Nutrition and Physical Activity   20

Need for Collaboration Between Education and Health   21

Whole School, Whole Community, Whole Child (WSCC) Model   22

Applying the WSCC Model   28

Best Practices   29

Role of Teachers   30

Summary   30

Review Questions   31

Chapter 3 Health Education 33

Growth and Development 34

Improving Health Behavior 37

Learning Styles 40

Comprehensive School Health Education 42

Summary 46

Review Questions 49

Chapter 4 Physical Education 51

Defining Physical Activity 52

Defining Physical Education 53

Standard 1 55

Standard 2 56

Standard 3 59

Standard 4 60

Standard 5 61

Summary 62

Review Questions 63

Part II How to Integrate Health and Physical Education Into the Classroom 65

Chapter 5 Advocating for a Healthy, Active School 67

Advocacy in the Classroom 68

Advocacy in the School 69

Advocacy Ideas for Parents and the Community 71

Advocacy Tips for Using a Media Source 71

Advocacy Tips for Policymakers and Administrators 72

Summary 74

Review Questions 75

Chapter 6 Creating a Healthy Classroom 77

Classroom Health for Every Day 78

Classroom Health Throughout the Year 82

Dimensions of a Healthy Classroom 84

Back-to-School Supply List 94

Unhealthy Teaching Practices 95

Summary 95

Review Questions 96

Chapter 7   Creating an Active Classroom   97

Activity Breaks and Brain Breaks   98

Integrating Movement Into Academic Lessons   99

Equipment Needs for an Active Classroom   99

Class Management and Organization   99

Inappropriate Practices   102

Safety   103

Class Behavior Management   103

Summary   105

Review Questions   106

Labs   107

Chapter 8   Integrating Health Education Into the Classroom   113

National Standards for Academic Performance   114

National Health Education Standards (NHES)   114

Brainstorm Integration Ideas   115

Link Health Education Standards With Academic Standards   115

Develop Grade-Specific Interdisciplinary Activities   116

Develop an Integrated Activity Plan   119

Summary   121

Review Questions   122

Labs   123

Chapter 9   Integrating Physical Education Into the Classroom   143

National Standards for Academic Performance   144

National Standards for K-12 Physical Education   144

Brainstorm Integration Ideas   145

Link Physical Education Standards With Academic Standards   146

Develop Grade-Specific Interdisciplinary Activities   146

Develop an Integrated Activity Plan   149

Summary   151

Review Questions   152

Labs   153

Chapter 10 Best Practices in the Classroom and Beyond 163

Planning Ahead 164

Teaching Methods That Work 164

Assessment of Learning 169

Learning Environment 171

Professional Development 172

Supporting Policies That Encourage Wellness 173

Summary 174

Review Questions 175

Appendix A: National Health Education Standards 177

Appendix B: National Standards and Grade-Level Outcomes for K-12 Physical Education 181

Glossary 203

References 207

Resources 211

Index 215

About the Authors 223

About SHAPE America 225

A Note From SHAPE America

Imagine a world in which every child you have taught or will ever teach leaves your classroom equipped not just with the foundational knowledge and skills to tackle the academic rigors of middle school and beyond but also with the ability and the desire to be physically active for a lifetime.

That's the world we envision at SHAPE America – Society of Health and Physical Educators, the leading professional organization for health and physical educators: that every child leaves school with the skills, knowledge, confidence, desire, and opportunity to enjoy a healthful, physically active lifestyle.

And while SHAPE America advocates for physical education and health to be taught by state-licensed or state-certified teachers, we recognize that elementary classroom teachers are often asked to teach subjects in which they have limited background. We also appreciate that elementary classroom teachers care about their teaching and the welfare of their students,

and that they are well trained in child development and general teaching methods. That is why SHAPE America chose to collaborate with these excellent authors and publisher in bringing this book to you, the elementary classroom teacher in practice or in training: to ensure that you have the best tools with which to integrate health and physical education into your daily teaching. The skills-based content of the book is correlated with the National Health Education Standards, SHAPE America's National Standards for K-12 Physical Education, and relevant Common Core State Standards.

It is our hope that this book will help you develop physically active—and physically literate—students, and that you become an advocate for health and physical education in the process. If you ultimately are tasked with including health and physical education into your daily curriculum, you can do so with confidence that you are providing the best instruction and experience possible for your students.

—E. Paul Roetert, CEO, SHAPE America – Society of Health and Physical Educators

50 Million Strong by 2029

Approximately 50 million students are currently enrolled in America's elementary and secondary schools (grades pre-K to 12). SHAPE America is leading the effort to ensure that by the time today's preschoolers graduate from high school in 2029, all of America's students will have developed the skills, knowledge and confidence to enjoy healthy, meaningful physical activity.

Preface

As school budgets shrink across the United States, elementary classroom teachers are being asked to teach subjects in which they have limited expertise. Teaching health education and physical education might seem like a daunting task for someone who does not have specialist training; a teacher might worry, for example, that she isn't athletic enough to teach physical education, or that her affinity for junk food disqualifies her from any sort of authority in the area of health. Although expertise in these topics is desirable, it is possible for the non-specialist to offer quality health and physical education to elementary students. In fact, teaching health and physical education gives the elementary classroom teacher the power to help children grow in every aspect of their being.

Health education and physical education may feel like a tremendous responsibility to a classroom teacher, who likely already feels as if there are not enough hours in the day to address high-stakes academic requirements. There can be a lot of pressure when it comes to standardized test scores and yearly progress reports from administrators, parents, and even politicians. What is a teacher to do?

Health and Physical Education for Elementary Classroom Teachers: An Integrated Approach equips students with the essential knowledge and skills needed to teach these subjects without specialist training. Written for undergraduate elementary education students and for in-service elementary teachers charged with teaching health and physical education, this unique textbook is skills-based and designed to provide ample opportunities to practice the concepts taught. All content is correlated with the National Health Education Standards (Joint Committee on National Health Education Standards, 2007), the National Standards for K-12 Physical Education (SHAPE America, 2013), and relevant state-specific academic standards, including Common Core State Standards. Most important, the book's integrated approach emphasizes the practical ways that health and physical education can be built into the existing academic curriculum.

By learning essential knowledge and using the strategies developed in this book, you will be able to skillfully navigate health and physical education! You will discover how to integrate health and physical education into every aspect of the school day. Are your students breathing bus fumes while waiting to be picked up? Are the hallway water fountains clean and working? Are your students rested, focused, and ready to learn? By creating a healthy school environment for students, you will maximize your students' academic achievement. You will learn how to seamlessly incorporate health education and physical education into the core subject areas while meeting state and national standards. You will reap the benefits of becoming an advocate for student health with colleagues, administrators, and parents.

Features

Throughout the textbook, you will find informative web sites, tips for best practices, tables filled with innovative strategies, and other resources on how to incorporate health, wellness, and physical education/activity during your school day. Each chapter includes the following elements:

- Objectives
- Summary
- Review questions

Chapters also contain boldfaced important terms, and you can find a list of those terms and their definitions in the glossary in the back of the book. Cited references and valuable sources of further information are listed in the book's References and Resources sections, respectively.

Labs have been included in chapters 7, 8, and 9. These labs are designed to help you brainstorm the process of integration into practice. The labs are critical to the textbook and the reader because they connect the textbook's content with practical ways to apply it in a classroom setting.

Organization

The text is organized into two main parts, each dedicated to different components of incorporating health and physical education into the elementary classroom. Part I, Role of Health and

Physical Education in the Classroom, focuses on the important background concepts needed to form foundational knowledge for health education and physical education. Chapter 1 provides an overview of the health risk behaviors inherent with today's generation of children, describes health disparities that contribute to differences in quality of health among groups, and explains why it is important for classroom teachers to take an active role in their students' health. Chapter 2 focuses on the coordinated school health approach. It describes how academic achievement is related to health behaviors and establishes why the National Health Education Standards are significant. Chapter 3 describes how physical growth and brain development in children are related to health. It identifies theories that can be used to change health behavior and provides an overview of comprehensive school health education. Chapter 4 provides an overview of the need for physical education and physical activity in elementary schools. It describes the many benefits of physical activity and characteristics of a high-quality physical education program.

Part II, How to Integrate Health and Physical Education Into the Classroom, emphasizes the strategies necessary to build health, physical education, and physical activity into the curriculum and school day. Chapter 5 describes how classroom teachers can advocate for healthy and active schools. It also incorporates ideas for advocacy with parents, administrators, and the community. Chapter 6 identifies habits that promote everyday health in the classroom. Indicators of school violence and bullying, signs of depression and suicide, and indicators of child abuse and neglect are just of few of the important topics discussed in this chapter. Chapter 7 describes ways to incorporate physical activity into the classroom. Strategies for incorporating activity breaks, dancing to music, and movement into academic lessons are the focus of this chapter. Chapter 8 outlines how to incorporate the National Health Education Standards into the academic curriculum. Using the Common Core is also described. Illustrations and labs are provided in this chapter. Chapter 9 is similar to chapter 8 but with a

focus on physical education rather than health. The chapter details how to incorporate the National Standards for K-12 Physical Education into academic curriculum. And, like chapter 8, chapter 9 also discusses the Common Core and includes labs. Chapter 10 summarizes practical approaches to teaching health and physical education in the classroom. Teaching methods, assessment tools, and evaluation strategies are described in this chapter.

eBook available at HumanKinetics.com

Web Resource

Students who purchase *Health and Physical Education for Elementary Classroom Teachers: An Integrated Approach* receive access to a student web resource that will enhance learning. The web resource includes the following learning aids from the book in order to allow downloading for studying and completing assignments:

- Review questions
- Important terms and their definitions
- Labs
- Websites listed in Resources
- Sidebars

The web addresses in the web resource's version of the Resources and sidebars are links that you can click on so that you don't have to manually key in the address.

The following icon is displayed by content from the book that can also be found on the web resource.

The web resource also features sample integrated activity plans that demonstrate how health and physical education can be incorporated into the academic curriculum. Two activity plans are given for every health education and physical education standard, for a total of 26 plans.

The school setting provides an incredible opportunity for changing the health and overall trajectory for children everywhere. Our goal is to empower the classroom teacher to make a positive difference in students' health, well-being, and future.

Acknowledgments

A lot of work and dedication go into writing a textbook, but the author's writing is only a part of the work that goes into the development and production of a final product. The authors are thankful for the support, guidance, and patience of family and friends throughout this process. The authors would also like to acknowledge the hard work and diligence of the following people; without them this project would not be possible. A heartfelt thank-you goes to Sarah Toth for her careful editing, writing, and development of ancillary materials throughout the book. Thanks to Jacqueline Blakley, developmental editor for Human Kinetics. She did an amazing job of keeping an incredibly complex process running smoothly, and she gave great suggestions on improving our textbook. Finally, we'd like to acknowledge the future teachers who will use this book. We believe you are the best advocates for a healthy, active classroom. Our hope is that you will empower your students to be healthy and physically literate for life.

SHAPE America thanks Cindy Allen, PhD, professor in the Health Science Department and director of student teaching and field experience at Lock Haven University, for reviewing the content in this book.

Accessing the Web Resource

You will notice a reference throughout *Health and Physical Education for Elementary Classroom Teachers* to a web resource. This online content is available to you for free upon purchase of a new print book or an e-book. All you need to do is register with the Human Kinetics website to access the online content. The steps below will explain how to register.

The web resource offers learning aids from the book such as review questions, lab assignments and blank forms from the book, and sample integrated lesson plans for each national health education and physical education standard. We are certain this material will be useful to you as you study and learn the book's content.

Follow These Steps to Access the Web Resource

1. Visit www.HumanKinetics.com/HealthAndPhysicalEducationForElementaryClassroomTeachers.
2. Click the first edition link next to the corresponding first edition book cover.

3. Click the Sign In link on the left or top of the page. If you do not have an account with Human Kinetics, you will be prompted to create one.
4. After you register, if the online product does not appear in the Ancillary Items box on the left of the page, click the Enter Pass Code option in that box. Enter the following pass code exactly as it is printed here, including capitalization and all hyphens: **EVANS-2TFB-WR**
5. Click the Submit button to unlock your online product.
6. After you have entered your pass code the first time, you will never have to enter it again to access this online product. Once unlocked, a link to your product will permanently appear in the menu on the left. All you need to do to access your online content on subsequent visits is sign in to **www.HumanKinetics.com/HealthAndPhysicalEducationForElementaryClassroomTeachers** and follow the link!

Click the Need Help? button on the book's website if you need assistance along the way.

Part I

Role of Health and Physical Education in the Classroom

Chapter 1

Healthy Bodies, Healthy Minds

Objectives

- Define the six dimensions of health, and explain how they interact to affect overall health.
- Understand how the health of Americans has changed since the 1900s.
- Describe the *Healthy People 2020* objectives for schools and school-age children.
- Identify the six categories of risk behaviors monitored by the Centers for Disease Control and Prevention (CDC).
- Define health disparities that contribute to differences in quality of health between groups.
- Determine what behaviors students could change in order to improve their overall health.
- Explain why classroom teachers should take an active role in their students' health.

When health is absent, wisdom cannot reveal itself, art cannot manifest, strength cannot fight, wealth becomes useless, and intelligence cannot be applied.

Herophilus

In the United States, more than 55 million K-12 students spend about 6 hours in the classroom each day. Therefore, the school setting provides ample opportunity for changing the health and overall trajectory for children. This book aims to empower you to use classroom time to make a positive difference in your students' health, well-being, and future.

The relationship between health and academic achievement is undeniable. Healthy students are better learners and are better behaved. Children who come to school without breakfast, without a good night's sleep, and having had no physical activity during the previous day are not ready to learn or able to focus. If students are habitually absent and fall behind academically during the elementary years, it may hinder their academic success in middle and high school.

To understand why incorporating health into the classroom is so critical, you must first understand the evolution of health and its history. This chapter examines the modern definition of health as well as the complex dimensions that make up the contemporary view of health. The chapter then provides an overview of the history of health, its role in modern society, and the present common health behaviors and determinants of health that may impact you and your students.

Defining Health in the 21st Century

People commonly define health as physical fitness and the absence of disease. This tendency is rooted in the medical model of health, which defines good health as having low levels of disease, illness, and infirmity. Many definitions of health exist. A broader definition of **health** is *a state of mental, physical, and social well-being.* This definition supports the concept that a person's health is influenced by multiple factors and cannot be based solely on the presence or absence of disease and illness. A person's health depends on both the individual strength of and the interactions among these six dimensions: physical, intellectual, emotional, social, spiritual, and environmental (figure 1.1). Maintaining a balance among all six dimensions is key to achieving a high overall state of health.

- **Physical health** refers to the well-being of the physical body. It is the most visible dimension of health and can be influenced by multiple variables, including genetic makeup, exposure to infectious agents, access to medical care, and personal health-related behaviors such as tobacco use, levels of physical activity, and nutritional habits. Observable characteristics (including height, weight, and energy level) are often associated with this aspect of health and wellness.

- **Intellectual health** is the ability to interpret, analyze, and act on information. Intellectual health also spans a person's ability to reason. Intellectual health can influence a person's overall wellness by controlling the ability to recognize, understand, and utilize information about health.

- **Emotional health** involves a person's feelings and how they are expressed. An emotionally healthy person practices self-control and self-acceptance and can express both positive and negative emotions in productive, socially acceptable ways that are not self-destructive or threatening to others. Poor emotional health can be characterized by poor management of negative feelings and emotions, which can lead to stress-related illnesses as well as susceptibility to infection and heart disease.

- **Social health** is characterized by the ability to navigate social environments while maintaining healthy relationships with others. People live and work in a variety of social environments, including homes, workplaces, schools, and neighborhoods. The ability to navigate these environments effectively is a critical part of social health. Maintaining strong personal relationships, communicating with respect for and acceptance of others, and recognizing ways to enrich relationships are all indicative of strong social health.

- **Spiritual health** involves the ability to deal with day to-day life in a manner that leads to realizing one's full potential, finding meaning and purpose of life, and experiencing happiness from within. The definition of spiritual health is not confined to sacred terms or practices. Rather, spiritually healthy people have developed a strong sense of personal values and the capacity to integrate these values (including

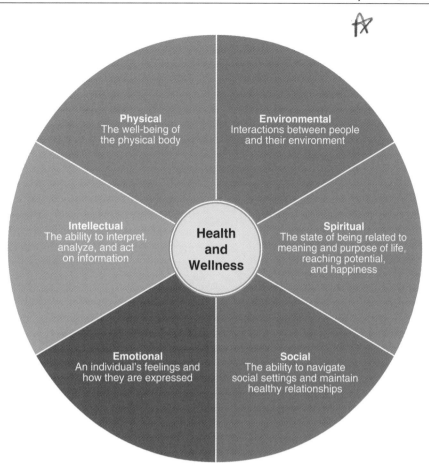

Figure 1.1 The six dimensions of health.

trust, honesty, and integrity) into their practices of everyday living. In general, religion is a way in which spirituality is practiced; it is an organized practice of beliefs. Religion provides ways to give life meaning and deeper purpose while providing organization and structure as an impetus to action. The words "health" and "heal," which refer to putting separated things back together or to be made whole, are related to the concept of "holy." Poor spiritual health may contribute to feelings of isolation and may cause a person to struggle in maintaining productive relationships. Research has demonstrated that people who have strong religious faith and people who are active in a church or religious community reap better overall health (Rew & Wong, 2006). Specific elements of spiritual health proven to contribute to enhanced health are altruism, hope, forgiveness, feeling close to God, prayer, meditation, giving up hostility, loving relationships, and a supportive community.

• **Environmental health** includes preventing and controlling diseases or injuries related to the interactions between people and their environment. It encompasses all biological, chemical, and physical factors external to the body that impact behavior and over which a person has limited or no control. These factors include indoor and outdoor air quality, water quality, soil quality, toxic substances, hazardous wastes, and natural disasters. Daily life and health are affected through the air, water, food, and products people consume. Globally, environmental hazards are to blame for approximately a fourth of all disease (World Health Organization, 2013). Air pollution alone is responsible for 3.7 million deaths each year worldwide and is a leading environmental cause of cancer deaths (World Health Organization, 2013; 2014a). Arsenic, which is highly toxic and a known carcinogen, occurs in high levels in U.S. groundwater (World Health Organization, 2012). Lead exposure in young children is particularly devastating because it can lead to mental retardation, irreversible behavior problems, and even death (World Health Organization, 2014b). Children—who cannot choose their environments—are particularly vulnerable to the health-damaging effects of harmful physical and social environments, and childhood adversity often results in seriously diminished health in adulthood (Robert Wood Johnson Foundation, 2008).

These sobering facts are presented not to alarm you but to raise your awareness of the environments in which your students live, play, and go to school and the relationship to potential academic and behavioral outcomes. The key to environmental health is promoting wellness through healthy homes, communities, and schools. Children metabolize toxins at a slower rate than adults, so they are at higher risk for exposures found at schools, including mold, asbestos, radon, airborne metals, volatile compounds, and noise. In addition, vulnerable populations, such as minorities and low-income groups, bear more than their fair share of these environmental exposures. Outcomes related to the school environment can include respiratory illness, behavioral outcomes, mental health, physical activity, and academic performance (Marks, 2009). National objectives related to environmental health and specific to elementary, middle, and high school campuses include topics such as indoor air quality, mold problems, hazardous materials, pesticide exposure, and safe drinking water.

Sometimes, the term "environment" is used in a broader sense to describe larger systems in which the individual interacts. Social and lifestyle factors in a person's environment, such as crime, safety, abuse, food access, housing,

access to medical care, and transportation, are important issues in health.

History of Health in Culture

Now that you are familiar with the complexities of contemporary health, you are ready to dig in to its historical roots. History helps you to bring context and appreciation to what is happening in the current world so that you can intelligently create a better future. The following section explains how ancient ideas of public health shaped how disease prevention and health promotion are handled today.

Ancient Civilizations

In early cultures, medical lore was passed from generation to generation, and virtually all cultures turned to some type of physician or medicine man for health information, education, treatments, and cures. Egyptians were considered the healthiest people of their time, emphasizing personal cleanliness, using pharmaceutical preparations, and building drainage systems for sewage. Hebrews (1500s BC) formulated the book of Leviticus, one of the world's first written hygienic codes. This text dealt with various health-related responsibilities, including cleanliness and hygiene, protection against the spread of contagious disease, isolation of lepers, disinfection, and sanitation.

Ancient Greeks (1000-400 BC) were first to place almost as much emphasis on disease prevention as they did on treatment and control. Emphasis was placed on achieving balance between physical, spiritual, and mental aspects of an individual. Hippocrates, the famous Greek physician, is known as the father of medicine. He developed a theory of disease that was still taught in medical schools as a valid theory of disease causation as recently as the early 20th century. This theory stated that health results from balance while illness is a result of imbalance.

The Romans (500 BC-500 AD) built extensive aqueduct and underwater sewer systems. This feat of engineering brought an abundance of water from great distances and removed sewage from principal Roman cities. These systems were efficient enough to deliver at least 40 gal-

Environmental Health Begins at Home

Discover possible health hazards in your home. See www.cdc.gov/healthyhomes/byroom/index.html for room-by-room tips for a healthy home. Try this discovery with your students.

lons of water to each citizen in Rome every day. In addition, settling basins were placed along the aqueducts to allow sediment to be deposited, thereby filtering the water. Unfortunately, the aqueducts were lined with lead, and researchers believe that lead poisoning played a role in the Roman Empire's downfall. The Romans were also the first to build hospitals and develop both a public medical service (physicians assigned to certain towns or institutions) as well as a private practice.

Middle Ages

The Middle Ages (about 500-1500 AD) was a time of political and social unrest during which many advancements in health were lost. Cities were overcrowded, and little emphasis was placed on cleanliness, personal hygiene, or sanitation. Thus, the Middle Ages were characterized by great epidemics of communicable diseases including leprosy, bubonic plague, syphilis, and smallpox. In the 1300s, the bubonic plague (also known as the Black Death) resulted in more deaths than any war, famine, or natural disaster in history. In Europe, millions of lives were lost and entire cities were wiped out. More than 14 million people were killed by the plague in China. In Cairo, Egypt, the death tolls would rise as high as 10,000 to 15,000 per day. The plague epidemics brought changes in attitude toward hygiene, and people began to adapt their behavior in order to lessen their susceptibility. As a result, hospitals were organized, quarantines were established, guidelines were developed for food safety, and streets were regularly swept clean.

Renaissance and Enlightenment

The Renaissance (1500-1700 AD) was a time of exploration, expanded trade, and a renewed search for knowledge and learning. The printing press and microscope were invented, and realistic anatomical drawings were produced. Anatomy was studied systematically, diseases were classified, and occupational diseases were identified in the quest for medical knowledge. Surveys were developed in order to obtain information on diseases, and general health and mortality and morbidity data were assembled.

Despite growth in scientific advancements, public health was not substantially improved; diseases and plagues were still prevalent. In Italy, many cities instituted health boards to fight the plague. By the middle of the 16th century influenza, smallpox, tuberculosis, bubonic plague, leprosy, anthrax, and impetigo were identified as different diseases with varying causes. Although people believed that diseases were contagious, there was lack of consensus about particular causes and prevention. With this limited understanding and good intentions, community leaders, priests, and medical doctors attempted to educate people about health and disease. Treatment of ailments and diseases remained primitive. Bloodletting was prescribed for many maladies, and barbers performed dentistry.

The Age of Enlightenment (1700s) was characterized by revolution, industrialization, and growth, yet living conditions only worsened as a result of the pollution that industrialization created. Dietary deficiency was unrecognized as fundamental to health and well-being. Scurvy (caused by a severe deficiency of vitamin C) was responsible for the deaths of up to 2 million sailors between 1500 and 1850 (Rosen, 1993). The plague and epidemics remained problematic, but scientists had yet to discover that the diseases involved were caused by microscopic organisms.

In 1798, Edward Jenner discovered a vaccine procedure against smallpox. Smallpox was responsible for thousands of deaths each year, and survivors were frequently left disfigured and blind. People with smallpox were treated with remedies that added to their suffering, such as bloodletting, purging, lancing, and sweating. Jenner's success with the smallpox vaccine led to the eventual worldwide eradication of the disease in the 1900s.

History of Health in the United States

From the Egyptians' focus on personal hygiene to the invention of the microscope and the development of the first smallpox vaccine, public health practices have deeply embedded roots from the past. The following text explains how

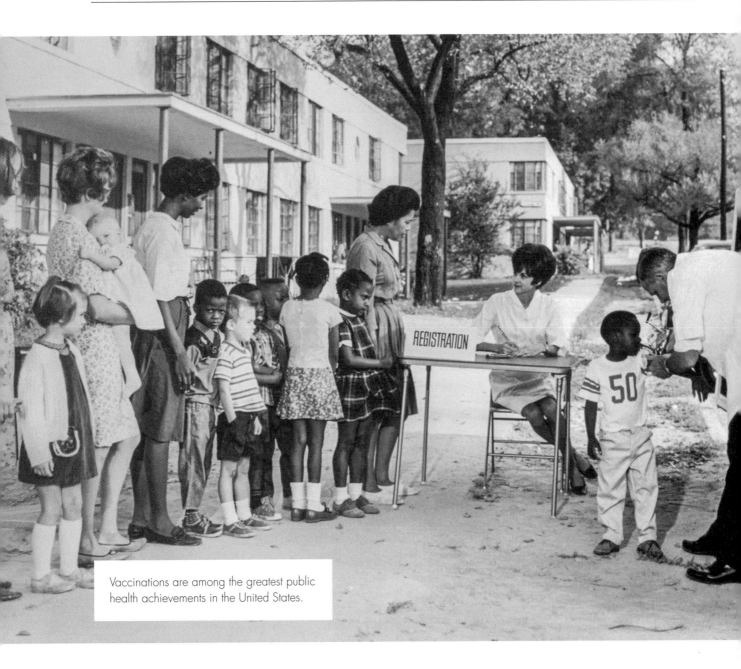

Vaccinations are among the greatest public
health achievements in the United States.

developing a better understanding of human
disease in the modern United States helped to
dramatically improve life expectancy and overall quality of life around the world.

18th Century

Throughout the 1700s, health conditions were
deplorable, mainly because of overcrowding,
poverty, and filth. These conditions allowed
communicable diseases such as smallpox,
cholera, and diphtheria to remain prevalent.
While some cities formed health boards to address health problems, the primary means of

controlling the spread of disease was through
quarantine and regulation of environmental
cleanliness. In 1789, Dr. Edward Wigglesworth
developed the first tables measuring life expectancy. In that year, life expectancy at birth was
only 28.15 years (Rosen, 1993).

19th Century

Health status improved a little in the 1800s,
but the Industrial Revolution worsened issues
of overcrowding, poverty, and filth, thereby
causing epidemics such as smallpox, tuberculosis, yellow fever, cholera, and typhoid to re-

main prevalent. In 1850, the rate of deaths by tuberculosis in Massachusetts reached 300 per 100,000 residents. Life expectancy actually decreased during this time. From 1820 to 1825, the life expectancy in New York decreased from 26.15 to 19.69. In 1870, Louis Pasteur discovered the first scientific approach to immunization. He also invented the process of heating raw milk to kill dangerous microorganisms in a process now known as pasteurization. In addition, he developed the food preservation method of canning, which increased the ability of food to be stored safely for long periods of time. Pasteur is known as the father of immunology.

The time from 1850 to 1880 was known as the miasma phase of public health. During this time, people thought that diseases were caused by inhaling poisonous vapors (called *miasmas*) that rose from rotting filth and refuse. It was a prevalent belief that cholera and other contagious diseases were attributed to impure air that arose from graveyards, sewage, human respiration, and decomposing vegetation. Public officials espoused that the elimination of smells would result in the elimination of disease. The approach to disease control was based on this idea, and efforts were therefore directed entirely toward general cleanliness.

The years between 1800 and 1900 became known as the bacteriological period of public health, initiated by Louis Pasteur, Robert Koch, and other bacteriologists whose work demonstrated that a specific organism causes a specific disease. Scientists discovered that bacteria and viruses caused diseases. Louis Pasteur discovered the fowl cholera bacillus and developed a method of inoculation against rabies.

These discoveries led to the greater protection of water and food sources as well as the elimination of insects and proper disposal of sewage. This improved sanitation effort prolonged children's lives and reduced infant deaths. Access to education during this time also played a significant role in improving children's health. Scientists wrote manuals and books to elucidate the causes of disease and methods of disease transmission. Schools began adding hygiene classes to the curriculum, and handwashing and sanitation practices became more commonplace.

20th Century

Improved public health services, medical care, and immunizations meant that many contagious diseases no longer threatened as they once did. Therefore, the public health focus began to shift to preventing chronic diseases as opposed to fighting infectious diseases. State health departments began to expand their programs in order to direct their efforts toward building up and maintaining the highest possible quality of personal health service to all citizens. Health began to be defined more in terms of longevity—how long a person would live—as well as quality of life. During the 1940s, antibiotics were introduced for widespread use. The first antibiotics were marketed in the 1920s, and in 1944 penicillin became commercially available. The Centers for Disease Control and Prevention (CDC) compiled the top 10 achievements that most impacted the nation's health in the 20th century (CDC, 1999). They are listed here and are not ranked in order of importance:

1. **Immunization/vaccines:** Routine immunization eradicated smallpox from the globe and eliminated polio in the Americas, and vaccines reduced some preventable infectious diseases to an all-time low, causing few people to experience the devastating effects of measles, pertussis, and other illnesses.

2. **Motor vehicle safety:** Advancements in engineering both in vehicles and highways, increased use of safety belts and motorcycle helmets, and a decrease in drinking and driving.

3. **Workplace safety:** Improved control of environmental hazards and reduction in job-related injuries.

4. **Control of infectious diseases:** Resulted from clean water, improved sanitation, and use of antibiotics.

5. **Declines in deaths from heart disease and stroke:** Decreases in tobacco use, management of elevated blood pressure, increased access to early detection, and better quality care.

6. **Safer and healthier foods:** Decreased microbial contamination, increased nutritional content, and food fortification processes.

7. **Healthier mothers and babies:** Improvements in hygiene and nutrition, antibiotics, greater access to prenatal care, and technological advances in maternal and neonatal medicine; since 1900, infant death rates have decreased by 90 percent, and maternal death rates decreased by 99 percent.

8. **Family planning:** Improved (and increased access to) contraception and reduced transmission of human immunodeficiency virus (HIV) and other sexually transmitted diseases.

9. **Fluoridation of drinking water:** Prevention of tooth decay and reduction in tooth loss.

10. **Tobacco as a health hazard:** Recognition led to reduced exposure to environmental (secondhand) smoke and a reduction in smoking prevalence and associated deaths.

Health Today in the United States

The leading causes of death among Americans have changed dramatically since the beginning of the 20th century. In the 1900s, the majority of deaths were caused by infectious or communicable diseases, including tuberculosis, cholera, and influenza. With improved sanitation, waste disposal, and medical discoveries, the number of deaths from infectious diseases has decreased and people are living longer lives. The leading causes of death in 1900 and 2010 are compared in table 1.1. Educators need to know that causes of death also vary by age (see table 1.2). The leading causes of death listed in table 1.1 are based on all deaths but not controlled for the age of the person who died. According to CDC data (CDC, 2010), in 2010 the leading cause of death for people from age 15 to 44 was unintentional injury. The term "unintentional injury" refers to a wide range of injuries, including suffocation, burns, drownings, work-related injuries, and motor vehicle accidents.

Many of the leading causes of death among adults today are the result of health behaviors and controllable risk factors including poor

diet, lack of physical activity, tobacco use, and excessive alcohol consumption. A physician might state on a death certificate that a person died of heart disease, yet the root causes of heart disease could be traced back to any number of these risky behaviors. Keeping in mind that healthy children are more likely to grow up to be healthy adults, the majority of adults who engage in risky health behaviors learned and initiated these behaviors during their adolescent years. To better prepare education professionals to educate children against these risks, the CDC identified these six priority health behaviors (CDC, 2011a), which are linked to the leading causes of illness and death among Americans:

1. Tobacco use
2. Poor eating habits
3. Alcohol and other drug use
4. Behaviors resulting in intentional or unintentional injury
5. Physical inactivity
6. Sexual behaviors that result in HIV infection, other sexually transmitted diseases, or unintended pregnancy

Healthy People

In 1979, the U.S. government published the document *Healthy People: The Surgeon General's Report on Health Promotion and Disease Prevention*. The **Healthy People** document confirmed the shift from infectious to chronic disease within the U.S. population and recognized the importance of personal health behaviors and

Youth Risk Behaviors in Your State

Go to the CDC's Youth Risk Behavior Surveillance System (YRBSS) website at https://nccd.cdc.gov/youthonline/App/Default.aspx?SID=HS and find out which health behaviors that youth in your state are most at risk for. Compare your state with another state. Are you surprised by what you found?

Table 1.1 Leading Causes of Death Among Americans in 1900 and 2010

1900 (20th century)	2010 (21st century)
Pneumonia	Heart disease
Tuberculosis	Cancer
Diarrhea/enteritis	Chronic lung diseases
Heart disease	Stroke
Liver disease	Unintentional injuries
Injuries	Alzheimer's disease
Cancer	Diabetes
Senility	Influenza and pneumonia
Diphtheria	Nephritis and other kidney disorders

Causes of death are listed in order of prevalence.
Source: U.S. Department of Health, Education and Welfare, Public Health Service, 1979, *Healthy people: The Surgeon General's report on health promotion and disease prevention* (Washington, DC: U.S. Government Printing Office).

Table 1.2 Leading Causes of Death Among Americans by Age in 2010

Ages 15–24	Ages 25–44
Unintentional injuries	Unintentional injuries
Homicide	Suicide
Suicide	Homicide
Cancer	Cancer
Heart disease	Heart disease
Congenital defects	HIV/AIDS
Stroke	Diabetes

Data from National Vital Statistics System, National Center for Health Statistics, CDC. Office of Statistics and Programming, National Center for Injury Prevention and Control, CDC. Available: www.cdc.gov/injury/wisqars/pdf/10LCID_All_Deaths_By_Age_Group_2010-a.pdf

lifestyle in relation to health outcomes. Approximately 50 percent of cases of premature illness and death in the United States are attributed to participation in risky health behaviors such as tobacco use, physical inactivity, alcohol and substance abuse, and unsafe sexual practices. In 2010, five major causes of death (heart disease, cancer, chronic lower respiratory diseases, stroke, and accidents) accounted for 63 percent of all deaths in the United States (Murphy, Xu, & Kochanek, 2012). Chronic diseases are of intense focus and are the overall drivers of medical care spending.

Since the publication of *Healthy People* in 1979, local, state, and federal agencies have committed to a long-term initiative to promote the health of the country. Every 10 years, the

U.S. Department of Health and Human Services (USDHHS) gathers and analyzes current data, reviews scientific trends and innovations, and uses this information to establish and monitor health objectives for the nation. These objectives cover a broad range of health problems among diverse ages and groups of Americans, and they allow individuals as well as communities to make and act on informed health decisions.

Health Disparities

As a result of the data generated through the CDC and many other federal, state, and local public, nonprofit, and private health agencies, much more is known about the health of certain groups of Americans. Health not only is a product of biology and medical care but also is influenced by significant factors such as income, education level, and neighborhood environments. Differences in health pertaining to these factors are known as **health disparities**. Health disparities are preventable differences in the burden of disease, injury, violence, or opportunities to achieve optimal health that are experienced by socially disadvantaged populations (defined by factors such as race, ethnicity, gender, education, income, and geographic location). A high amount of racial and ethnic disparity exists in connection with common and serious chronic diseases. Health disparities may result from multiple factors, including poverty, environmental threats, inadequate access to health care, individual and behavioral factors, and educational inequalities.

In a 2008 publication of The Robert Wood Johnson Foundation (RWJ; the largest charitable organization in the United States that is focused on health and health care), the foundation reported that in general, the poor and nearly poor are most affected by health disparities. African American and Hispanic populations experience higher poverty rates, but nearly half of poor Americans are whites. In every racial or eth-

nic group, significant amounts of economically disadvantaged people exist. Health disparities do not only affect the poor. Middle-class Americans experience worse heath than the affluent. Therefore, by reducing health disparities, those living in poverty as well as those in the middle class will benefit (RWJ, 2008).

Dropping out of school is associated with multiple social and health problems. For example, babies whose mothers have not completed high school are twice as likely as babies whose mothers have graduated from college to die before turning 1 year old. Overall, people with less education are more likely than those with more education to experience a number of health risks, such as obesity, substance abuse, and injury. Higher proportions of physical inactivity and smoking are consistently related to lower education attainment. On the other hand, higher levels of education are associated with a longer life and an increased likelihood of obtaining or understanding basic health information and services needed to make appropriate health decisions. Men and women who have graduated from college are likely to live 5 or more years longer than those who do not finish high school (RWJ, 2008). Life expectancy also varies by race and sex. Figure 1.2 provides

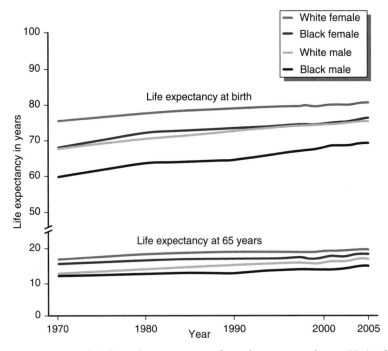

Figure 1.2 Life expectancy at birth and at 65 years of age by race and sex (United States, 1970-2005). Death rates used to calculate life expectancies from 1997 to 1999 are based on 1990 census data. Death rates used to calculate life expectancies from 2000 to 2005 are based on 2000 census data.
From CDC/NCHS, National Vital Statistics System.

further information on these variables related to health disparities in the United States.

Differences in the health of those that are disadvantaged socially or economically are holding the United States back from realizing optimal health. Overarching health goals for the country include the achievement of health equity, the elimination of health disparities, and the improvement of the health of all groups of people. The United States spends more on health care than any other country—more than twice compared to other industrial nations—but it consistently ranks near the bottom in life expectancy (RWJ, 2008). Health behavior and its consequences play out through the choices available to people in the contexts of family and society. Groups who have been historically constrained need barriers removed and opportunities created to make healthy choices.

Solving the complex social issues related to health disparities is a lofty and noble goal but is beyond the scope of most educators' reach. What teachers can take away from this information is awareness. In the United States people hold true to the belief that all people are *created equal* and have *equal value*. Unfortunately, not all people have *equal circumstances*, which may limit opportunity. Many children are born into poverty or raised in environments that negatively affect their health and ultimately their academic success. Empower your students and families affected by health disparities by connecting them with the school nurse, free and reduced lunch program, English as a Second Language services, and before- and after-school child care options. Other helpful suggestions include providing classroom computer access, flexible conference hours/days, nonelectronic means of communication, and verbal communication (for parents who cannot read or write). Above all, be flexible and aware of each child's individual circumstances while maintaining the same high academic expectations for all.

Determinants of Health

Many factors are involved in influencing a person's health. These factors are known as the **determinants of health**. Determinants include personal, social, economic, and environmental factors that determine the health status of individuals or populations. According to *Healthy People 2020* (2011), the determinants of health can be divided into these six broad categories:

- **Policymaking:** Policies affecting both individual and population health, including health laws on tobacco and seatbelt use, vaccinations, and infant screenings.
- **Social factors:** Interactions with family and friends, housing circumstances, transportation options, quality schools, public safety, and the availability of resources needed in order to meet everyday needs (food, housing, job opportunities, etc.).
- **Health services:** Access to and quality of available health services; lack of access to quality health care can lead to unmet health needs, delays in receiving appropriate care and an inability to get preventive services.
- **Individual behaviors:** Choices people make regarding health-related behaviors such as tobacco use, diet, physical activity, and handwashing.
- **Biology and genetics:** Factors with which a person is born (sex, inherited medical conditions, etc.), family history, any health problems acquired due to the process of aging.
- **Environmental conditions:** Pollutants, food contamination, microbial agents; for example, lead-based paints.

The focus of this text is on individual behaviors and their relationship to lifelong health and well-being.

Individual Behaviors and Health

Just as certain behaviors contribute to illness and death, research has shown that specific behaviors exist that contribute to health and wellness throughout the life span. These behaviors include being physically active, choosing a healthy diet, maintaining a healthy body weight, managing stress effectively, avoiding tobacco and drug use, limiting alcohol consumption, and preventing disease and injury.

Physical Activity

In 2008, the U.S. Department of Health and Human Services (USDHHS) published guidelines for physical activity participation for all Americans. Adults should perform at least 2 1/2 hours of moderate-intensity aerobic activity a week, or 75 minutes of vigorous activity. They should increase that to 5 hours of moderate or 2 1/2 hours of vigorous aerobic activity a week for additional health benefits. They should also perform muscle-strengthening activities involving all major muscle groups on two or more days a week. The recommendations for children are slightly different. Children should engage in an hour of physical activity each day. Most of that activity should be moderate or vigorous aerobic activity and should include vigorous-intensity activity at least three days a week. Children should engage in muscle-strengthening and bone-strengthening activity at least three days a week (USDHHS, 2008).

Physical activity contributes to overall health and wellness in a variety of ways, including improved strength, flexibility, cardiovascular health, metabolism, levels of body fat, and emotional well-being as well as decreased risks for chronic disease. To enjoy these benefits, people need to engage in the recommended amounts of physical activity while also incorporating various types of physical activity (listed in figure 1.3). The link between low levels of physical activity and health risks are clear. For example, a person's risk of obesity and type 2 diabetes increases as the number of hours spent watching TV increases (Grøntved & Hu, 2011).

Healthy Diet

Choosing a healthy diet is critical to maintaining health throughout the life span. In late 2015, the U.S. Department of Agriculture (USDA) released new dietary guidelines for all Americans. The 2015 guidelines provide five overarching recommendations that provide guidance for healthy eating. These include following a healthy eating pattern across the lifespan; focusing on variety, nutrient density, and amount; limiting calories from added sugars and saturated fats and reducing sodium intake; shifting to healthier food and beverage choices; and supporting healthy eating patterns for all. The USDA still recommends that peo-

ple balance calories by eating smaller portions; increase consumption of fruits and vegetables and of whole grains so that each category makes up half of a plate; use low-fat milk and low-sodium foods; and drink water instead of sugary drinks (USDHHS and USDA, 2015). The MyPlate icon provides a graphic representation of the guidelines (figure 1.4). It serves as a simple, quick reminder to create a healthy plate by prioritizing and emphasizing the important parts of a healthy, well-balanced plate: fruits and vegetables, lean protein, whole grains, and low-fat dairy including dairy substitutes (e.g., soy milk, almond milk).

Responsibility of Classroom Teachers

Classroom teachers are in a unique situation that allows them to influence and positively affect both the education and the health of students across the nation. Certain behaviors established during youth can influence the health of students as they move into adulthood. These behaviors include tobacco use, nutritional habits, levels of physical activity, alcohol and drug use, sexual behaviors, and behaviors that have the potential to result in violence or unintentional injury. According to the CDC, the academic success of America's youth is strongly linked with their health (figure 1.5). Factors including hunger, abuse, chronic illness, early sexual initiation, violence, and physical inactivity have all been linked to poor school performance or lower educational attainment (CDC, 2011b).

The childhood obesity epidemic in the United States is still on the rise. According to the 2011 National Health and Nutrition Examination Survey (NHANES), approximately 17 percent of young Americans ages 2 to 19 are obese. Between 1994 and 2008, the prevalence of obesity among Mexican-American boys and girls rose from 27.5 percent to 44.2 percent; rose from 27 percent to 49 percent among non-Hispanic black children; and rose from 20.5 percent to 31.2 percent among non-Hispanic white adolescents (CDC, 2011c).

Obesity is the result of an energy imbalance—namely, eating too many calories and getting too little physical activity. Despite this

Figure 1.3 The physical activity pyramid is a helpful guide for planning an active lifestyle.
Reprinted, by permission, from C.B. Corbin, G.C. Le Masurier, and K.E. McConnell, 2014, *Fitness for life*, 6th ed. (Champaign, IL: Human Kinetics), 96. Source: C.B. Corbin

knowledge, physical activity levels are shockingly low in U.S. school children; 81.8 percent of adolescents do not engage in recommended amounts of physical activity, and 69 percent of students do not attend daily physical education classes while in school. Nutrition in U.S. schools is also an issue of concern. According to the CDC's 2011 Youth Risk Behavior Survey (YRBS), 12 percent of youth did not eat fruit, 6 percent did not eat vegetables, and 11 percent

drank a can, bottle, or glass of soda three or more times per day during the 7 days preceding the survey (CDC, 2011b).

As a teacher, you should be committed to the overall health, well-being, and academic success of the children you influence. You have a subtle but powerful impact on students' health behaviors by what you teach and how you model healthy habits in and out of the classroom. Supporting a nationally publicized

Figure 1.4   The USDA's MyPlate makes it easy to remember how to make healthy food choices.
USDA's Center for Nutrition Policy and Promotion.

health awareness week (e.g., National Youth Violence Prevention Week in March) can be effective. However, these strategies alone tend to breed indifference to the important health topics during the remainder of the year. Instead of using the teach-it-once-and-forget-it approach, teachers can use developmentally appropriate health content to teach the reading, writing, and arithmetic curriculum throughout the school year. Role modeling becomes particularly important to children as they transition from babies to active, energetic youth. Being a role model sets the stage for what is considered normal and acceptable behavior. Modeling healthy eating habits, physical activity, and appropriate responses to stress can have a powerful effect on students' health decision-making behaviors. Having a positive attitude and placing a high value on healthy habits can affect students' attitudes as well. It sets up an environment in which health topics can be openly discussed and healthy habits are encouraged.

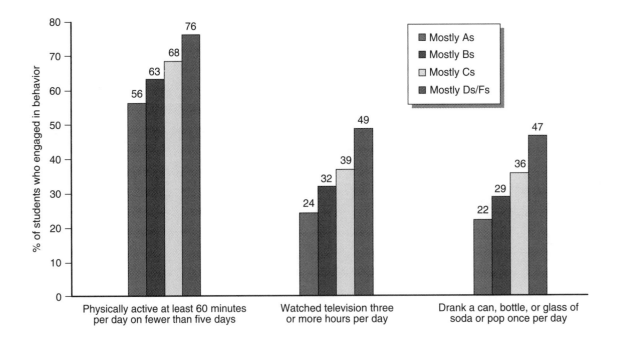

Figure 1.5   Percentage of high school students who engaged in obesity-related health risk behaviors in the previous seven days by type of grades earned (2009 YRBS).
Adapted from Centers for Disease Control and Prevention (2011). Adolescent and School Health: YRBSS I Brief.

Summary

The health of Americans has changed dramatically since the 1900s. Public health efforts have led to reductions in communicable diseases. However, diseases of behavior are more prevalent in the modern era. Chronic ailments such as cancer, heart disease, and diabetes plague millions of Americans and are considered consequences of poor diet, lack of physical activity, and other volitional behaviors. Today's complete definition of health encompasses not only the physical dimension but also the spiritual, emotional, social, intellectual, and environmental dimensions.

Now that you are more familiar with what encompasses health education, read in the next chapter about federal policies that impact the health and nutrition of students. The chapter also teaches you about a comprehensive approach to ensuring that student health is an important part of the curriculum.

Review Questions

1. What are the six dimensions of health? List and define them.

2. How have the leading causes of death in Americans changed throughout history?

3. What are the current leading causes of death in the United States?

4. How much exercise is recommended by the U.S. Department of Health and Human Services? List three of the benefits of exercising regularly.

5. What are 3 of the 6 categories of risk behaviors identified by the CDC? Name and describe them.

6. Why is incorporating health in the academic environment important?

Chapter 2

Coordinated School Health: A Team Approach

Objectives

- Describe how health is related to the mission of schools.
- Explain why the implementation of school wellness policies may be limited.
- Discuss the Child Nutrition and WIC Reauthorization Act of 2004 and its effect on school health today.
- Describe the components of the Whole School, Whole Community, Whole Child (WSCC) model of school health, and identify the role of each component.
- Identify a minimum of three barriers to quality health instruction.
- Describe how academic achievement is related to risky health behaviors.
- Establish why the National Health Education Standards are significant.
- Determine practical applications and best practices of the WSCC model of school health.

Today's students are less likely to graduate from high school than their parents were, making the U.S. the only industrialized country where that is the case.

Anna Habash, Education Trust

The primary mission of U.S. schools is the education and academic success of young people, which has been strongly linked to their health. Chapter 1 discusses the rising levels of childhood obesity, low levels of physical activity, and poor nutrition habits among U.S. school children. These health-related factors, as well as hunger, chronic illness, physical and emotional abuse, substance abuse, and violence, can all lead to poor academic performance along with lower school attendance, grades, test scores, and ability to pay attention in class. As you learned in chapter 1, health risk behaviors can be placed into these six categories: tobacco use, unhealthy diets, inadequate physical activity, drug and alcohol abuse, violence and unintentional injuries, and sexual behaviors.

On the positive side, studies have consistently shown that physical activity and higher levels of physical fitness are linked to enhanced concentration and attention, improved classroom behavior, fewer disciplinary problems in school, better attendance, and improved performance on standardized tests. Coordinated school-based health initiatives (including several national programs) are a critical means to improving both educational performance and the well-being of young Americans and the adults they will become.

National School Policies Focusing on Nutrition and Physical Activity

The **National School Lunch Program** (NSLP) is a federally funded meal program for public schools and nonprofit private schools. The NSLP was established in 1946 to address the nation's malnutrition problems among young Americans. Commonly known as the free or reduced-price lunch program, the NSLP provides nutritious lunches to millions of students every day at low or no cost. The lunches must meet certain standards such as containing at least one third of children's daily nutritional requirements. By federal law, students who are unable to afford the full price of school lunches must be provided a free or reduced-price lunch. Children from families with annual incomes between $30,615 and $43,586 are eligible to receive reduced-price lunches. Children from families with annual incomes at or below the poverty level of $30,615 are eligible for free lunches (USDA, 2013). For more than 60 years, this important federally funded program has ensured that children are being fed while at school. However, the NSLP has changed little over the last several decades, and updates to the program have been needed.

On June 30, 2004, President George W. Bush signed into law the **Child Nutrition and WIC Reauthorization Act of 2004**, which expanded the definition of WIC (Supplemental Nutrition Program for Women, Infants and Children) to include education in order to help make positive changes in physical activity habits. Begun by the federal government in 1972, WIC provides grants to states for supplemental foods and nutrition education for low-income pregnant, breastfeeding, and nonbreastfeeding postpartum women, and to infants and children up to age 5 who are found to be at nutritional risk. The Child Nutrition and WIC Reauthorization Act of 2004 expanded the definition of WIC foods that would promote the health of the WIC population as indicated by relevant science, public health concerns, and cultural eating patterns. The act expanded the availability of nutritious meals and snacks to more children and improved the quality of food in schools.

This law also required that all school districts participating in the NSLP establish local **wellness policies** by July 1, 2006. These wellness policies addressed healthy eating and physical activity. Local wellness policies are an important tool for parents, local education agencies (LEAs), and school districts in promoting student wellness, preventing and reducing childhood obesity, and providing assurance that school meal nutrition guidelines meet the minimum federal school meal standards. School wellness policies should include, at a minimum, nutrition education goals, physical activity goals, nutrition standards for all foods available at school, goals for other school-based activities designed to promote student wellness, and a plan for measuring implementation of the local wellness policy.

However, writing a wellness policy does not ensure policy implementation. Some policies contain weak or vague language, which limits implementation. Schools may also lack the resources and time to enact wellness policies. Because of variation between schools, districts, and states, the impact of policy on student health may be limited.

Section 204 of the **Healthy, Hunger-Free Kids Act of 2010** (Public Law 111-296) expanded the scope of wellness policies, effective the 2011-2012 school year, in these two major ways:

- Additional stakeholders are now being brought in for development, implementation, and review of school wellness policies.

- Public updates (available to parents, students, and others in the community) on the content and implementation of wellness policies are now required.

The Child Nutrition Division of the U. S. Department of Agriculture's Food and Nutrition Service provided an overview of the requirements for local school wellness policies along with recommended actions for the 2011-2012 school years. The new regulations, created by the Healthy, Hunger-Free Kids Act of 2010, required schools to serve fruits and vegetables to students every day; provide only fat-free or low-fat milk; serve more whole grains; and decrease their use of salt, saturated fat, and trans fat. Schools were also required to limit calories according to the age. For children in kindergarten through fifth grade, calorie limits for breakfast and lunch are set at 500 and 650, respectively, while middle and high school students are limited to 600 and 850 calories, respectively.

Need for Collaboration Between Education and Health

Education not only empowers students with knowledge to improve health behaviors but also potentially increases income and access to quality health care. Research shows that coordinated school efforts not only reduce health risk behaviors but also increase academic performance (CDC, 2012). Students who do not engage in risky health behaviors achieve higher grades, and students with higher grades are less likely to participate in risky health behaviors. Although the relationship between academics and health is clear, causation has not yet been established. Take a look at figure 2.1, which displays results from the 2009 Youth Risk Behavior Survey showing the grades and health-risk behaviors of high school students.

The strong link between academic performance and healthy behaviors lends testimony to the potential impact of coordinated school health initiatives. Many children and youth spend a considerable amount of time in school during their formative years. Coordinated school health programs are a critical means to improving both education performance and the well-being of young people and the adults they will become.

For decades, the efforts of schools to establish and maintain a cohesive approach to providing education and preventive programs and services on health were underfunded, underserved, and largely ignored. Because of the lack of coordination, schools and essential public and private programs serving mental health, social services, recreation, and youth development remained disengaged. This problem has led to overlap and duplication in educational efforts, wasteful spending, and widespread gaps in important educational opportunities. In the late 1980s, the idea of coordinated school health (CSH) emerged in response to these issues.

Give Your Wellness Policy a Checkup

The Wellness School Assessment Tool (WellSAT; see www.wellsat.org), developed through grants from the Robert Wood Johnson Foundation and Rudd Foundation, assists schools in assessing the quality of their school district's wellness policy. Stakeholders can perform an online assessment, which generates personalized guidance and resources for making improvements based on that assessment.

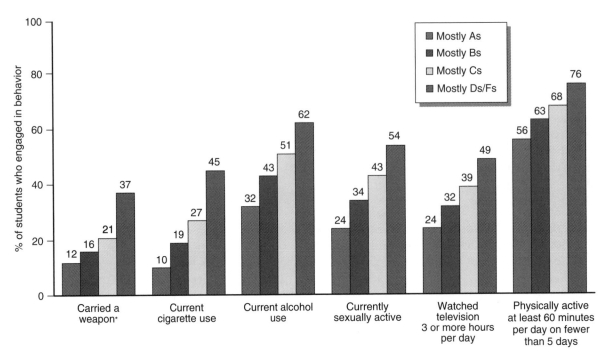

*This means that 12% of students with mostly As carried a weapon and 37% of students with mostly Ds or Fs carried a weapon.

Figure 2.1 Percentage of high school students who participated in health-risk behaviors by types of grades earned.

Reprinted, by permission, from D.A. Birch and D.M. Videto, 2015, *Promoting health and academic success: The whole school, whole community, whole child approach* (Champaign, IL: Human Kinetics), 67: Adapted from United States Youth Risk Survey 2009.

No single best definition exists for **coordinated school health (CSH)**, because programs are often tailored to meet the needs of each state, school, and community. CSH is a systematic approach to improving the health and well-being of all students so that they can fully participate and be successful in school. The process involves bringing together school administrators, teachers, staff, students, families, and community members to assess health needs, set priorities, plan, implement, and evaluate all health-related activities within the confines of the school setting. Necessary ingredients common to high-quality CSH are strong leadership, collaboration, commitment of resources, consistent health-related messaging, and safe facilities.

CSH typically integrates health promotion efforts across eight interrelated areas that already exist to some extent in most schools. These components include health education, physical education, health services, nutrition services, counseling, psychological and social services, healthy and safe school environments, staff wellness, and family and community in-

volvement. These components exist to promote lifetime fitness, address all aspects of health, bring focus to the prevention and management of chronic diseases, furnish healthy meals and food choices, and involve caregivers in health promotion.

Whole School, Whole Community, Whole Child (WSCC) Model

Recently, a more holistic approach focusing on the whole child has evolved from the CSH model. ASCD (formerly known as the Association for Supervision and Curriculum Development) and the CDC developed a model for improving student learning and health in U.S. schools. The **Whole School, Whole Community, Whole Child (WSCC) model** combines elements of the traditional coordinated school health approach with ASCD's Whole Child framework, aiming to provide students with improved knowledge, attitudes, and behaviors related to health, and increased educational and social outcomes. The Whole Child framework focuses attention on the child with a schoolwide collaborative approach, ensuring that each student is healthy, safe, supported, engaged, challenged, and poised for success. Learning and health are interrelated; students are active participants in both.

The WSCC model (figure 2.2) provides a framework for integration and collaboration between education and health in order to improve student cognitive, physical, social, and emotional development. Whereas the tradition-

al coordinated school health model contained 8 components, the WSCC contains 10. Healthy and Safe School Environment has been broken into two distinct components: Social and Emotional Climate and Physical Environment. In addition, Family/Community Involvement has been separated into the categories of Family Engagement and Community Involvement. These changes highlight the importance of both the school physical and psychosocial environments and the influence of community and family support on the healthy development of students.

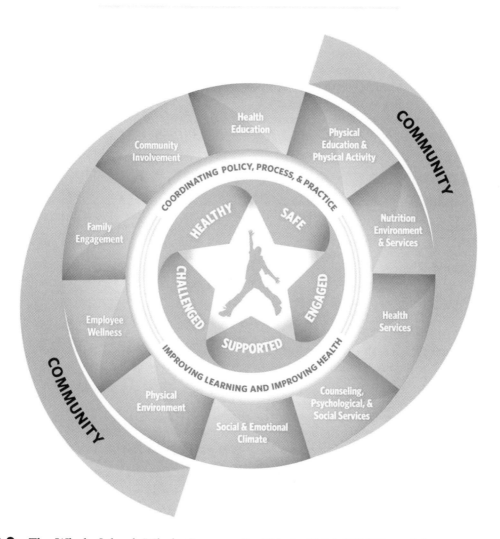

Figure 2.2 The Whole School, Whole Community, Whole Child (WSCC) model.
Reprinted from ASCD, 2014, *Whole school, whole community, whole child: A collaborative approach to learning and health.*

The following sections take a closer look at the 10 WSCC components.

Health Education

Health education provides students with opportunities to acquire the knowledge, attitudes, and skills necessary for making health-promoting decisions, achieving health literacy, adopting health-enhancing behaviors, and promoting the health of others. Topics include alcohol and other drug use and abuse, healthy eating and nutrition, mental and emotional health, personal health and wellness, physical activity, safety and injury prevention, sexual health, tobacco use, and violence prevention.

Health education curricula should address the **National Health Education Standards (NHES)**. Figure 2.3 lists all eight standards. These written indicators were developed to establish, promote, and support health-enhancing behaviors for students at all grade levels—from pre-kindergarten through grade 12. The standards provide a framework for teachers, administrators, and policymakers in designing or selecting curricula, allocating instructional resources, and assessing student achievement and progress. The standards provide students, families, and communities with concrete expectations for health education, an important factor in their implementation and success.

A variety of barriers contribute to a lack of quality health instruction at the elementary level. These barriers include minimal teacher preparation program requirements in health, lack of health education topics on standardized student tests, absence of administrative support for health instruction, and little or no teacher in-service training related to health. School administrators and teachers are held accountable for academic achievement but not for health. As a result, when it comes to allocating instructional time and resources in schools, academics frequently take priority over health.

Physical Education and Physical Activity

Physical education is a school-based instructional curriculum for students to gain the necessary skills and knowledge for lifelong participation in physical activity. Physical education

---

Figure 2.3 National Health Education Standards (NHES)

Standard 1 Students will comprehend concepts related to health promotion and disease prevention to enhance health.

Standard 2 Students will analyze the influence of family, peers, culture, media, technology, and other factors on health behaviors.

Standard 3 Students will demonstrate the ability to access valid information, products, and services to enhance health.

Standard 4 Students will demonstrate the ability to use interpersonal communication skills to enhance health and avoid or reduce health risks.

Standard 5 Students will demonstrate the ability to use decision-making skills to enhance health.

Standard 6 Students will demonstrate the ability to use goal-setting skills to enhance health.

Standard 7 Students will demonstrate the ability to practice health-enhancing behaviors and avoid or reduce health risks.

Standard 8 Students will demonstrate the ability to advocate for personal, family, and community health.

Reprinted from Joint Committee on National Health Education Standards, 2007, *National Health Education Standards: Achieving Excellence.* (Washington, DC: American Cancer Society).

is characterized by a planned, sequential K-12 curriculum that provides cognitive content and learning experiences in a variety of activity areas. Quality physical education programs should assist students in achieving the **National Standards for K-12 Physical Education** (figure 2.4), as set forth by SHAPE America – Society of Health and Physical Educators. The outcome of a quality physical education program is a physically literate person who has the knowledge, skills, and confidence to enjoy a lifetime of healthful physical activity.

Health Services

These services are designed to ensure access to primary health care services, promote appropriate use of primary health care services, prevent and control communicable disease and other health problems, provide emergency care for illness or injury, promote and provide the best possible sanitary conditions for a safe school facility and school environment, and provide educational and counseling opportunities for promoting and maintaining individual, family, and community health. Qualified professionals such as physicians, nurses, dentists, health educators, and other allied health personnel provide these services.

Nutrition Environment and Services

Schools should provide access to a variety of nutritious and appealing meals that accommodate the health and nutrition needs of all students. School nutrition programs reflect the **U.S. Dietary Guidelines for Americans** and other criteria for achieving integrity in nutrition (Office of Disease Prevention and Health Promotion, 2015). The school nutrition services offer students a learning laboratory for classroom nutrition and health education, and they serve as resources for linking with nutrition-related community services. Qualified child nutrition professionals provide these services. States that prohibit junk food consumption, evaluate their nutrition, prohibit food as a reward, and provide funding for staff training have better overall academic performance and higher test scores (Vinciullo & Bradley, 2009).

Counseling, Psychological, and Social Services

These services are provided to improve students' mental, emotional, and social health and include individual and group assessments,

---

Figure 2.4 National Standards for K-12 Physical Education

Standard 1 The physically literate individual demonstrates competency in a variety of motor skills and movement patterns.

Standard 2 The physically literate individual applies knowledge of concepts, principles, strategies and tactics related to movement and performance.

Standard 3 The physically literate individual demonstrates the knowledge and skills to achieve and maintain a health-enhancing level of physical activity and fitness.

Standard 4 The physically literate individual exhibits responsible personal and social behavior that respects self and others.

Standard 5 The physically literate individual recognizes the value of physical activity for health, enjoyment, challenge, self-expression and/or social interaction.

Reprinted from the Society of Health and Physical Educators (SHAPE America), 1900 Association Drive, Reston, VA 20191, www.shapeamerica.org.

Connect With Your Local Farmers

The USDA provides resources for schools interested in developing or growing a farm to school initiative. Fact sheets, grant opportunities, videos, webinars, and planning toolkits are just a few of the valuable resources you will find on this website: www.fns.usda.gov/farmtoschool/farm-school.

interventions, and referrals. Organizational assessment and consultation skills of counselors and psychologists contribute not only to the health of students but also to the health of the school environment. Professionals such as certified school counselors, psychologists, and social workers provide these services.

Employee Wellness

Schools can provide opportunities for school faculty and staff members to improve their health status through activities such as health assessments, health education, and health-related fitness activities. These opportunities encourage staff members to pursue a healthy lifestyle that contributes to their improved health status, improved morale, and a greater personal commitment to the school's overall coordinated health program that transfers into creation of a positive role model for students. A personalized lifestyle intervention program for teachers (that includes health screenings, health education, peer support, and supportive health policies) can result in improved health habits of faculty and staff members who are involved. Health promotion and worksite wellness programs and activities have been shown to improve productivity, decrease absenteeism, and reduce health insurance costs.

Physical Environment

The **physical environment** includes the physical and aesthetic surroundings and the psychosocial climate and culture of the school. Factors that influence the physical environment include the school building and the area surrounding it;

any biological or chemical agents that are detrimental to health; and conditions such as temperature, noise, and lighting. Aesthetic characteristics (such as landscaping, architecture, color, artwork, acoustics, views, and natural lighting) and accommodations (such as climate control, indoor air quality, cleanliness, size of classrooms, hallway traffic flow, and elbow room) are components of the physical environment that influence the comfort and security of students and staff. Researchers have found that excessive noise and overcrowding can affect the academic performance and health of students and faculty. An example of the impact of physical conditions is the substantial body of evidence that is available to support the use of good handwashing practices in reducing infectious diseases, improving school attendance, and reducing student and staff illness.

Social and Emotional Climate

The **social and emotional climate** includes the physical, emotional, and social conditions that affect the well-being of students and staff. It is the collective attitudes, values, beliefs, and behaviors of the entire school community, and it has been linked to student achievement. Research shows that a feeling of connectedness to school is a major contributor to healthy social and emotional development, academic success, and potential protection against risky behaviors (such as sexual, violent, and drug-related behaviors; absenteeism; suspensions; and psychiatric problems). It is therefore imperative that a school climate evoke feelings of connectedness, inclusion, safety, and security, as well as a high expectation of success for every student.

Health is a social issue, and students are influenced by the social environment of their schools. Students learn through observing others, imitating behaviors, and social reinforcement. The social and emotional climate of schools can support or impede healthy choices. Some of the most vulnerable students are those who are socially isolated. Having close friends and experiencing connectedness with others is critical to student health and development. These relationships provide students with nurturance, reassurance of self-worth, and help in coping with stress, and they counteract the effects of loneliness. States with policies prohibiting harassment of students by fellow students and encouraging the prevention of harassment at school were found to have higher test scores and lower dropout rates when compared to states without similar health-promoting policies.

Family Engagement

Schools must actively solicit parent and family involvement. Attitudes, behaviors, and expectations within families impact the health behavior and academic performance of students. Family relationships provide students with support systems and identity. Children reared in strong families are more likely to be healthy and have opportunities for physical activity, balanced diets, emotional support, and stress reduction. In addition, the way children feel about themselves is determined largely by the way their parents treat them. Families have a primary influence on the health choices that

The social and emotional climate of schools can support or impede healthy choices.

students make. Children observe their parents' habitual patterns related to eating, drinking, smoking, and seatbelt use. For example, if parents smoke, it is more likely that their children will smoke. Because of this powerful and dynamic relationship, family engagement must be an integral part of school health initiatives.

Community Involvement

An integrated school, parent, and community approach can enhance the health and well-being of students. Communities dictate social norms or behavior standards, either formally or informally, which are associated with student health behaviors. For example, alcohol consumption may be forbidden, or involvement in sports may be encouraged in the community. School health advisory councils, coalitions, and broadly based constituencies for school health can build support for school health program efforts and engage community resources and services to respond more effectively to the health-related needs of students. Strong, connected communities are more effective in supporting positive health behaviors and shunning negative ones. Community support breeds increased child well-being, less youth delinquency, and improved child development.

Applying the WSCC Model

The WSCC model is envisioned as a strategy to achieve a healthy school community by bridging components of the existing school environment. The first step in coordinating this process is gaining administrative support and commitment. To do so, meet with the appropriate administrators and educate them on the WSCC model and how the process can benefit the health of students, faculty, and staff. Next, establish a health council comprised of teachers, parents, and students who have a commitment to health and wellness in their school. Then, identify a school health coordinator (usually someone who is a strong advocate for health and wellness with good organizational skills and leadership qualities).

Once you have a team in place, a critical step in identifying avenues for linking school

health and academic outcomes is to collect needs assessment data. Gather demographic information about the student population. In other words, ask the question *Who are they?* The answer includes information on age, ethnicity, socioeconomic status (SES), and percent of students on free or reduced lunches. These data can help inform what strategies will best meet the needs of students and the school. You can obtain academic performance data through the district's website or the state department of education.

Conduct a **windshield tour**. Windshield tours are conducted by driving through the community and recording important observations about the school, neighborhood, and physical environment. Observations may also include parks and other recreational areas, nearby businesses, and health care facilities. Does the community include safe areas for children to play and exercise? Does it have enough sidewalks and fencing?

Complete **key informant interviews**. Key informant interviews are in-depth interviews of key people in the community who have knowledge about the topic of interest. The interviews are loosely structured, relying on a list of issues to be discussed. Interview a few teachers, students, parents, and administrators to get a good idea of the health needs of the school community. Focus groups are another qualitative method of collecting information on the needs and interests of a population.

Once all of the needs assessment data have been gathered, meet with your team to analyze and interpret the results. What are the health needs of students, faculty, and staff? How can families be involved in the process? Now you have a better snapshot of the school community.

Next, taking each component of the WSCC model, develop goals and objectives for each. Goals and objectives may be composed of updating or changing policies and procedures or be more comprehensive, such as curriculum development or writing a grant to purchase new equipment for the school kitchen.

The next step is to implement the strategies you have developed for each of the components of the WSCC model. Lastly, complete a thorough evaluation. Monitor whether you achieved your goals and objectives. Build in a

Implementing WSCC in Your School

The steps to implementing the WSCC model that are discussed here are explained in greater detail in *Promoting Health and Academic Success* (Birch & Videto, 2015). This resource was written by several of the people involved in developing the WSCC and offers a thorough guide to understanding the new model and implementing it, including a detailed appendix describing assessment tools (many of which are free).

year-end event to celebrate and advertise your successes. Invite parents, community members, and local organizations that had a hand in the various strategies implemented throughout the year.

Best Practices

In order to further explain the role of best practices in improving the health and wellness of a school community, this section presents two important dimensions that have gained national attention over the past two decades. They are (1) the growing incidences of bullying in America's schools and (2) efficiency levels of school security and emergency preparedness.

Bullying can threaten students' physical and emotional safety and can impact their ability to learn. According to the National Center for Education Statistics (2013), more bullying behavior occurs in middle school (grades 6, 7, and 8) than in high school. Additionally, middle school students, and particularly sixth graders, were more likely to be bullied on the bus, and sixth graders were most likely to be injured as a result of bullying. There are a number of strategies school experts recommend for bullying prevention:

- Focusing attention on improving the school's social environment
- Gaining the support of both staff and parents for bullying prevention

- Forming a multi-disciplinary team to coordinate bullying prevention activities
- Conducting assessments in the school to determine how often bullying occurs and where it happens
- Training staff in bullying prevention
- Establishing and enforcing anti-bullying rules and policies
- Increasing adult supervision where bullying tends to occur the most
- Intervening consistently and appropriately in bullying situations
- Consistently focusing class time on bullying prevention
- Continuing these efforts over time

Because of increasing school violence over the past two decades and the impending threat of natural disasters, emergency preparedness has become extremely important. Although there are no federal laws requiring that school districts have emergency preparedness plans, an estimated 95 percent of school districts reported that they have a plan (U.S. Government Accountability Office, 2007). To help guide the development of these plans, the Office of Safe and Drug-Free Schools has prepared guidelines for school systems (Office of Safe and Drug-Free Schools, 2004). The guidelines focus on four stages of planning: mitigation and prevention, preparedness, response, and recovery.

- Mitigation and prevention: The goal of mitigation and prevention is to reduce the effect of an event and decrease the need for an emergency response. Schools must identify situations they could encounter based on geographical trends and school incident data, as well as other appropriate factors.
- Preparedness: Schools should identify a school crisis team comprised of teachers, parents, local police and public health officials, and other interested community stakeholders. A comprehensive plan should be developed and formalized; components of a plan might include logistics on lockdowns, evacuations, and relocations. Scheduled practice of the plans through drills is needed to ensure that gaps are identified and the school is ready for a disaster event.

- Response: This stage is when the crisis team is activated and the plan is initiated. It is important during this stage that mental health professionals are available as a resource for parents and children.
- Recovery: The purpose of this stage is to reestablish a return to normalcy for the students and staff.

Additional information about this entire process can be found on the U.S. Department of Education's website at www.ed.gov/admins/lead/safety/emergencyplan/crisisplanning.pdf.

Role of Teachers

Second only to the family, schools are perhaps the largest potential influence on student health. Consider that the average elementary student spends roughly 6 hours a day at school, and most elementary classrooms remain self-contained for the majority of the school day. This exclusive setting creates a unique opportunity for the elementary teacher to influence student health. The role of the elementary teacher is an undeniable force in the physical, social, and emotional health of students.

Strong scientific evidence links student health with academic success. It makes sense for teachers to be active participants in promoting student health in order to fulfill the schools' ultimate mission of education. Optimal health ensures optimal learning conditions. Poor student performance can be caused by health-related issues such as sleep deprivation, hunger, illness, physical and emotional abuse, access to health care, lack of health insurance, air pollution, and even dental hygiene. Health-risk behaviors such as physical activity, poor diet, substance abuse, violence, and unintentional injury are implicated in a plethora of academic problems. Good health is a solid foundation for readiness and learning.

One of the greatest challenges for beginning teachers is classroom management. Creating

an environment conducive to learning includes addressing student behavior. The previously mentioned health issues and health-risk behaviors are implicated in student misbehavior. If their fundamental health needs are not being met, children cannot learn. The full spectrum of student behaviors—such as inability to pay attention during class or chronic absenteeism—is affected by student health.

Fortunately, teachers do not have to go it alone when it comes to student health. Numerous school health programs, funding sources, and policies exist to facilitate health and learning. Using a coordinated effort, educators may build partnerships with health professionals and other stakeholders in the community. The key is to focus on prevention and to minimize risk behaviors while children are still young. Students can avoid health-risk behaviors and be taught to engage in health-promoting behaviors. In turn, with an emphasis on health, educators may realize the dream of closing the educational achievement gap for good.

Summary

Schools play a vital role in the health of students and therefore the nation. Health and academic achievement are closely related. When risky behaviors are reduced, academic performance increases. Federal laws require schools to ensure healthy environments for children, and many approaches exist to fulfilling those laws. Getting involved with a coordinated school health plan—particularly one that follows the Whole School, Whole Community, Whole Child (WSCC) model—is an important way that classroom teachers can create a healthy environment for their students. National standards for health and physical education as well as best practices provide benchmarks for teachers as they do this work.

Review Questions

1. Can you describe the link between student health and academic achievement?

2. What is the Child Nutrition and WIC Reauthorization Act of 2004, and how does it relate to student health and wellness in schools?

3. What are the components of the Whole School, Whole Community, Whole Child (WSCC) model?

4. How can you utilize the WSCC model to improve student health and wellness? Describe three ways to do so.

5. Name a health-risk behavior. What is its potential influence on academic achievement?

6. Why are elementary schools an ideal setting for impacting the health of children?

7. Why does quality health instruction not exist in some elementary schools, and how can this problem be remedied?

8. Choose a National Health Education Standard. What are three ways that it could be implemented in a self-contained elementary classroom?

Chapter 3

Health Education

Objectives

- Describe normal growth and brain development in children.
- Describe normal physical development and health in children.
- Identify theories that can be used to change health behavior.
- Define self-efficacy and how it applies to health behavior.
- Analyze the relationships between student health, health instruction, and academic achievement.
- Describe the goals and content areas of comprehensive school health education.
- Identify challenges and facilitators to health education.

Health is where we live, where we learn, where we work, where we play and where we pray. Health is in everything we do.

Regina M. Benjamin,
former U.S. Surgeon General

Imagine a nation where children are healthy, fit, and ready to learn; where youth are prepared with the necessary skills to make good decisions and avoid injuries and disease; and where adult health is the natural outgrowth of knowledge, skills, and behaviors established from childhood. Imagine a nation where young people are aware of the influences of media and technology on their lives; where they are prepared to be wise consumers of goods and services to enhance personal health; they are skilled in decision making and goal setting to achieve their greatest potential; and they possess the skills to advocate for themselves, their families, and their communities.

This scenario does not reflect the current reality in the United States. Today's U.S. youth face greater risks for being injured in motor vehicle accidents, acts of violence, sexually transmitted diseases, teen pregnancy, and suicide. According to the Centers for Disease Control and Prevention (CDC), in the United States one third of children and teens are overweight or obese, one fifth of all high school students are smokers, and one third of female adolescents are pregnant before reaching age 20 (CDC, 2009; CDC, 2012). In addition, motor vehicle accidents cause 30 percent of deaths among young people, 22 percent of youth experience severe mental illnesses, and only about 40 percent of students eat breakfast every day (CDC, 2009; CDC, 2012). The U.S. Department of Health and Human Services (USDHHS) reports that in 2010 there were 754,000 victims of child neglect and physical, sexual, or emotional abuse; 1,560 children died from this abuse (USDHHS, 2011).

Health education can bridge the divide between reality and the ideal. It encompasses a framework that makes this scenario a possibility for everyone. In addition, elementary teachers can take the initiative in the process by providing the vehicle in which health education is delivered to children.

Health education is a blend of planned and sequential learning experiences based on appropriate theories and research that provide learners the opportunity to acquire the information, skills, and practice necessary to make good health decisions. It addresses all physical, emotional, mental, and social aspects of health. Today's health education instruction fo-

cuses on attitudes, behavior, and skills related to the knowledge transferred from teacher to student. In this way, knowledge is more likely to be integrated into positive attitudes and useful behavior change. Today's health education instruction uses a more skills-based approach than in years past. Skills-based health education incorporates the development of knowledge, attitudes, and skills, using a variety of learning experiences, with an emphasis on participatory methods. The development of life skills is a key component of contemporary health education. **Life skills** are a set of psychosocial competencies and interpersonal skills that help youth make informed decisions, solve problems, think critically, communicate more effectively, and manage their lives in a healthy and productive way. Before teachers jump right in to health instruction, they must have a solid understanding of the growth and development of children and a little bit of background in the process of health behavior change.

Growth and Development

Children make substantial leaps in growth and development during their elementary school years. These leaps include changes in hormonal brain chemistry; motor development that affects coordination; and physical growth that

Free Health-Related Lesson Plans

KidsHealth in the Classroom (http://classroom.kidshealth.org) offers educators free health-related lesson plans for all grades and subject areas. Each Teacher's Guide includes discussion questions, activities, and reproducible handouts and quizzes, which are all aligned to national health education standards. The site has a section called How the Body Works that tailors activities to teach children about their own growing bodies.

can be affected by external factors such as poor nutrition, chronic stress, and lack of opportunity for exercise. An example of an external factor is when a child has frequent or prolonged experiences such as abuse or neglect without positive adult interaction; this chronic stress becomes toxic to the child's overall health. However, when adults are present to support a child's experiences and help the child's stress levels come down, stressors may be tolerable and the child can maintain good overall health. The developing brain's ongoing adaptations are the result of both genetics and experience. Classroom teachers should have a basic understanding of human development and growth in order to plan and implement age-appropriate health education experiences in the classroom.

Brain Development and Learning

During the early elementary years, children develop reasoning skills, language, coordination and motor skills, memory, and social skills. Teachers can foster these growing brain skills through creative and innovative teaching strategies. Using games that incorporate movement can greatly enhance the learning of new material. For example, children need abundant opportunities to memorize academic content. Bending, twisting, balancing, and other forms of nonlocomotor movement are easy to incor-

porate into the classroom setting and make the learning more engaging. Using rhymes, music, and storytelling are also fun and generate more pathways in the brain for learning that is more likely retained.

During the later elementary school years, the child's brain activity is mostly in the posterior regions of the brain, where the areas for auditory, visual, and tactile functioning are contained. Hands-on learning experiences, such as learning labs and small group projects, are best for this age group. Also, generally children of this age group are more interested in peer interactions. Children who have good relationships with classmates are less lonely, less depressed, and report enjoying school more. Provide opportunities for group interaction. Give students a scenario and, in small groups, have them demonstrate problem solving for a solution. Create opportunities for children to make choices, and ask them to explain their reasons.

Frontal lobe maturity continues during early adolescence. Assuming the children have a healthy support system at home and in school, they become better able to control more primitive methods of reacting (e.g., fighting or arguing) in favor of behaviors that are adaptive. Preadolescent children begin to see the world through the eyes of others; they become better at relating to their peer group and those in their surroundings. Teachers are in a unique place to help parents and adolescents understand this

Movement Activities Help Kids Learn

Children learn best through moving their bodies. As sensory learners, children should be encouraged to move, use their imaginations, and engage their muscles, all in a safe place where they are mentally and emotionally connected. The cerebellum, which is responsible for balance, posture, and muscle coordination, is also involved in memory, language, and decision making. When connected to movement, information is more easily recalled and retained. Exercising the cerebellum through movement enhances neural pathways that lead to the cognitive areas of the brain. A good reference for activities to keep children moving while learning is the book titled *Active Bodies, Active Brains: Building Thinking Skills Through Physical Activity*, by Mary Ellen Clancy (2006). This book is a guide for classroom teachers who want to help their students become better movers and thinkers. This book explains the current theories behind the movement–learning connection and provides activities that promote this connection in students.

transitory period. If you are teaching preadolescent children, emphasize inferential skills and higher-order thinking. As the frontal lobe of the brain becomes more refined, preadolescent children are expected to think about their behaviors and the consequences related to those behaviors. Unfortunately, this is the time when they are more apt to take risks and be impulsive, too. This behavior is linked to changes in hormonal development as well as maturity of certain areas of the brain. Taking these developmental changes into consideration can greatly enhance the quality of learning your students experience in your classroom.

Physical Development and Health

An elementary-aged child goes through an amazing transformation not only in brain chemistry and growth but in physical development as well. It is wise to be aware of the following physical changes, which may affect self-concept, relationship development, and ultimately learning.

- **Height and weight.** The first period of rapid growth for boys and girls is infancy. Between ages 5 and 7, their growth is steady. According to most authorities, the adolescent growth spurt begins at the approximate age of 9 for girls and 11 for boys; girls reach their peak in development typically by age 14, while boys reach maximum gains by about age 16. Weight gain is then steady until growth is complete. Body proportions change during puberty; hips widen in females, whereas the shoulders broaden in males.

- **Muscular growth and development.** Fitness data show that between ages 5 and 12, boys are slightly stronger than girls. This difference before puberty may be linked to social factors and not physiology. Boys are more likely engaged in physical activities that encourage upper- and lower-body strength development (wrestling, running, and jumping), whereas girls are typically involved in more sedentary activities (playing with dolls, playing house, reading books). However, once puberty begins, boys show significant increases in overall muscular strength while girls begin to gain body fat.

- **Body composition.** Body composition is the relative amount of body mass that is lean or fat. Obesity among U.S. children is growing at an alarming rate. Obese children have difficulty performing simple motor tasks, such as skipping, walking up stairs, and climbing. Therefore, they are more likely to be teased and bullied and may have trouble seeking out friends. Body composition is both genetic and environmental. Overweight children have a 70 percent chance of becoming overweight or obese adults. This number increases to 80 percent if at least one parent is overweight or obese. Obesity in adulthood increases the risk of diabetes, high blood pressure, high cholesterol, asthma, arthritis, and a general poor health status. Children often exhibit wide variations in growth patterns. High body fat can bring about an earlier than normal adolescent growth spurt. Both weight and height change as the body grows. Body fat and muscular development also change, and significant gender differences exist in the pattern of change. Parents should consider the weight of their children to be an important indicator of health, and they should ensure periodic checks by a health practitioner to see that the child is on an appropriate path of weight gain and body composition based on their growth trajectory.

- **Skeletal growth and development.** Children have immature skeletons that are growing at varying rates based on age, nutrition, stress, and key interactions in brain and hormonal chemistry. As kids reach puberty, bone growth accelerates. Physical activity stimulates healthy bone growth in youth. Bone growth occurs best during weight-bearing activity. Exercise during childhood can have a critical effect on bone health that can last a lifetime. Physical activity is a potent stimulus for bone mineralization (the deposition of minerals important to the density and strength of bone). Children and adolescents are susceptible to different types of injuries than adults and are vulnerable to growth-related overuse injuries. If a student complains of an injury, teachers should contact the parents and recommend a visit to a health care practitioner to rule out joint or growth plate injuries.

Once teachers understand the basics of human growth and development, the next step is to become familiar with the mechanics of how health behavior can be changed.

Exercise during childhood can have a critical effect on bone health that can last a lifetime.

Improving Health Behavior

Health behavior is simply the choices people make that influence health status. These choices can include negative or positive behaviors. Some positive behaviors might include eating fruits and vegetables, washing hands frequently, sleeping for 8 hours each night, and exercising regularly. All of these behaviors can impact health. Health education borrows theories from the field of psychology and education and applies them to health behavior.

When applying health behavior theory to young children, it is essential to consider that children are products of their environments. Many of their health choices are made for them, so be careful not to place blame or criticize. Children have little to no control over what foods are purchased, adult supervision, housing, neighborhood crime rates, bedtime, availability of appropriate car seats, and the scheduling of routine doctor or dentist appointments. Parents and caregivers typically control these factors.

How can positive health behavior change occur in a home environment that is not conducive to health? Families must be involved in the process. In order to gain support for positive health behavior change, elementary teachers and parents must be in a two-way partnership. Parents should be encouraged not only to meet their basic obligations but also to become involved in school health programs, home learning activities, health policy, and advocacy.

Health behavior change is a collaborative and empowering process.

One essential factor that affects human behavior is **self-efficacy**. Self-efficacy is the extent of one's belief in one's own ability to complete tasks and reach goals. Self-efficacy plays a critical role in how people think, feel, and behave. Students with a strong sense of their own effectiveness are more likely to challenge themselves with difficult tasks and be intrinsically motivated. These students devote great time and energy into their commitments, and they often attribute failure to things that are in their control rather than blame others. Students with high self-efficacy recover quickly from setbacks, and they are able to achieve personal goals. Conversely, students with low self-efficacy tend to think they cannot be successful and are less likely to make the effort needed to accomplish a goal or task. Therefore, students in this category may have lower aspirations, which may result in poor academic performance. The school setting provides the perfect platform for learning academic and social skills, solving problems, communication, and relationship development. In a social setting, levels of self-efficacy become evident. Children are particularly sensitive to how their peers view them. A child with high self-efficacy likely has confidence in her relationship with peers, but a child with low self-efficacy might feel unaccepted and withdraw.

The four sources of self-efficacy are

- mastery experiences,
- vicarious experiences,
- verbal persuasion, and
- emotional states.

Teachers can use strategies to build self-efficacy in many ways. For example, having successful experiences with a presentation or exam boosts self-efficacy (an example of *mastery experience*), while failures tend to erode it. Observing a peer succeed at a task can strengthen beliefs in one's own abilities (an example of a *vicarious experience*). Teachers can boost self-efficacy with *verbal persuasion*—praise and feedback to guide the student through the task or motivate them to make their best effort. Using incentives to reward the achievement of health goals is another way to support self-efficacy

among children. Lastly, a positive level of emotional stimulation (*emotional state*) can contribute to strong performances. Teachers can help by reducing stressful situations and lowering anxiety about events such as tests or presentations. Throughout school, parents and teachers can have a profound effect on self-efficacy. The goal of health education is to increase student self-efficacy by facilitating the acquisition of knowledge and developing the skills needed in order to achieve and maintain healthy behaviors.

So, you know that children with high self-efficacy are going to be more successful at achieving their goals—in this case, their health-related goals. Another important element to adopting health behaviors is through modeling behaviors they see. **Social cognitive theory** (SCT) refers to a psychological model that focuses on the idea that learning occurs in a social setting and that much of what is learned is gained through observation. SCT adheres to some basic assumptions about learning and behavior. One assumption is called reciprocal determinism, whereby personal, behavioral, and environmental factors influence one another in a bidirectional way. So, a person's behavior is a product of an ongoing interaction between cognitive, behavioral, and contextual factors. Another assumption is that people can influence their own behavior and the environment in a purposeful, goal-directed way. A third assumption within SCT is that learning can occur without an immediate change in behavior. A strength of SCT is that it provides a framework for classroom interventions designed to improve students' learning. So, if a student sees the teacher walking around the track during recess, then eating an apple and drinking water during lunchtime, the child is more likely to adopt those healthy behaviors.

Now that you can acknowledge the role of self-efficacy and the social environment (SCT) in successfully changing health-related behaviors, you can also characterize behavior change as occurring through a series of stages. The **transtheoretical model of behavior change** (TTM) is a way to categorize a person by stage based on readiness to change a particular behavior. The concept of readiness is important because if a person is not ready to change a behavior, then change is unlikely to occur.

Table 3.1 lists the stages through which people progress during behavior change and the characteristics that accompany each stage. The stage helps to determine what kind of intervention would be most effective. For example, if smokers are not aware that smoking can lead to serious health problems, they are unlikely to attempt to give up smoking right away and an intervention aimed at providing information about the negative effects of smoking may help them move to the next stage.

Think about a health behavior that you would like to change. Would you like to exercise more, increase your fruit or vegetable intake, or reduce your consumption of salt? Use table 3.1 to determine what stage best describes your efforts. What would it take to move you to the next stage? Teachers can use the TTM as a way to engage their students in making behavior changes. For example, after staging your students, use table 3.1 as a guide in moving them to the next stage in increasing physical activity.

People are motivated at different times to perform positive health-related behaviors, and attitude can affect this phenomenon. The **theory of planned behavior** attempts to predict how a person's attitudes about a behavior may affect the intention to engage in that behavior. Health educators posit that behavior is often established by intention, which is determined by attitude toward the behavior (good or bad), subjective norm (perception of social pressures to perform or not perform behavior), and perceived behavioral control (perception of ease or difficulty in performing behavior). For example, the likelihood of John intending to change behavior in order to lose weight is based on three factors: his attitude toward the behavior change, **subjective norms** of friends and family, and whether or not John feels he has control over the process and outcome. If John is trying to lose weight, he must believe that healthy eating and exercise will result in weight loss. He must also have confidence that losing weight will result in him looking and feeling better. Another factor that will influence John's intention is how subjective norms affect his decision making and his perception that he must comply with them. If he has health-minded friends and family and believes that they want him to

lose weight, he is more likely to comply with healthful eating and exercising. Lastly, John must think he is capable of accomplishing the tasks necessary to lose weight (self-efficacy). According to the theory of planned behavior, attitudes, intentions, subjective norms, perceived behavioral control, and self-efficacy are the main ingredients for health behavior change. These components are closely related to and overlap with constructs in other health behavior theories.

Lastly, the **health belief model** (HBM) is a psychological model that seeks to explain and predict health behaviors by focusing on people's attitudes and beliefs. The model suggests that people's beliefs about health problems, perceived benefits and barriers to the behaviors that will prevent the health problem, and self-efficacy explain whether they will engage in a health-promoting behavior. According to the model, a cue to action must also be present in order to trigger the health-promoting behavior. See table 3.2 for the components of the HBM.

Teachers can use constructs of the HBM to assist their students in making positive changes to their health. For example, you may aim to increase perceived susceptibility to and perceived seriousness of a health condition by providing education about prevalence and incidence of a disease, having students complete a family health history, and citing facts about the consequences of the disease. You could also have students complete an activity such as a cost–benefit analysis of engaging in a health-promoting behavior (benefits and barriers). The activity could include information about the various behaviors to reduce risks of the disease, identify common perceived barriers, and describe incentives to engage in health-promoting behaviors. In addition, you could provide cues to action to remind and encourage students to engage in health-promoting behaviors.

The fields of education and psychology have made important contributions in understanding and guiding health behavior change. Teachers with a sound understanding of human behavior and the theories that explain it are better armed with the skills needed to individualize health education instruction in the classroom.

Table 3.1 Stages of Readiness to Change Behavior and Strategies to Facilitate Change

Stage of change	Characteristics	Strategies
Precontemplation	No intention of change within next 6 months, perhaps from a lack of information or failure during past attempts	■ Read about the many benefits of physical activity. ■ Describe ways that inactivity may be affecting loved ones. ■ Discuss physical activities you enjoy and where in the community those activities could take place. ■ Reassess stage monthly.
Contemplation	Intend to take action within 6 months; aware of pros and cons of changing	■ List pros/cons of not changing behavior. ■ Describe barriers to physical activity and possible solutions. ■ Make small changes in normal daily routines to integrate physical activity. ■ Keep a log of daily activity. ■ Reassess stage monthly.
Preparation	Plan to act within 1 month; have a plan of action	■ Analyze activity log, and plan to replace 15 minutes of inactive time with physical activity. ■ List activities you enjoy, and find friends/classmates with similarities. ■ Discuss with parents how they can reward you for meeting your goals. ■ Reassess stage monthly.
Action	Outwardly change behavior within last 6 months; highest risk for relapse	■ Commit to doing at least 30 minutes of activity each day. ■ Try a new activity you think you may enjoy. ■ Reflect on the benefits you have already received by doing physical activity. ■ Reassess stage monthly.
Maintenance	Successful behavior change for 6 or more months; less temptation and more confidence	■ Create a contract, and continue setting short-term goals for physical activity. ■ Discuss what to do if you are not meeting your goals. ■ Find ways to make physical activity fun and refreshing.
Termination	No temptation and 100% self-efficacy	

Learning Styles

Learning is the process that occurs in order to understand and remember new information. It is reflected in the way people respond to social, environmental, emotional, and physical stimuli. **Learning styles** are defined as the way in which information is processed.

A popular interpretation of research on learning is founded on Howard Gardner's theory of multiple intelligences. Gardner proposed several types of learning intelligences (verbal-linguistic, logical-mathematical, visual-spatial, naturalistic, bodily-kinesthetic, musical, interpersonal, intrapersonal) that people exhibit in unique and subtle ways (figure 3.1).

Table 3.2 Components of the Health Belief Model (HBM)

Concept	Definition	Application
Perceived susceptibility	One's opinion of chances of getting a condition	Define population(s) at risk, risk levels; personalize risk based on a person's features or behavior; heighten perceived susceptibility if too low.
Perceived severity	One's opinion of how serious a condition and its consequences are	Specify consequences of the risk and the condition.
Perceived benefits	One's belief in the efficacy of the advised action to reduce risk or seriousness of impact	Define action to take; how, where, when; clarify the positive effects to be expected.
Perceived barriers	One's opinion of the tangible and psychological costs of the advised action	Identify and reduce barriers through reassurance, incentives, assistance.
Cues to action	Strategies to activate readiness	Provide how-to information, promote awareness, give reminders.
Self-efficacy	Confidence in one's ability to take action	Provide training, guidance in performing action.

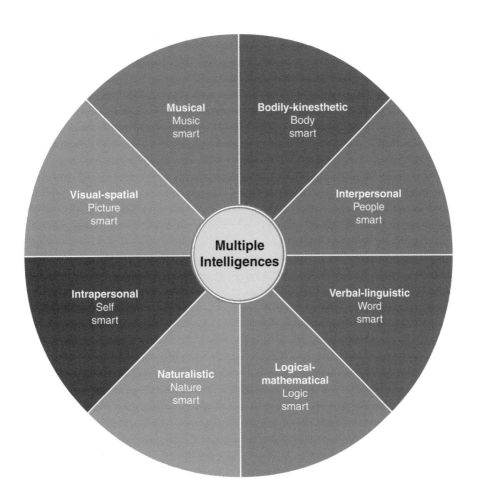

Figure 3.1 Gardner's multiple intelligences.

Many teachers would agree that students learn in a variety of ways, and that a classroom that offers a variety of learning opportunities increases the likelihood of success. Students gain benefits when their teachers recognize their strengths and weaknesses as learners. So, for example, if given an essay to write on the achievements of the public health system since 1900, a logical-mathematical learner could use a graphic organizer to categorize and organize thoughts before writing. An outline is a written version of a graphic organizer. However, a visual-spatial learner might want to draw or design the subject of the piece, then write or create the written draft. Details in the drawing would lead to details in the writing. If teachers know their students' learning styles, they can better adapt material to best teach to each learner. Elementary teachers must take into consideration the variety of learning styles when planning for effective health instruction. See table 3.3 for a summary of the characteristics of these learning styles.

Comprehensive School Health Education

The evidence is undeniable that teachers play a key role in the health knowledge and, consequently, the health behavior of students. Research shows that pre-service teacher preparation in health education leads to an increase in health instruction and health content in the elementary classroom. This is encouraging since this increase is directly correlated with positive health behavior change in children. Let's take a look at how to begin the journey of providing your students with a strong foundation in health education that increases their chances for a lifetime of improved health outcomes.

U.S. health and education authorities have long advocated for **comprehensive school health education (CSHE)** in schools. CSHE is a planned, sequential health education curriculum with appropriate scope and sequence that addresses the mental, emotional, physical,

Table 3.3 Characteristics of Learning Styles

Category	Type	Characteristics
Bodily-kinesthetic	Body smart	Learn best through manipulating and doing; may work best standing up and moving rather than sitting still.
Interpersonal	People smart	Learn best through relating to others by sharing, comparing, and cooperating.
Verbal-linguistic	Word smart	Learn best through reading, writing, listening, and speaking.
Logical-mathematical	Logic smart	Learn by classifying, categorizing, and thinking about patterns, relationships, and numbers.
Naturalistic	Nature smart	Learn best by working with nature; enjoy learning about living things and natural events; often excel in the sciences and are passionate about environmental issues.
Intrapersonal	Self smart	Learn best by working alone and setting individual goals; independent and organized.
Visual-spatial	Picture smart	Learn best by drawing or visualizing things using the mind's eye; are good spellers; learn best from pictures, diagrams, other visual aids; tend to be fast readers.
Auditory-musical	Music smart	Often learn using rhythm or melody, especially by singing or listening to music; are easily distracted by noise; can spell better out loud than in writing.

and social dimensions of health and enables students to become healthy, productive citizens. A quality health education curriculum is designed to give students the knowledge, skills, and attitudes to maintain and improve their health, prevent disease, and reduce health-related risk behaviors. Another characteristic of CSHE is that the content is a separate curriculum taught by personnel with the appropriate training in health education. CSHE traditionally includes 10 content areas that should comprise the health curriculum. In other words, this is what should guide the development of unit and lesson plans for the coverage of health topics in your classroom. The number of lesson plans will be based on the needs of the students as well as the time needed to devote to each health topic. Table 3.4 lists the 10 content areas and examples of topics for each content area for grades K to 6.

Table 3.4 Ten Content Areas of Health Education

Content area	Potential topics for grades K-3	Potential topics for grades 4-6
Mental and emotional health	Expressing feelings Managing feelings Respect Positive self-image Role models Making friends Listening to others Resisting peer pressure Conflict resolution Being a responsible family member	Effective communication Conflict resolution Developing good character Responsible decision making How to listen Role models Being a responsible family member Family communication Listening in families Problems in families Positive self-image Caring for self Caring for others
Promoting health and preventing disease	Covering coughs and sneezes Washing hands Immunizations Checkups Brushing and flossing teeth Skin care Sun safety Lice Eye care Ear care	Personal hygiene Dental hygiene Preventing infectious diseases Preventing/managing diabetes Preventing/managing asthma Sun safety Reducing health risks Health care services
Promoting physical activity	Safety Movement Physical fitness Heart rate Injury prevention	Promoting health through movement Benefits of physical activity Influences on activity level Developing fitness Safety Flexibility Cardiovascular and respiratory fitness Warming up Cooling down Healthy body composition Injury prevention

(continued)

Table 3.4 *(continued)*

Content area	Potential topics for grades K-3	Potential topics for grades 4-6
Promoting healthy eating	Food safety Washing hands Nutrition Food groups Nutrients Meals and snacks Shopping for food Storing food Drinking water Digestive system	The digestive process Following dietary guidelines Healthy snacks Food labels Food packaging Food choices Storing food Meal planning Nutrients Importance of water Disease prevention through food Improving eating through behavior change Preventing foodborne illness Maintaining a healthy weight Recognizing eating disorders
Growth and sexual development	Growth and development Circulatory system Nervous system Respiratory system Muscular system Skeletal system Respect for self and others Family roles Owner's manual to body care Puberty 101: mood swings, developmental changes	Growth and development Owner's manual to body care Puberty Changing bodies Changing minds Respect for self and others Family roles Responsibility HIV/AIDS Pregnancy and childbirth Male and female reproduction
Community and consumer health	Looking at medicine labels Our community Doctors Pharmacists Nurses Paramedics Firefighters Police officers	Being an informed consumer Spending time and money wisely Reading medicine labels Using medications correctly Prescription medications Over-the-counter medications Health services in our community Health career development Evaluating health information Developing health literacy
Environmental health	Reducing waste Recycling Sanitation workers Clean water Clean air	Connections between the environment and personal health Reducing waste Recycling Preventing pollution of air, water, and soil Conserving resources Reducing, reusing, and recycling Conserving water Conserving energy Advocating for a healthy environment

Table 3.4 *(continued)*

Content area	Potential topics for grades K-3	Potential topics for grades 4-6
Preventing alcohol and drug abuse	Safely using medicine Being safe around medicine Difference between over-the-counter and prescription medicines Dangerous substances Choosing friends Problem solving and goal setting	Responsible drug use: prescription drugs, over-the-counter drug use/abuse and dependency Inhalants Protective factors to resist alcohol, tobacco, and drugs Evaluating how alcohol and tobacco are harmful Evaluating the media's promotion of tobacco and alcohol Alcohol, tobacco, and drugs in the news Resisting peer pressure to use alcohol, tobacco, and drugs
Preventing intentional injury and violence	Conflict resolution Expressing feelings Managing feelings Respect Listening to others Positive self-image Role models Making friends Avoiding weapons Dealing with bullies Emergency preparedness	Risk and protective factors associated with youth violence Preventing school violence Violence and maltreatment at home Protecting yourself from gangs and weapons Bullying, cyberbullying Effective communication Conflict resolution How to listen Role models Positive self-image
Injury prevention and safety	Wearing seatbelts Riding in the backseat Getting help in emergencies Staying safe at home Pedestrian safety Using a buddy system Wearing helmets Water safety Fire safety Electrical safety Staying away from poison Preventing dog bites Basic first aid	Emergency preparedness Universal precautions Fire safety Preventing accidents in the water Motor vehicle safety Being home alone Pedestrian and bike safety Calling someone in an emergency Staying safe during severe weather and natural disasters Preventing illness during hot/cold weather

Health Education Challenges

Even with the known strong link between academics and student health, health education is not a high priority in many classrooms. Few states currently require and support CSHE. Because of political and financial pressures, most states use existing classroom teachers, physical educators, school nurses, and other professionals within the school community to teach the health education content. Most elementary teachers consider health to be an important subject—and even an enjoyable subject to teach—but they do not provide consistent health instruction, nor do they have the appropriate training to do so. Those that do teach health content often exclude primary prevention and address only the immediate health needs of students such as bullying, lice, germs, and handwashing. Because schools are required to maintain passing scores in core academic content for federal educational agencies, more time is spent on those required areas, and programs including health education and physical education are commonly de-emphasized or superficially addressed. Perhaps the biggest obstacle to teaching health is lack of instructional time. Health instruction is frequently neglected for the benefit of other core subjects such as math and reading. Elementary teachers often report that major barriers include a lack of adequate planning time, limited access to appropriate health curriculum resources, and lack of funding. A final challenge to teaching health education may be political, religious, or cultural values within a community that are inconsistent with health education goals. For example, it may initially be a challenge to introduce topics related to growth and sexual development if the general attitude of administrators or parents is one of denial that sex is an issue in the community. Teachers need to inform administrators and parents of any potentially controversial topics that may be addressed in the classroom.

Health Education Facilitators

Today, quality health education curricula reflect a growing body of research that emphasizes teaching functional knowledge, shaping personal beliefs and social norms that support healthy behaviors, and developing the skills needed to practice and maintain healthy behaviors. Figure 3.2 lists characteristics that should serve as a foundation for good K-12 health education programming.

Elementary teachers have the responsibility of planning, implementing, and evaluating health instruction based on the needs and interests of students. Health education also includes a variety of components, ensuring its effectiveness. It not only focuses on health behavior outcomes but also addresses group norms, social influences, and peer pressure. Not only should there be adequate instructional time for learning and skill reinforcement, there should also be ample time for students to practice in order to synthesize what they have learned. This practice also helps to build self-efficacy, self-advocacy, and confidence in social situations. Elementary teachers should take care to provide student materials and health information that are age appropriate and developmentally tailored. In addition, teachers should use strategies that make health information personal, engaging, and culturally sensitive. Health education also depends on teachers participating in ongoing professional development to ascertain continued competence in health instruction.

Elementary health instruction that is skills based, developmentally appropriate, and consistent is a critical foundation for student health. Teacher preparation is the key to guaranteeing fortified health education. One of the most important factors in providing health instruction is pre-service preparation in health content and teaching methodology. The good news is that if you are reading this book, there is a strong possibility you are enrolled in a training program preparing you to do so. Also related is ongoing training through health in-service opportunities and collaboration with colleagues. Policy and administrative support are crucial to health education efforts. Another enabler to health education is ensuring that teachers are skilled at accessing health-related resources and know how to integrate health content into other core subject areas. Doing so saves valuable instructional and planning time. Community health professionals and experts are potential health education facilitators who may be available to serve as instructional consultants or guest speakers in the classroom or at parent–teacher organization meetings.

Summary

Health education provided by elementary teachers is necessary for the health and academic achievement of U.S. children. Health education is a set of experiences that help students acquire skills and information necessary for making good health-related decisions. In order to implement effective health education, elementary teachers should have an understanding of growth and development in children as well as the theories related to health behavior change. Health instruction, health behavior, and academic achievement enjoy a symbiotic relationship. Comprehensive school health education (CSHE) is a planned and sequential health education curriculum that addresses all dimensions of health. It encompasses 10 content areas: mental and emotional health, promoting health and preventing disease, promoting physical activity, promoting healthy eating, growth and sexual development, community and consumer health, environmental health, alcohol and drug prevention, preventing intentional injury and violence, and injury prevention and safety. Elementary teachers are responsible for the health education of their students and may encounter a variety of barriers and facilitators to health education.

Figure 3.2 Characteristics of Health Education Programming

Focuses on clear health goals and related behavioral outcomes. Instructional strategies and learning experiences are directly related to behavioral outcomes.

Uses research-based and theory-driven approaches. Instructional strategies and learning experiences are built on theoretical approaches (e.g., social cognitive theory and theory of planned behavior) that effectively influence health-related behaviors among youth. The most promising curriculum goes beyond the cognitive level and addresses health determinants, social factors, attitudes, values, norms, and skills that influence specific health-related behaviors.

Addresses individual values, attitudes, and beliefs. Fosters attitudes, values, and beliefs that support positive health behaviors. It provides instructional strategies and learning experiences that motivate students to critically examine personal perspectives, thoughtfully consider new arguments that support health-promoting attitudes, and generate positive perceptions about protective behaviors and negative perceptions about health-risk behaviors.

Addresses individual and group norms that support health-enhancing behaviors. Provides instructional strategies and learning experiences to help students assess the level of risky behavior among their peers, corrects misperceptions of peer and social norms, emphasizes the value of good health, and reinforces health-enhancing attitudes and beliefs.

Reinforces protective factors and increases perceptions of personal risk and harmfulness of engaging in specific unhealthy practices and behaviors. Provides opportunities for students to validate positive health-promoting beliefs, intentions, and behaviors. It provides opportunities for students to assess their vulnerability to health problems, actual risk of engaging in harmful health behaviors, and exposure to unhealthy situations.

Addresses social pressures and influences. Provides opportunities for students to analyze personal and social pressures to engage in risky behaviors.

Builds personal competence, social competence, and self-efficacy by addressing skills. Builds essential skills (communication, refusal, assessing accuracy of information, decision making, goal setting, self-control, and self-management) that enable students to build their personal confidence, deal with social pressures, and avoid or reduce health-risk behaviors.

Provides functional health knowledge that is basic, accurate, and directly contributes to health-promoting decisions and behaviors. Provides accurate, reliable information for usable purposes so that students can assess risk, clarify attitudes and beliefs, correct misperceptions about social norms, identify ways to avoid or minimize risky situations, examine internal and external influences, make behaviorally relevant decisions, and build personal and social competence. A curriculum that provides information for the sole purpose of improving knowledge of factual information will not change behavior.

(continued)

Figure 3.2 *(continued)*

Uses strategies designed to personalize information and engage students. Includes instructional strategies that are student centered, interactive, and experiential. Learning experiences correspond with students' cognitive and emotional development, help them personalize information, and maintain their interest and motivation while accommodating diverse capabilities and learning styles.

Provides age-appropriate and developmentally appropriate information, learning strategies, teaching methods, and materials. Addresses students' needs, interests, concerns, developmental and emotional maturity levels, experiences, and current knowledge and skill levels. Learning is relevant and applicable to students' daily lives.

Incorporates learning strategies, teaching methods, and materials that are culturally inclusive. Materials are free of culturally biased information but include information and activities that are inclusive of diverse cultures and lifestyles (such as gender, race, ethnicity, religion, age, physical/mental ability, appearance, and sexual orientation).

Provides adequate time for instruction and learning. Provides enough time to promote understanding of key health concepts and practice skills. Behavior change requires a sustained effort. A short-term curriculum, delivered for a few hours at one grade level, is generally insufficient to support the adoption and maintenance of healthy behaviors.

Provides opportunities to reinforce skills and positive health behaviors. Builds on previously learned concepts and skills and provides opportunities to reinforce health-promoting skills across health topics and grade levels. It can include incorporating more than one practice application of a skill, adding skill-boosting sessions at subsequent grade levels, or integrating skill application opportunities in other academic areas.

Provides opportunities to make positive connections with influential others. Links students to other influential people who affirm and reinforce health-promoting norms, attitudes, values, beliefs, and behaviors. Instructional strategies build on protective factors that promote healthy behaviors and enable students to avoid or reduce health-risk behaviors by engaging peers, parents, families, and other positive adult role models in student learning.

Includes teacher information and plans for professional development that enhance effectiveness of instruction and student learning. Implemented by teachers who have a personal interest in promoting positive health behaviors, believe in what they are teaching, are knowledgeable about the content, and are comfortable and skilled in implementing expected instructional strategies. Ongoing professional development and training are critical for helping teachers implement a new curriculum or implement strategies that require new skills in teaching.

Adapted from Centers for Disease Control and Prevention, *Characteristics of an effective health education curriculum.* Available: www.cdc.gov/HealthyYouth/SHER/characteristics/

Review Questions

1. Describe normal growth and development in children.

2. Choose a health behavior that you would like to change in yourself, and explain how one of the theories discussed in this chapter could be used to obtain this goal.

3. What is self-efficacy, and how does it relate to health behavior?

4. Why is health education important?

5. Imagine you are a first-year teacher. What types of barriers might you face when trying to implement health education into your classroom? How can these barriers be overcome?

6. List the 10 content areas of comprehensive school health education, and provide an example of a topic for each.

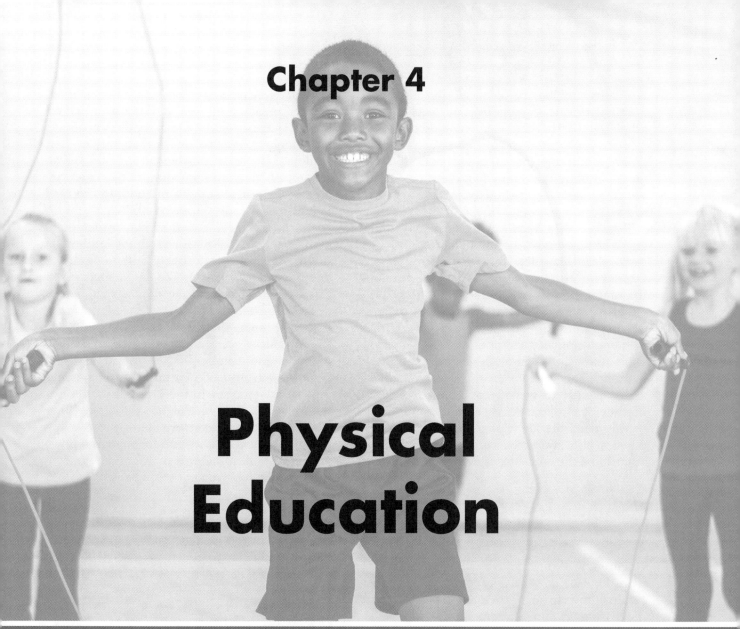

Chapter 4

Physical Education

Objectives

- Define physical activity.
- List the benefits of physical activity.
- Define physical education.
- Describe a quality physical education program.
- Define physical literacy.
- Identify the five National Standards for K-12 Physical Education.

Movement is essential to memory, emotion, language and learning. The so called higher brain functions evolved from movement and depend on it.

John Ratey

A quality elementary physical education program is a critical component to teaching the whole child. The U.S. elementary school curriculum is packed with subjects to enhance the child's knowledge (mind), but schools often neglect the body that will carry the mind of the child. If schools want children to have essential life skills to address all of the challenges they will face in life, then having a healthy mind and a healthy body go hand in hand.

Physical education today is not the old PE class from years ago. In addition to developing motor, fitness, and social skills, today's elementary physical education programs include playing games for understanding, participating in interdisciplinary activities, climbing on rock walls, and using technology devices to enhance learning. The focus is on the development of skills needed to provide a foundation for a lifetime of movement. As the classroom teacher, you need the knowledge of what a quality physical education program looks like and how you can be the educator of the whole child.

Defining Physical Activity

Children need physical activity. Human bodies were built to move. Classroom teachers must rethink how to organize the school day and move from teaching students sitting in desks all day to creating an active learning environment. It is time for active education.

Physical activity is any body movement that results in energy expenditure (SHAPE America, 2015). This movement is not limited to playing sports. Physical activity is any movement—walking, dancing, jumping, climbing trees, riding a bike, playing hide and seek, walking the dog, washing the car, hiking a trail—the list is endless. Physical activity is an easy addition to any classroom, and it comes with many benefits.

Benefits of Physical Activity for Children

Regular physical activity has numerous benefits for children. Beyond the health benefits for a better quality of life, students who are physically active have better classroom behavior, increased mental alertness, and improved self-esteem. Those benefits alone should encourage all schools to increase physical activity of their students. However, this benefit may get the attention of school administrators the most: Increasing physical activity in children can lead to better academic achievement.

Dr. John Ratey, a well-known professor of clinical psychiatry at Harvard and author on brain research, wrote a book about exercise and the brain. In *Spark: The Revolutionary New Science of Exercise and the Brain* (2008), Ratey described exercise as the single most powerful tool to optimize the functions of the brain. He stated that exercise elevates the brain-derived neurotrophic factor (BDNF), a protein that supports survival of neurons and encourages growth of synapses in the brain; it is vital for learning, memory, and higher thinking. Other research studies have revealed a positive impact of physical activity and school-based physical education in the area of attention, concentration, and achievement test scores.

Recommendations

According to the United States Department of Health and Human Services (USDHHS) *Physical Activity Guidelines for Americans*, children

Positive Benefits of Physical Activity on Academic Performance

There is growing evidence that physical activity has positive benefits on academic performance. After participating in physical activity, studies have indicated that children are better able to stay focused, remain on task, and complete tasks faster and more accurately, which leads to an improvement in overall academic performance.

For more information, go to http://activelivingresearch.org/sites/default/files/ALR_Brief_ActiveEducation_Jan2015.pdf.

and adolescents should participate in 60 minutes or more of physical activity daily (US-DHHS, 2008). The best approach is for the entire school to address the 60 minutes with opportunities for activity before, during, and after school. Schools should develop a plan to provide physical activity programs along with providing high-quality daily physical education classes for these recommended minutes.

To address the recommendation of 60 minutes, schools are encouraged to implement a comprehensive school physical activity program (CSPAP). This program is a systemic approach in which schools use five different opportunities for students to meet the recommended physical activity minutes each day and to develop students to have the knowledge, skills, and confidence to be physically active for a lifetime. The five components of the CSPAP are high-quality physical education, physical activity during school, physical activity before and after school, staff involvement, and family and community engagement.

The program designed to get the entire school involved in CSPAP is the **Let's Move! Active School (LMAS)** campaign. LMAS is a comprehensive program used by school champions (teachers, administrators, and parents) to create an active environment in the school. An active school incorporates physical activity before, during, and after school for at least 60 minutes every day. LMAS provides opportunities in the five components of CSPAP and a clear roadmap to guide school champions to meet their goals in the five components through a simple six-step process. This process helps school champions to build a team, make a plan, access free resources and program materials, and get other necessary help for achieving their goals (Lets Move! Active Schools, 2013).

Defining Physical Education

Physical education is different from physical activity. According to SHAPE America (2015), "Physical education is an academic subject that provides a planned, sequential, K-12 standards-based program of curricula and instruction designed to develop motor skills, knowl-

edge and behaviors for healthy, active living, physical fitness, sportsmanship, self-efficacy and emotional intelligence" (p. 3). High-quality physical education programs in schools can help foster lifelong habits of physical activity and improve the health of children. The goal for a physical education program is "to develop physically literate individuals who have the knowledge, skills and confidence to enjoy a lifetime of healthful physical activity" (SHAPE America, 2014, p. 11). A **physically literate person** has learned the skills necessary to participate in a variety of physical activities; knows the implications and the benefits of involvement in the various types of physical activities; participates regularly in physical activity; is physically fit; and values physical activity and its contributions to a healthful lifestyle.

Physical education has these four essential components:

- Policy and environment
- Curriculum
- Appropriate instruction
- Student assessment

Specifically, *policy and environment* means advocating for 150 minutes of instructional periods per week with a qualified physical education specialist who provides a developmentally appropriate program with adequate equipment and facilities. *Curriculum* includes a written plan for how standards-based outcomes will be attained by schools or school districts. *Appropriate instruction* is defined as allowing all students to have maximum practice opportunities for class activities in well-designed lessons that facilitate student learning. Quality programs also include *student assessments* throughout the curriculum. These assessments are aligned with state standards and the National Standards for K-12 Physical Education as well as program assessments (SHAPE America, 2015).

Developmental Appropriateness

Teaching to the developmental level of your students is easier said than done. Teachers have to make constant decisions about content so that the progression of tasks is appropriate

motivation/
self efficacy--

(Graham, 2008). Very similar to what you recognize when teaching academic lessons in your classroom, students' skill abilities vary greatly. Your job will be to plan appropriate activities that are not too hard or too easy for your students. This task is challenging, but understanding the importance of addressing this issue will create a better learning environment. See "Developmentally Appropriate Physical Education Resources" for some recommended resources that can help you.

Physical Literacy

Literacy is a general term used to represent basic knowledge, understanding, and application of reading and writing. Margaret Whitehead (2001) is a leading educator credited with defining the term "physical literacy." **Physical literacy** is "the ability to move with competence and confidence in a wide variety of physical activities in multiple environments that benefit the healthy development of the whole person" (Mandigo, Francis, Lodewyk, & Lopez, 2012, p. 28; Whitehead, 2001). In 2013, SHAPE America added the term "the physically literate individual" to replace "the physically educated individual" in the National Standards for K-12 Physical Education.

Schools can address physical literacy by providing high-quality physical education. Students need to move with competence and confidence in a wide variety of physical activities. The best method for accomplishing this goal is for elementary schools to hire degree-certified physical education teachers who have the training to provide a strong physical education program for the school. A physical educator has the knowledge and training necessary to identify and teach critical elements needed for proficiency in fundamental skills and movement concepts. To develop physical literacy in their elementary students, the physical educator and the classroom teacher must work as a team. If the school does not have a degree-certified physical educator in the school, the classroom teacher is responsible for providing the physical education requirements for students. Having this responsibility means that classroom teachers must know and understand the five National Standards for K-12 Physical Education.

Motor development is the overall goal of the first two standards. Fitness development is the goal of third standard. Social development is the main goal of Standards 4 and 5. Quality physical education programs address all 5 standards.

 Developmentally Appropriate Physical Education Resources

The following resources are helpful for planning appropriate activities for your students.

- *Best Practices for Physical Activity: A Guide to Help Children Grow Up Healthy* at www.nemours.org/content/dam/nemours/www/filebox/service/preventive/nhps/paguidelines.pdf
- Play and Children's Learning at www.naeyc.org/play

Including students with disabilities can also be a challenge in a physical activity setting. An excellent free resource for you is Discover Inclusive Physical Education: A Guidebook for Educators. This document can be found at www.nchpad.org/fppics/Discover%20Inclusive%20Physical%20Education-Final.pdf.

Standard 1

National Standard 1 states, "The physically literate individual demonstrates competency in a variety of motor skills and movement patterns" (SHAPE America, 2014, p. 12). The foundation skills for a physically literate individual include fundamental skills (nonlocomotor/nonmanipulative skills, locomotor/transport skills, manipulative skills) and movement concepts. **Nonlocomotor/nonmanipulative skills** are skills that do not require moving from one place to another or using the hands and fingers. They include twisting, turning (in place), leaning, stretching, curling, bending, swinging, balancing, and weight transfer. **Locomotor/transport skills** move the body from one place to another. They include walking, jogging, running, hopping (one foot), jumping (two feet), skipping, galloping, sliding, leaping, chasing, fleeing, and dodging. **Manipulative skills** mostly involve using the hands or feet, but other body parts can also be used. They include throwing, catching, kicking, punting, dribbling, volleying, and striking (Graham, Holt/Hale, & Parker, 2012; Pangrazi & Beighle, 2013).

The best practice for teaching motor skills and movement patterns is to break down each one into critical elements for each phase of the skill (preparation, execution, and follow-through). **Critical elements** are the key observable components of a motor skill. Appropriate cues are created to help students focus on the critical elements and practice skills correctly. Two examples of this practice are shown in table 4.1.

Teachers can create their own charts of critical elements to use as handouts for the students; or the charts can be posted at skill stations in the classroom, gym, or field. Using this method to teach skills gives you and your students specific elements to focus on during skill instruction. It also aids in giving feedback and assessments; you can list specific elements that help improve skill development.

After analyzing the skill and breaking it down into critical elements and cues, brainstorm common performance errors and possible factors to address to help correct the errors. Be prepared for students to make errors when performing motor skills. Thinking through possible errors and possible solutions helps to create a successful learning environment. Table 4.2 lists common errors and some factors to consider in correcting them.

Table 4.1 Critical Elements and Cues for Phases of Skipping and Overhand Throw

Phase	Critical elements	Cues
Skipping		
Preparation	■ Eyes are forward; body faces forward. ■ Feet are slightly staggered at shoulder width.	
Execution	■ Step on one foot, then hop on that same foot; repeat on the other foot. ■ While skipping, swing arms opposite of the hopping leg.	Step Hop
Follow-through	Land lightly on the balls of the feet. Skipping is a continuous skill.	
Overhand throw		
Preparation	■ Have the throwing arm in an L-shaped position. ■ Open the chest with the elbow of the nonthrowing arm pointed toward the target.	L Open
Execution	■ Step in opposition with your toe. ■ Close the chest.	Step Close
Follow-through	■ Cross your arm in front of your body. ■ All of your body weight is on the front leg.	

Table 4.2 Common Errors and Considerations for Correcting Them

Common error	Factors to consider
Missing one or more of the critical elements of the skill	Breaking down the skill into parts
Equipment creating a problem (too large/small or too light/heavy)	Modifying equipment
Missing the target due to distance—too far away	Making the space larger or smaller
Missing the target due to distance—too challenging	Changing the goal (intent) of drill
Hard to complete task due to size of group	Increasing or decreasing the number of people
Defender makes practice too difficult	Changing the conditions of performance
Lack of scoring	Changing the rules to remove goalie

For example, you might observe that some students are not swinging arms in opposition to the hopping leg when skipping. Because the students are missing one or more critical elements of the skill, the remedy is to break the skill into parts (see first row of table 4.2). You could repeat the cues for the critical elements that include the *hop*. Break the skill down further, having the student perform the skill in slow motion. This breaking down of skills allows the student to concentrate on the opposite arm swing while it is exaggerated in slow motion. Consider a case where students performing the overhand throw are not stepping in opposition. Again, you would repeat the cues for the critical elements that include the *step*. Break the skill down further by having the student put all of the body weight on the leg that you do not want him to step on. Have him shift weight forward to the opposite foot to correct the error.

Several errors will be listed for each skill. Your job as a teacher is to think through the errors before teaching the skill in order to be better prepared to help correct the errors.

After identifying the critical elements and possible errors of skills, plan for the teaching progression of the skills. After completing the progression steps needed, identify the plan to check student progress. This will give you the information needed to know when students are ready to move to the next step in the sequence. You can use task challenges or assessments to check student progress. Using a chart like the one in table 4.3 can help in more effective lesson preparations.

Teachers need to be aware of the scope and sequence of all motor skills and movement patterns. An excellent resource is *National Standards & Grade Level Outcomes for K-12 Physical Education* (SHAPE America, 2014).

Take a look at the sequence for locomotor skills in Standard 1 by reviewing K-5 Grade-Level Outcomes (table 4.4). Standard 1 Outcome S1.E1 addresses hopping, galloping, running, sliding, skipping, and leaping. Notice that according to the standard all kindergarten students should be taught most of the locomotor skills, but they are not expected to show a mature form until later grades. Hopping, galloping, jogging, and sliding should be mastered by the end of the first grade, followed by skipping (second grade) and leaping (third grade). This document is an excellent resource for all teachers, because it details a progressive scope and sequence of all skills needed for becoming a physically literate student.

Standard 2

National Standard 2 states, "The physically literate individual applies knowledge of concepts, principles, strategies and tactics related to movement and performance" (SHAPE America, 2014, p. 12). Movement concept skills are also important and are divided into these three categories:

- **Space awareness**
- **Effort**
- **Relationship**

Table 4.3 Sample Teaching Progression and Assessments for Skipping and Overhand Throw

Step	Teaching progression (basic technique—drills—game play)	Challenges/assessments
Skipping		
1	Stand facing the direction of travel and practice, stepping on one foot and then rolling up on the toes of that foot.	Can the students step and roll correctly?
2	Add the hop to step 1.	Can the students step, hop?
3	Focus on the arms swinging in opposition during execution of the skip.	Can the students swing arms in opposition while correctly performing skipping?
4	Perform exaggerated skips where the steps are long and the hops are high.	Can the students skip using proper form? Increase the distance between skips using proper technique.
5	Perform quick skips where the steps are short and the hops are low.	Can the students skip using proper form? Increase the speed of the skips using proper technique.
Overhand throw		
1	Prepare the throwing arm using the L cue.	Can the students show the difference in an L and the arm being in an inappropriate V position?
2	Open the body where the elbow of the nonthrowing arm is pointing toward the target.	Can the students turn the body to show the open ready position?
3	Throw a ball to a stationary target focusing on stepping in opposition to the throwing arm.	Can the students use the L and open step?
4	Throw a ball to a stationary target working on closing the shoulders and trunk to help produce force and proper follow-through.	Can the students throw using proper form to a stationary target? As students consistently hit the target using proper technique, increase the distance from the stationary target.
5	Throw to a moving target using correct form.	Can the students throw using proper form to a moving target? As students consistently hit the target, increase the distance from the moving target.

Movement concepts are important to understand separately as well as apply during motor skill instruction.

The category that classroom teachers can easily identify is the understanding of *space awareness* (where the body moves). To teach this concept, you need to explain space in the following terms:

- Location (self-space, general space)
- Direction (forward/backward, left/right, up/down, clockwise/counterclockwise)
- Level (low, medium, high)
- Pathways (straight, curved, zigzag)
- Extension (small/large, far/near)

Table 4.4 Sample Grade-Level Outcomes for Standard 1

Standard 1	Kindergarten	Grade 1	Grade 2	Grade 3	Grade 4	Grade 5
Demonstrates competency in a variety of motor skills and movement patterns.						
***S1.E1 Locomotor* Hopping, galloping, running, sliding, skipping, leaping**	Performs loco-motor skills (hopping, galloping, running, sliding, skipping) while maintaining balance. (S1.E1.K)	Hops, gallops, jogs, and slides using a mature pattern. (S1.E1.1)	Skips using a mature pattern. (S1.E1.2)	Leaps using a mature pattern. (S1.E1.3)	Uses various locomotor skills in a variety of small-sided practice tasks, dance, and educational gymnastics experiences. (S1.E1.4)	Demonstrates mature patterns of locomotor skills in dynamic small-sided practice tasks, gymnastics, and dance. (S1.E1.5a) Combines locomotor and manipulative skills in a variety of small-sided practice tasks and games environments. (S1.E1.5b) Combines traveling with manipulative skills for execution to a target (e.g., scoring in soccer, hockey, and basketball). (S1.E1.5c)

Reprinted from SHAPE America. (2014). *National standards & grade-level outcomes for K-12 physical education* (Champaign, IL: Human Kinetics), 26.

To help students understand personal space, have them explore all of the previous terms through moving in various ways while not interfering with others' personal space (Graham, Holt/Hale, & Parker, 2012; Pangrazi & Beighle, 2013).

Movement concepts in the *effort* category include concepts of how the body moves. Effort is focused on the quality of the movement. Those concepts (Graham, Holt/Hale, Parker, 2012; Pangrazi & Beighle, 2013) are listed here:

- Time or speed (fast/slow)
- Force (strong/light)
- Flow (bound/free)

Movement concepts in the *relationship* category include concepts involving relationship of the body, relationships with objects and others, and relationships with people. *Relationship of the body* includes round (curved), narrow, wide, twisted, and symmetrical/asymmetrical. *Relationship with objects and others* includes over/under, on/off, near/far, along/through, in front/behind, meeting/parting, surrounding, around, and alongside. *Relationship with people* includes leading/following, mirroring/matching, unison/contrast, solo, partners, between groups, within groups, and alone in a mass (Graham, Holt/Hale, & Parker, 2012; Pangrazi & Beighle, 2013).

Look at a Standard 2 progression by reviewing the Grade-Level Outcomes for a *space awareness* concept (table 4.5). Standard 2 Outcome S2.E2 involves pathways, shapes, and levels. According to the chart, kindergarteners are introduced to pathways first (straight, curved, and zigzag). In first grade, teachers should be covering traveling in levels as well as traveling over, under, around, and through objects. In second grade, children should be able to combine shapes, levels, and pathways into simple travel, dance, and gymnastics sequences. By the end of the third grade, students should be able to recognize locomotor skills specific to a wide variety of physical activities. Space awareness changes in the fourth and fifth grades. Fourth graders should be able to combine movement concepts with skills in small-sided practice tasks, gymnastics, and dance environments. Fifth grade is similar to the outcome for fourth grade, but games are added along with student self-direction.

By the end of fifth grade, "students should be able to demonstrate, through their performance of movement tasks, an understanding of how their bodies move in space and should be starting to apply this understanding to some specific contexts, namely dance, gymnastics, and games (Mitchell & Walton-Fisette, 2016, p.

55). An excellent resource for classroom teachers who will be teaching physical education to their students is the textbook *The Essentials of Teaching Physical Education* (Mitchell & Walton-Fisette, 2016).

Standard 3

Along with teaching movement skills and concepts, classroom teachers need to also address the fitness needs of the children. National Standard 3 states, "The physically literate individual demonstrates the knowledge and skills to achieve and maintain a health-enhancing level of physical activity and fitness" (SHAPE America, 2014, p. 12). Achieving and maintaining fitness is a daily process. Developing the knowledge and skills of physical activity and fitness concepts enables students to know what is expected in order to achieve and maintain their personal physical activity and fitness levels. A good fitness development resource for elementary classroom teachers is the SPARK curriculum. SPARK, which stands for Sports, Play, and Active Recreation for Kids, is an elementary physical education curriculum that

Table 4.5 Sample Grade-Level Outcomes for Standard 2

Standard 2	Kindergarten	Grade 1	Grade 2	Grade 3	Grade 4	Grade 5
Applies knowledge of concepts, principles, strategies and tactics related to movement and performance.						
S2.E2 Pathways, shapes, levels	Travels in 3 different pathways. (S2.E2.K)	Travels demonstrating low, middle and high levels. (S2.E2.1a) Travels demonstrating a variety of relationships with objects (e.g., over, under, around, through). (S2.E2.1b)	Combines shapes, levels and pathways into simple travel, dance and gymnastics sequences. (S2.E2.2)	Recognizes locomotor skills specific to a wide variety of physical activities. (S2.E2.3)	Combines movement concepts with skills in small-sided practice tasks, gymnastics and dance environments. (S2.E2.4)	Combines movement concepts with skills in small-sided practice tasks and games environments, gymnastics and dance with self-direction. (S2.E2.5)

Reprinted from SHAPE America. (2014). *National standards & grade-level outcomes for K-12 physical education* (Champaign, IL: Human Kinetics), 32.

includes health-related fitness activities as well as skill-related fitness activities (McKenzie, Rosengard, & Willison, 2006).

Organization and planning skills can aid in the development of fitness in elementary students. Teachers should organize activities with maximum participation of all students as the focus. Designing activities to be played in small groups is one way you can organize activities that promote fitness development. Combining a focus on a fitness component (cardiovascular endurance, muscular strength, muscular endurance, flexibility, or body composition) with motor skill activities can help students understand the important connection of motor skill development and fitness development. For example, the use of stations (odd stations for motor skills and even stations for fitness skills) enables excellent use of limited equipment as well as provides the perfect combination of work and active rest for students participating in the stations. The focus of the kicking fitness stations could be muscular strength exercises targeting leg muscles.

Table 4.6 presents a Standard 3 progressive sequence for a fitness concept. Standard 3 Outcome S3.E3 addresses fitness knowledge. The progression of fitness knowledge moves from kindergarten students recognizing the heart rate increases with activity to fifth graders understanding the difference between skill-related and health-related fitness. As you might expect, the knowledge outcomes are clearly different in the K-5 **grade band**. This knowledge is critical in order for students to make informed decisions about their personal fitness.

Standard 4

Developing social skills is also important in a quality physical education program. National Standard 4 states, "The physically literate individual exhibits responsible personal and social behavior that respects self and others" (SHAPE America, 2014, p. 12). A quality program works to help children develop the social skills needed in order to interact well with others as well as apply those skills, such as displaying

Table 4.6 Sample Grade-Level Outcomes for Standard 3

Standard 3	Kindergarten	Grade 1	Grade 2	Grade 3	Grade 4	Grade 5
Demonstrates the knowledge and skills to achieve and maintain a health-enhancing level of physical activity and fitness.						
S3.E3 Fitness knowledge	Recognizes that when you move fast, your heart beats faster and you breathe faster. (S3.E3.K)	Identifies the heart as a muscle that grows stronger with exercise/play and physical activity. (S3.E3.1)	Recognizes the use of the body as resistance (e.g., holds body in plank position, animal walks) for developing strength. (S3.E3.2a) Identifies physical activities that contribute to fitness. (S3.E3.2b)	Describes the concept of fitness and provides examples of physical activity to enhance fitness. (S3.E3.3)	Identifies the components of health-related fitness. (S3.E3.4)	Differentiates between skill-related and health-related fitness. (S3.E3.5)

Reprinted from SHAPE America. (2014). *National standards & grade-level outcomes for K-12 physical education* (Champaign, IL: Human Kinetics), 34.

good sporting behavior. Students must accept personal responsibility for their behavior. This behavior involves following rules, respecting others, accepting peers of all ability levels, accepting feedback from others, displaying good sporting behavior, and focusing on playing safely. Standard 4 is a standard all teachers want to see in their classroom and gyms, but they often do not specifically design activities to address these important social skills.

A quick review of the Standard 4 sequence for the concept of working together is revealed in table 4.7. Standard 4 Outcome S4.E4 is all about students working together. This is a concept that every elementary classroom teacher uses in the classroom each day. The expectation is that kindergarten students can learn to share equipment and space with their classmates. First and second graders are expected to work independently with others in small and large groups (first grade) and in partners (second grade). By third grade, students should be able to work cooperatively and to recognize their peers' successful work. All fourth graders should be inclusive of their peers no matter what skill level they have, and by fifth grade students work well with others by accepting, recognizing, and involving all skill groups in activities.

Standard 5

National Standard 5 states, "The physically literate individual recognizes the value of physical activity for health, enjoyment, challenge, self-expression and/or social interaction" (SHAPE America, 2014, p. 12). Helping students find joy in movement is a critical component to developing physically literate individuals. Some teachers steal the joy of movement by constantly telling students to sit down, stop moving around, or be still. Some even use physical activity to punish students when they break a rule, such as run a lap for being late, drop down and do push-ups for talking back, or wall sit for being out of your seat. All teachers should focus on helping students value physical activity. Helping students find the joy of movement starts with your own attitude toward activity. Teaching Standard 5 offers excellent life lessons, such as education on the health benefits of physical activity, the challenge to persevere when activities are difficult, the need to display positive self-expressions, and the importance of interacting socially.

Table 4.7 Sample Grade-Level Outcomes for Standard 4

Standard 4	Kindergarten	Grade 1	Grade 2	Grade 3	Grade 4	Grade 5
Exhibits responsible personal and social behavior that respects self and others.						
S4.E4 Working with others	Shares equipment and space with others. (S4.E4.K)	Works independently with others in a variety of class environments (e.g., small & large groups). (S4.E4.1)	Works independently with others in partner environments. (S4.E4.2)	Works cooperatively with others. (S4.E4.3a) Praises others for their success in movement performance. (S4.E4.3b)	Praises the movement performance of others both more- and less-skilled. (S4.E4.4a) Accepts players of all skill levels into the physical activity. (S4.E4.4b)	Accepts, recognizes, and actively involves others with both higher and lower skill abilities into physical activities and group projects. (S4.E4.5)

Reprinted from SHAPE America. (2014). *National standards & grade-level outcomes for K-12 physical education* (Champaign, IL: Human Kinetics), 36.

Table 4.8 shows a specific Standard 5 progression involving self-expression and enjoyment. This set of outcomes is interesting because it is hard to objectively assess enjoyment. However, the outcome expectations give you specific things to look for across the K-5 band. In kindergarten, students should be able to identify enjoyable activities and discuss the enjoyment of playing with friends. First graders can describe positive feelings that they have when playing in certain activities and discuss the reasons they enjoy the activities. Self-expression is the focus in the second grade as students identify physical activities that allow them to use self-expression. Reflection on the enjoyment of a favorite activity is the expectation of third graders. All fourth graders should be able to rank activities depending on their enjoyment of playing the activity or game. By the end of the fifth grade, students should be able to analyze physical activities according to enjoyment and challenge level and to identify the positive and negative feelings about the activities.

The National Standards for K-12 Physical Education are broad. The Grade-Level Outcomes provide the details that teachers need to address the standards. Teachers who use these outcomes will help their students to have the opportunity to become physically literate.

Summary

Developing physically literate individuals is not an easy task. This task involves a schoolwide effort. Physical activity should be offered before, during, and after school. Classroom teachers should create an active classroom environment. Administrators should demand more accountability of the physical education program to address the National Standards for K-12 Physical Education and their accompanying Grade-Level Outcomes. Students need your help so that they can have the skills to participate in physical activities, know the benefits of participation, participate regularly, be physically fit, and value a healthy lifestyle. The physical literacy of your students is up to you.

Table 4.8 Sample Grade-Level Outcomes for Standard 5

Standard 5	Kindergarten	Grade 1	Grade 2	Grade 3	Grade 4	Grade 5
Recognizes the value of physical activity for health, enjoyment, challenge, self-expression and/or social interaction.						
S5.E3 Self-expression/enjoyment	Identifies physical activities that are enjoyable. (S5.E3.Ka) Discusses the enjoyment of playing with friends. (S5.E3.Kb)	Describes positive feelings that result from participating in physical activities. (S5.E3.1a) Discusses personal reasons (i.e., the "why") for enjoying physical activities. (S5.E3.1b)	Identifies physical activities that provide self-expression (e.g., dance, gymnastics routines, practice tasks/games environment). (S5.E3.2)	Reflects on the reasons for enjoying selected physical activities. (S5.E3.3)	Ranks the enjoyment of participating in different physical activities. (S5.E3.4)	Analyzes different physical activities for enjoyment and challenge, identifying reasons for a positive or negative response. (S5.E5.5)

Reprinted from SHAPE America. (2014). *National standards & grade-level outcomes for K-12 physical education* (Champaign, IL: Human Kinetics), 37.

Review Questions

1. What are three benefits of physical activity?

2. What is the difference between physical education and physical activity?

3. What are the four essential components to a quality physical education program?

4. What is physical literacy?

5. Describe the five National Standards for K-12 Physical Education.

Part II

How to Integrate Health and Physical Education Into the Classroom

Chapter 5

Advocating for a Healthy, Active School

Objectives

- Define advocacy.
- Describe why classroom teachers are in the perfect position to be advocates for healthy, active schools.
- Describe the need for advocating for a healthy, active school.
- List advocacy ideas that a classroom teacher could use in the classroom.
- List advocacy ideas to use in the school.
- List advocacy ideas to use with parents and in the community.
- List advocacy tips using a media source.
- List advocacy tips for policymakers and administrators.

Healthy citizens are the greatest asset any country can have.

Winston Churchill

The word "advocacy" is often misunderstood. Some people think that advocacy is someone else's job. Others think that you have to be an extremist in order to be an advocate. Neither of those perceptions is correct. Advocacy is something all people do—whether they know it or not—which means that you, too, are an advocate. This chapter defines advocacy, explains your role as an advocate, and gives you tools for advocating more effectively.

Advocacy can be defined in many ways:

- An action directed at changing the policies, positions, or programs of an institution

- Pleading for, defending, or recommending an idea before other people

- Speaking up, drawing a community's attention to an important issue, and directing decision makers toward a solution

- Putting a problem on the agenda, providing a solution to that problem, and building support for acting on both the problem and the solution

- Influencing the decision-making process at any and all administrative levels

Actions in the previous definitions of advocacy include *changing, pleading, defending, recommending, speaking, drawing, directing, putting, providing, building,* and *influencing*. The most important action word not listed here is *participating*. Through active participation, **advocacy** is a powerful set of action-based strategies through which people are engaged in the decision-making processes that affect their lives and the lives of others.

Teachers are in the perfect position to be advocates for healthy, active schools. Classroom teachers are role models for students and should be aware that they are advocates even without trying to be. Students watch everything that the teacher does, says, wears, eats, and drinks. Knowing this fact, you can use this powerful position to change opinions and behavior toward a healthier direction.

Chapters 1 through 4 give numerous reasons U.S. communities need to create healthier, more active schools. These reasons include the increase of health issues of students, specifically obesity and diabetes; low levels of physical activity and poor nutrition habits of young peo-

Advocating for More Physical Activity in School

Educating the Student Body: Taking Physical Activity and Physical Education to School (www.iom.edu/Reports/2013/Educating-the-Student-Body-Taking-Physical-Activity-and-Physical-Education-to-School.aspx) is an excellent resource for advocating for healthy, active schools. Sponsored by the Institute of Medicine, this resource includes a video, action guide, printable material, and the report itself. Included is an interactive website that provides creative ideas for getting busy kids active for 60 minutes each day before, during, and after school.

ple; and the positive link between academic achievement and wellness. Knowing about the growing need for wellness, classroom teachers should try to find strategies to advocate for healthy, active living not only to their own students but also in the school and surrounding community.

The following ideas are not organized in order of priority. They are suggestions for classroom teachers to help start them on a journey of daily advocacy efforts for a healthy, active school.

Advocacy in the Classroom

The classroom is an excellent venue in which the teacher has control of everything the students see and hear. It is a powerful forum, so as a teacher you must use it wisely and appropriately. The walls, boards, desks, and floor become places where positive messages can be displayed. Pictures, posters, signs, favorite sayings, words of the day, and longer messages can be on visual display. Another example of a positive visual message is displaying a collage of pictures of children playing or demonstrating good behaviors. This kind of visual display is a great motivational tool to encourage others to participate so that they, too, can have their picture taken.

Keep in mind that everyone likes praise. Promoting healthy practices by giving extrinsic awards may concern some people, but everyone needs a boost of motivation in order to make good choices. Students seeing other students getting an award may be encouraged to demonstrate the same healthy behavior. Examples of awards can be as simple as a pat on the back, a certificate, or a name listed on the wall.

Another great motivational idea is increasing the activity in the classroom. Teachers can encourage students to get out of their seat, especially when the students are tired. Have the students move from an activity space to their desks, then back to another area. Movement is innate but many classroom teachers have shut it down by always telling students to sit down or stay still. Asking them to sit still does not send a positive message about being physically active. You can choose to have your students get up and be active while still paying attention to academics.

Teachers need to be careful with the messages they send to students. Some teachers have used exercise as punishment, which creates a negative association with the exercise; it leaves the impression that if you are performing this exercise, it is a punishment later in life. Punishing by removing activity is also not appropriate. Alternative consequences could be not receiving positive behavior rewards, not being allowed to choose special activities when work is completed, or moving to a timeout to think about what was the inappropriate behavior and how to change it to exit timeout.

Practicing good health habits in the classroom is another way to be a positive wellness advocate. Practicing the correct way to cough, sneeze, brush and floss teeth, and wash hands are just a few habits that you can encourage during the school day. Examples include encouraging students to follow correct coughing and sneezing procedures in class, allowing time to disinfect desks—especially during flu season, and in February (in the United States, Children's Dental Health Month) have dentists come to class and provide free toothbrushes and floss and demonstrate the proper techniques to use them.

Teachers can bring in motivational speakers to the classroom. Children see many people as role models. Some adults are not healthy role models, but many others are. Identify local role models, then ask them to come to your classroom to speak to your students during the school year. Having guest speakers who can motivate your students can help promote a healthy, active lifestyle. Examples include high school athletes, community athletes, and community leaders in all professional areas.

As students leave for the day, consider assigning home*play* work that involves the students engaging in activity at home. Examples include counting the number of steps it takes to walk around the house, collecting leaves in the neighborhood and bringing them to class for a discussion on trees, and checking the heart rate of the family while playing an activity together.

The classroom is a powerful place to be an advocate. Remember that simply by being in the role of a teacher, you are advocating something every day.

Advocacy in the School

Just like the classroom walls, the walls throughout the school (e.g., hallways) are perfect places to send wellness messages. Displaying student work (such as artwork or assignments) that models healthy behaviors beyond the walls of your classroom is an excellent advocacy project that impacts more than just your own students. Examples include drawings of others performing healthy, active behaviors; reports on sport heroes; pictures of healthy nutrition choices; and posters discouraging bullying. The school intercom is a great medium for providing healthy tips or quotes for the day. Instead of the principal or a teacher reading the tip or quote, have a student read it, using the power of voice to encourage others to listen and learn.

Joining with other classroom teachers to work on a healthy and active project can increase the motivation and participation of the students. For example, recycling trash collected in school can be a worthy project that enhances the beauty of the campus as well as helps students participate in a healthy project. Competing in a walk-a-thon or other active event to promote health awareness is another example. Teachers may collaborate to promote heart health by distributing heart-healthy recipes in the month of February (American Heart Month) and have heart-healthy food and snacks in school.

Another school advocacy idea is to create a school wellness calendar for the year and have the entire school celebrate each of them. Table 5.1 shows an example.

Teachers need wellness, too. During each month, with your fellow teachers take turns leading employee wellness events. Encouraging the faculty and staff to create walking groups before and after school is a perfect way to start this process. Others may be interested in other forms of wellness events. Examples include aerobics, weightlifting, or yoga classes; professional development hours in stress management or

nutrition education; and opportunities to play team sports within the school or district.

Find Other National Health Observances

National health observances are listed on the website www.healthfinder.gov/nho/default.aspx. This site also lists many more health issues. In addition, it includes toolkits that you can download and use to promote the health awareness in your classroom.

Table 5.1 Sample School Wellness Calendar

January	National Hobby Month
	National Drug Fact Week
February	American Heart Month
	National Children's Dental Health Month
March	National Nutrition Month
April	Sports Eye Safety Month
	World Health Day (First Monday of April)
	Earth Day and Environmental Health
May	National Physical Fitness and Sport Month
	National Physical Education and Sport Week (First week of May)
June	National Great Outdoors Month
	National Safety Month
July	Eye Injury Prevention Month
August	Children's Eye Health and Safety Month
	National Immunization Awareness Month
September	Fruits and Veggies—More Matters Month
	National Childhood Obesity Awareness Month
	FEMA National Preparedness Month
October	Health Literacy Month
	National Bullying Prevention Month
November	American Diabetes Month
December	Safe Toys and Gifts Month
	National Influenza Vaccination Week

Advocacy Ideas for Parents and the Community

Parents and caregivers of elementary children need to hear from the teacher. Having a weekly or monthly newsletter is an excellent advocacy tool. You can educate both the students and their parents and caregivers with this newsletter. With today's technology, your newsletter can be sent electronically at no cost to you or the school. Some teachers may prefer to use a website. Knowing your community and what they have access to will determine how you share your messages. Here are some examples of newsletter topics: Choose a health topic to focus on each month, and include an article on it; provide information on healthy snacks for school and for the family; and give tips on how to cook healthy meals for children, perhaps providing healthy recipes of the month.

PTA/PTO meetings are great places to share information. A wellness topic or wellness speaker could provide a lecture. A cooking class could be provided for parents and caregivers to help teach healthy cooking skills or provide a testing table of healthy foods and recipes. Having a parent–child activity night in the gym after PTA/PTO could also be a great advocacy event.

Report cards are great sources of information. Teachers could add healthy behaviors to the report card. Examples include excellence in proper handwashing, good manners while eating, and good display of sporting behavior.

Teachers can create positive relationships with community members by hosting events in the community. Examples include organizing an event that demonstrates healthy activities where everyone in the community can participate, and sponsoring a 5K or 10K that the community can participate in as a group for a worthy fundraising event. Bringing community leaders into the school and making them part of the wellness program in the school will reap benefits for everyone involved.

Parents and caregivers need to be educated and involved in the school wellness process. Having this involvement will enable healthy, active living to go beyond the school hours. A school is stronger with a supportive community.

Advocacy Tips for Using a Media Source

Teachers may be asked to promote a school wellness event by giving an interview on a specific topic. The following tips may be helpful to teachers preparing for an interview.

Interviews can be produced in several formats: visual (TV, public appearances), auditory (radio, podcast), or written (local paper, social media). Special considerations are needed for all of these formats.

Visual Interviews

- **Do** wear grey, brown, or navy blue.
- **Don't** wear busy patterns, stripes, plaids, or checks.
- **Do** wear natural tone makeup.
- **Don't** wear large jewelry.
- **Do** talk in ordinary conversational tones.
- **Don't** talk with added *ums* and *uhs*.
- **Do** look at the interviewer.
- **Don't** talk to the camera.

Auditory Interviews

- **Do** talk in ordinary conversational tones.
- **Don't** talk with added *ums* and *uhs*.
- **Do** speak with passion.
- **Don't** allow your emotions to get in the way of making a point.
- **Do** answer the questions thoroughly.
- **Don't** rush your answer.
- **Do** be descriptive since there is not a visual (radio).
- **Don't** confuse the audience with scientific jargon.

Written Interviews or Statements

- **Do** state who you are, what you are doing, and why.
- **Don't** be mysterious or anonymous.
- **Do** use a headline that is short and grabs attention.
- **Don't** create a headline that is negative.
- **Do** be factual.
- **Don't** stretch the truth.

- **Do** be clear and concise by using simple words and sentences when using social media.
- **Don't** overstate your point or you will lose your audience in social media.
- **Do** use pictures if you have the chance.
- **Don't** use pictures of students without parent permission.

Advocacy Tips for Policymakers and Administrators

At times a classroom teacher may need to present an idea to a policymaker or administrator in order to create a change in a policy or to get permission to complete an advocacy project. It might be as easy as going in to the principal's office and requesting permission to be involved in a project or event. It may be a meeting with the school leaders to encourage the implementation of the school wellness plan. The idea may need a full faculty vote, such as when encouraging the school to remove unhealthy vending choices or eliminating donut and cookie sales from school fundraising choices.

Some advocacy ideas may involve school district policies that need to be changed, such as

SHAPE America Advocacy Resources

The SHAPE America website provides great advocacy resources. One in particular is the position statement on recess for elementary school students. You can find it at www.shapeamerica.org/advocacy/positionstatements/pa/loader.cfm?csModule = security/getfile&page-id = 4630. For other advocacy resources, go to www.shapeamerica.org/advocacy/positionstatements/pa/index.cfm.

adding time for recess in the school day. Some school boards may allow you to walk up and discuss your ideas on the day of a meeting, but others may require that you be added to the agenda in order to speak to the board.

Speaking in front of a group can be frightening for some people, and few educators have taken courses in advocacy. Tables 5.2 and 5.3 help educate all teachers on how to talk to people outside of the school.

To find information on your local, state, or national policymaker, go to www.congress.org. Then, type in your zip code.

When writing a letter to a policymaker, use the following guidelines:

- State your purpose for writing in the first paragraph of the letter. If your letter pertains to a specific piece of legislation, identify it accordingly (e.g., House bill: H.R. ____, Senate bill: S.____).
- Address only one issue in each letter; and, if possible, keep the letter to one page.
- Be friendly. Get to know your policymaker. Try to maintain contact throughout the year.
- Be courteous. Do not threaten or try to coerce. Put yourself in their place to try to understand his or her problems, outlooks, and aims.
- Be accurate and factual. You can establish trust and credibility with the correct facts.
- Handwritten letters are the best. Do not send a form letter or a postcard.
- Thank-you letters are a great follow-up! The importance of showing gratitude cannot be overemphasized.

When sending an e-mail message, do the following:

- Type a specific bill number or issue in the subject line.
- Include your name and home address.
- Follow the same advice as for writing letters.

Table 5.2 How to Present Your Message in 15 Minutes to Your Policymaker in a Personal Visit

Time (min.)	Description	Considerations
0-3	Introductions	Be on time. Establish connections.
3-10	Message	Deliver four clear points. Give personal stories. Provide state-specific facts and statistics. Engage the member.
10-13	Request	Designated spokesperson makes request. Ask for specific actions. Stay on topic.
13-15	Listen	Listen to the response. Record stance and any requests for follow-up.

Table 5.3 How to Present Your Message in 5 Minutes to Your Policymaker in a Phone Call

Time (min.)	Description	Considerations
0-2	Introductions	Identify yourself.
2-3	Message	Deliver four clear points. Be brief.
2-3	Request	Make request. (Be specific about bill numbers.) Ask for specific actions.
4-5	Listen	Listen to the response. Record stance and any requests for follow-up.

When addressing correspondence, use the following guides:

- Addressing to a Senator:

  The Honorable (Full Name)

  __(Rm.#)__(name of) Senate Office Building

  United States Senate

  Washington, DC 20510

  Dear Senator,

  [Close with your name and home address.]

- To a Representative:

  The Honorable (Full Name)

  __(Rm.#)__(name of) House Office Building

  United States House of Representatives

  Washington, DC 20515

  Dear Representative,

  [Close with your name and home address.]

- Note: When writing to the Chair of a Committee or the Speaker of the House, it is proper to address them as:

  Dear Mr. Chairman or Madam Chairwoman,

  or

  Dear Mr. Speaker,

Summary

Advocacy is a continuous process that involves educating students, faculty, staff, administration, parents, and community members throughout the year about the importance of achieving health and wellness in schools. Little things that a classroom teacher does, such as giving a pat on the back, displaying a picture, or hanging a poster for a health event, may be the motivating tools to get others involved in a wellness movement at school.

Success is often measured by wins and losses; however, true success is being competitive year after year. Advocacy success is often harder to measure. It may take months to change behavior and years to change a policy. No matter how long it takes, teachers who care about their students' health will fight the good fight. Administrators should support teachers in this fight. If this happens in a school, everyone wins.

Review Questions

1. Define advocacy.

2. Why should a classroom teacher be an advocate for healthy, active schools?

3. Name two advocacy ideas that a teacher could use in the classroom.

4. Name two advocacy ideas that could be used in the school.

5. Name two advocacy ideas that could be used with parents and caregivers and in the community.

6. Name two advocacy tips for visual interviews and two advocacy tips for auditory interviews.

7. Name five advocacy tips for policymakers and administrators.

Chapter 6

Creating a Healthy Classroom

Objectives

- Identify habits that promote everyday health in the classroom.
- Discuss how you can use the National Health Observances calendar in your classroom.
- Describe the signs of depression, suicide, and self-injury behavior in children.
- Identify indicators of child abuse and neglect.
- Discuss the importance of digital literacy and Internet safety.
- Describe the indicators of school violence and bullying and how to prevent it.
- Identify how to prevent disease transmission in your classroom.
- Define standard precautions.

True enjoyment comes from activity of the mind and exercise of the body; the two are united.

Alexander von Humboldt

As an elementary education major you may have taken courses that include how to appropriately manage your classroom, learning tips about collecting papers, distributing supplies, how to monitor unfinished assignments, and other essentials skills necessary for doing your job. This chapter provides tips that not only strengthen your students' academic experience but also support the health and wellness framework you are building for your classroom. The following strategies will help to foster a trusting and safe environment for you and your students.

Classroom Health for Every Day

Teachers know that the best reward for a job well done is a feeling of pride and accomplishment. This feeling is known as **intrinsic reward**, the internal payoff for accomplishing a goal. An **extrinsic reward** is something external and tangible given for an accomplishment. The intrinsic reward of satisfaction is worth far more than any extrinsic reward. **Incentives** are a form of extrinsic reward and may include anything that motivates someone to do something. Giving classroom incentives for individual students and the entire class can be an effective way to encourage positive behavior or celebrate accomplishments. It can be challenging to find incentives for good behavior that are no- or low-cost and healthful. Too many times pizza parties and cupcakes are the go-to incentives, but they send mixed messages to your students about health. Health experts advise that food should not be used as a reward or punishment. Schools should build on a healthy framework. Don't undo this work by using candy and other nutrition-poor foods as rewards in your classroom. Today's kids are already overwhelmed with unhealthy food choices. They face high risks of being overweight with chronic health conditions moving into adulthood. They need to be encouraged to make wise choices about food and healthy eating. Giving food as a reward in class causes difficulty and confusion for them. Psychologically, providing food based on performance or behavior connects food to mood. This practice can encourage children to eat when they are not hungry and can instill lifetime habits of rewarding themselves with food behaviors associated with unhealthy eating. Awarding children food during class also reinforces eating outside of meal or snack times.

Another important consideration is to avoid punitive practices connected to exercise, such as having students sit out at recess. This type of punishment prevents students from an important source of physical activity during the school day and from developing social skills. Children need the opportunity to blow off steam and socialize. It is not age appropriate for them to sit at a desk all day. When all students have recess, they have a better chance of being focused, better behaved, and ready to learn afterward. In fact, exercise is good for you, too. Grab a hula hoop or a ball, and join in as you model that exercise is fun.

As a teacher, it makes sense to follow health and physical education standards in instruction to help students attain related skills. However, make sure the classroom environment is conducive to health and wellness. Do not be hypocritical by giving out candy or junk food as classroom rewards or punish students by having them sit out of recess. Fortunately, effective and healthy ways exist to encourage positive behavior while setting an appropriate example of wellness. The following are ways to incentivize students for behavior, effort, and accomplishments that support health and wellness and foster connectedness in the classroom and school.

Recognition

- **Smile:** Treat each student with respect and kindness by making eye contact and smiling warmly. This gesture is a simple way to let your approval shine.

- **Friendly gesture:** A quick high five, pat on the back, thumbs-up, or handshake can go a long way in validating a student's efforts.

- **Spoken praise:** Identify a few students each class period, and find ways to individually praise something they did well. By the end of the week, every student in your class will have been praised. Remember to focus on the specific deed or achievement rather than on a general trait about the person. For example, instead of saying, "Katie, you are so smart," point out an accomplishment, saying, "Katie, give yourself a pat on the back for an awesome 19 out of 20 on your addition test!" Be available before and after school in case a student needs help or simply needs to talk to you. Praise students for good work as well as effort in completing tasks and assignments. You never know when your words of praise and encouragement will be the only ones a student hears all day.

- **Written praise:** Students thrive on a quick note to affirm positive behavior or accomplishments. It takes only a minute or two to jot a few warm words such as "Thank you, Kyle, for helping me sharpen pencils this morning. I felt rushed after my meeting ran late, and you were right there to help. I am lucky to have you in my class!" Keep a cheery notepad on your desk to remind you to find opportunities to build your students' confidence through the written word each day. In addition, on parent night, give parents index cards and pens to leave a written note of encouragement in their child's desk for them to find the next day.

- **Public announcements:** Recognizing a child's achievement on the schoolwide morning announcements is effective. A photo recognition board in a prominent location in the school is another way to publicly acknowledge a job well done.

- **Home communication:** Try calling, e-mailing, or sending a note to parents or guardians commending accomplishment. This incentive also reinforces the importance of health and wellness at home.

- **Class chant or cheer:** When students reach goals (such as reading a certain number of books or learning their 7s multiplication tables) give a class "Hip-hip hooray" or sing "For He's (or She's) a Jolly Good Fellow." The student being recognized can take a lap jogging around

Children need recognition for achievements in and out of the classroom.

the classroom and slapping five with class-mates during the cheer. When combined with sign language or clapping to a beat, this recognition is also a great way to incorporate physical activity into the classroom.

- **Assembly:** Every Friday have a class assembly during which each student gets to tell what she or he is most proud of that week; then the class applauds, snaps, gives a thumbs-up, or shows other signs of approval. It takes only a couple of seconds for each child, and it also gives them practice with speaking in front of a group.

Privileges

- Become a helper to the custodian, librarian, another teacher, or the office staff.
- Have lunch with a favorite person, fellow student (even one in another class or grade), principal, or teacher.
- Have an additional physical education period with another class. (Partner up with another teacher for this one.)
- Listen to the radio or a CD with headphones for a specified period of time.
- Be the leader for the first activity in gym class.
- Get an extra recess.
- Have additional computer time.
- Go on a field trip.
- Bring a special guest or buddy. Students may invite someone to visit the classroom, read a book, or give show and tell. This person may be anyone—a grandparent, older sibling, principal, or even the mayor.

School Supplies

- Pens, erasers, notepads or notebooks
- Stencils, stamps
- Highlighters, chalk (or sidewalk chalk), markers
- Puzzles, brain teasers, crossword puzzles

Sports Equipment

- Paddleball, flying disc, spongy ball
- Water bottle
- Hula hoop, jump rope

Lunchtime

Each day at lunchtime you have a wonderful opportunity to reinforce healthy habits with your students. Start by washing hands. Next, read the menu or have a student read the menu. Talk about the types of foods offered. Encourage your students to eat or sample their fruits and vegetables. You may want to give out inexpensive green stickers (the small round ones that are used for garage sales) to students who try the fruits and vegetables offered at lunch each day.

Lunchtime is also a great time for students to practice social skills and manners. Teach them how to make polite conversation using an appropriate volume, not to talk with their mouths full, how to use a napkin, and how to clean off their spot at the table when they are finished. Be clear about your expectations, and help students make strides socially. Make these rules clear at the beginning of the school year, and reinforce them with signage in the classroom that you reinforce with them periodically.

Remember that children are impressionable and imitate the adults around them. Like it or not, your students are influenced by your food and drink choices during the day. Are you eating cake left over in the teachers' lounge or drinking a couple of sodas each day in class? Do you drink water or eat an apple every day for a snack? Your students are taking note. When you are eating or drinking something healthy, point it out to them. You might be surprised by the results.

Finally, lunchtime is not a time for punishment. Isolation or having a silent lunch (where talking is not allowed) is not appropriate. On the contrary, this meal is an important socialization opportunity for children and a component of overall health.

Water and Bathroom Breaks

Only a few elementary classrooms are equipped with their own sink, water fountain, and toilet. You need to plan ahead of time for your students to meet their handwashing, hydration, and bathroom needs during the school day.

Water is essential to survival. The amount of water that elementary-aged children need each day varies from 1 to 3 liters. Children spend a large portion of their waking hours in the classroom. It is vital that they have access to water regularly. This is especially important after physical education or recess. Unfortunately, in the interest of time some teachers skip water breaks during the day or limit each child to one or two sips at the water fountain. This is not enough water for students to maintain optimal health and may lead to dehydration, fatigue, and illness. Encourage your students to bring a reusable water bottle from home so that they may drink water throughout the day. Remind your students to take the water bottles home and wash them daily. It is not safe to reuse empty bottled-water bottles. Put reusable water bottles on your classroom supply list at the beginning of the year to get your students off to a great start. Check school and district policy for approval.

Allow your students to use the restroom when they feel the need. It will be several times a day, especially if they are drinking enough water. Using the restroom is an essential bodily function that should not be ignored. It is not a privilege, and access should never be taken away as a punishment. Health consequences of delaying restroom needs could lead to urinary tract infections or impacted bowels. Also, be sensitive that some girls as young as third grade may already have begun menstruation.

Celebrations

Celebrations and special occasions can be opportunities for teachers to create a healthy classroom. Holidays and birthdays may be some of the biggest challenges to healthy eating. Experts strongly encourage schools to offer healthy food choices at classroom parties. It is best to provide written rules at the beginning of the school year concerning your policy about outside food. It could be that your school or district has already established a related policy. If not, clearly communicate that birthdays should be celebrated outside of class and that only healthy snacks and drinks will be allowed for class parties or holiday celebrations (e.g., no cupcakes or soda). Discuss this topic throughout the year with your room parent, especially when the holidays and the end of the school year are approaching. Be prepared that even with the best intentions, some well-meaning but uninformed parent may randomly show up at your class with a box of donuts at snack time. It happens. Be gracious, but stick to your resolve. You are there to be an advocate for your students' health. For healthy alternatives during in-class celebrations, rewards, fundraising, and snacks, check out www.tpchd.org/files/library/3379ffef0bb808ad.pdf.

Field Trips

Field trips can be a fun way to reinforce academic and health concepts. Similar to celebrations, parents and caregivers should be encouraged to pack a healthy lunch or snack if one is needed for the trip; send them reminders before the field trip. If a venue is providing the food during the field trip, check well in advance to make sure that healthy food and drink offerings are served and that allergy needs are addressed.

Field trips also provide an important opportunity to talk about safety. You are responsible for your students' safety at all times. Students should know their full names, phone numbers, and addresses before going on a class trip. Young students may require nametags or writing emergency contact information directly on their forearms with a permanent marker. Be sure to buckle up during transport. Remind students to stick with a buddy, and make sure that they have plenty of chaperones. If you plan to be outdoors, have students wear hats and sunscreen and have a plan to keep everyone hydrated on a hot day.

More Ideas for Classroom Celebrations

The Alliance for a Healthier Generation is a nonprofit organization dedicated to children's health. Their goal is to reduce the prevalence of childhood obesity and to empower kids to develop lifelong, healthy habits. Go to www.healthier-generation.org to find out more. Also, check out their ideas for healthy celebrating in schools at www.healthier-generation.org/_asset/nvgd8g/13-6162_HSPHealthyCelebration.pdf.

Once you have established a daily routine that is conducive to health, take a look at the school year. Many elementary teachers have monthly themes that are seasonal or related to holidays. Consider how you can keep health at the forefront of your classroom throughout the year.

Classroom Health Throughout the Year

Consider using the U.S. National Health Observances calendar (see http://healthfinder.gov/NHO) as a framework to promote health and increase awareness in your classroom. The possibilities are endless; use your imagination, and create a monthly calendar of two to four activities you plan to incorporate into your curriculum. The following text provides a suggestion for each month of the school year.

September: FEMA National Preparedness Month

Children like to be prepared and know what is going to happen in all aspects of their lives. Severe weather or impending disasters can be scary. Empower students, and help them to reduce anxiety by having a plan and supplies in case of emergency. Encourage families to meet together and develop a family plan for emergencies. Go to www.ready.gov/kids/make-a-plan for practice pages to use in class.

October: National Bullying Prevention Month

Create a weeklong event that culminates with students creating a story, poem, artwork, or video on the topic of bullying prevention. For more ideas on how to promote a bully-free school, go to www.pacer.org/bullying/nbpm. Focus on making friends and accepting others. Give your students the tools to stand up for themselves and others.

November: American Diabetes Month

Use the core curriculum to develop lessons on various aspects of diabetes-related topics. For example, in science teach how the body's organs are affected by diabetes. In math, have students compare rates of diabetes around the world. In language arts, have students list risk factors for diabetes, then create a crossword puzzle on those terms and definitions. Culminate the set of lessons on diabetes with a newsletter that students create. Distribute the newsletters to other classes and home to families to raise awareness and educate.

Another option is to create a No Soda November challenge for your students. Sugary sodas contribute to diabetes risk. Challenge your students to drink only milk, water, or 100-percent fruit or vegetable juice during the month of November. Who can go the longest without soda? Can you make it for a week or the whole month or even give it up for good? Track student progress with a class chart or individual charts. Invite other classes or the students' families to join in the challenge.

December: National Influenza Vaccination Week

Use the CDC website (www.cdc.gov/flu) to teach about how communicable diseases such as influenza are transmitted. In groups, have students conduct research about how vaccinations work and how they protect humans from getting diseases. Use this topic to teach the importance of handwashing and other preventive behaviors. Use glitter and petroleum jelly to show how germs can spread with a simple handshake.

January: National Drug Facts Week

During one week in January, incorporate information you find at www.drugfactsweek.drugabuse.gov. For younger students, use this time as an opportunity to teach risk and protective factors for drug use and abuse. Teach them about safe and unsafe things to eat or drink and to always check with an adult they trust if they are unsure. Visit a pharmacy or have a doctor, pharmacist, or nurse speak to your class about the safe use of medicines. Have students design posters on drug prevention and resources. Have students bring in articles and pictures about cigarettes, alcohol, and other drugs for a Facts About Drugs bulletin board. For older students, have groups create skits that explore why people use drugs (peer pressure, curiosity, rebellion, depression, trauma) and how they can get help.

February: American Heart Month

During February, try one or all of these ideas:

- Use the American Heart Association resources at www.heart.org/HEARTORG/ to develop tailored lessons about how to keep the body's hardest working muscle healthy.
- Teach the importance of knowing family health history, eating healthfully, and being active in promoting heart health.
- Integrate heart health topics into science, language arts, and social studies.
- Show your students how to find their pulse. Do some running in place to show students how to get their heart rates up.
- If your physical education teacher has the students participate in the American Heart Association's Jump Rope for Heart, grab a jump rope and jump right in.
- Have your students wear red on a given day or week to raise awareness for heart health.

March: National Nutrition Month

To encourage good nutrition, try one or all of these ideas during the month of March:

- Have students develop a healthy eating campaign composed of signage, bulletin boards, public service announcements, and newsletters.
- Host a Nutrition Question of the Day event for the entire school. Participating students put nutrition-related questions in a box in a designated area, then your students conduct the research to answer these questions. The answers get announced during the morning announcements.

- Work with cafeteria personnel to have a tasting event. For one week, offer a variety of fruits and vegetables cut into bite-sized pieces for students to try. This is a good way for kids to be exposed to new foods they might not otherwise try.
- Have students collect and share healthy recipes that go home with them at the end of the week, perhaps incorporating the fruits and vegetables that were tasted in the tasting event (see previous list item).

April: Earth Day and Environmental Health

To raise awareness about environmental health, try one or all of these ideas:

- Have students bring in a variety of clean packages from home. Discuss the materials that the packages are made from. Talk about waste and the throw-away mentality. How could these packages be reused or recycled?
- Take a trip to a local recycling plant or composting facility.
- Get a giant trash bag, and weigh how much waste your class throws away in a single day at lunchtime. Find a way to recycle paper used in your classroom. Compost food scraps with earthworms and dirt for your class garden.
- Challenge the students to pack a lunch in which everything is reusable (e.g., metal utensils, cloth napkins, lunch box, food without packaging) and nothing is wasted or thrown away. Weigh the waste (aim for no waste) for each student after the challenge. Chart the differences between students for a great lesson in math.

May: National Physical Fitness and Sports Month

Host a variety of activities throughout the month to promote movement among students, faculty, and families. Organize a gym night with fun activities for families. Partner with a local nonprofit group to host a fun run, with money collected being donated to a worthy cause. Host a student dance or skate night. Organize a jump rope marathon where jumping rope is counted as steps toward mileage; get the entire school involved, and track mileage on a bulletin board. Set a school goal of mileage, and have a pep rally or other fun event to celebrate meeting the challenge.

Dimensions of a Healthy Classroom

By now you know that health is more than merely the absence of disease. In chapter 1, you identified six dimensions of health. Given the vital connection between health and academic achievement, these dimensions can be expanded and applied directly to your elementary classroom.

Social Dimension of Health

Building trust and a close bond toward the school and teacher enhances a child's positive adjustment and self-identification and has been shown to decrease the likelihood of risky behaviors into young adulthood. Classroom connectedness is about feelings of safety (both emotional and physical), security, and positive relationships. Strategies for teachers may include sending home regular progress reports and having regular opportunities to communicate with parents (monthly parent chats, newsletters). Keeping a "Did You Know?" bulletin board in the hall for students to share important events also reinforces that students are valued members of the classroom family.

Disclose appropriate personal information that your students might find helpful or helps you describe a particular point during lessons.

May is a great time to celebrate National Physical Fitness and Sports Month with fun activities for students, families, and school staff.

Display a picture of yourself when you were their age. Share books you liked to read, hobbies, sports, and what your life was like when you were in their grade.

Children need recognition. Positive feedback validates behaviors or accomplishments that are valued by others. Praising behavior when a child exhibits self-control when angry, raises a hand instead of calling out, or shows compassion for a peer provides for a warm, comforting, and positive environment—all characteristics of classroom connectedness. Children need to know that they can make a difference. It is important to create a variety of developmentally appropriate opportunities to contribute, such as putting homework in the take-home folders, helping create a bulletin board, and being a helper for the day. Children can contribute outside of school through activities such as the Gran Club (a group of students who visit residents at a local nursing home once a week). Such activities reinforce being part of the community and allow children the opportunity to make a difference.

Mental and Emotional Dimension of Health

Mental health has historically been viewed through the lens of mental illness. However, today people acknowledge that good mental health also requires the skills necessary to cope with life's challenges. Educators must understand the role mental health plays in the school context because it is so pivotal to students' social, emotional, and academic success. It is estimated that one in five children will experience a major mental health issue during their K-12 experience (CDC, 2013). Failure to address the mental health needs of young people is linked to poor academic performance, behavioral problems, school violence, substance abuse, suicide, and other negative outcomes (CDC, 2013). A few of the typical mental health concerns are discussed in more detail here.

Depression

Depression is a serious health concern that affects people of all ages, including children and adolescents. Research indicates that the onset of depression is occurring earlier in life today than in past decades and often coexists with other mental health problems such as chronic anxiety and behavior disorders. Children who are under stress, have a family history of mental health issues, or have experienced a significant loss are at a greater risk for developing clinical depression.

Following are common symptoms of depression in children:

- Persistent sad and irritable mood
- Loss of interest or pleasure in activities once enjoyed
- Significant change in appetite and body weight
- Difficulty sleeping or oversleeping
- Difficulty concentrating
- Recurrent thoughts of death or suicide
- Frequent vague physical complaints (headaches, stomachaches)
- Outbursts of shouting, complaining, unexplained crying
- Chronic boredom or apathy
- Lack of interest in playing with friends
- Alcohol or drug abuse
- Withdrawal, social isolation, and poor communication
- Extreme sensitivity to rejection or failure
- Unusual temper tantrums, defiance, or oppositional behavior
- Increased risk-taking behavior

If one of your students exhibits signs of depression, document what you are seeing. Write down what behaviors you are observing, date it, and perhaps put it in the student's permanent file. Also record the action you are taking and any follow-up documentation. Talk to the school counselor. Discuss the issues you are seeing with parents and, if appropriate and with parental consent, arrange a counseling session for the student. The school nurse may also be able to provide resources. Consult your school administrator and school/district policy regarding your next steps.

Suicide

Suicide is the third leading cause of death among youth between 10 and 19 years of age

Children may exhibit signs of isolation and unhappiness if depression is occurring.

(CDC, 2013). Children who have experienced a personal loss; physical, sexual, or emotional abuse; or depression or other mental health issues have a higher risk of suicide. Children who are contemplating suicide frequently give warning signs of their distress. Parents, teachers, and friends are essential in identifying the signs.

Warning signs of suicide in children and adolescents include the following:

- Suicide note or journaling about wanting to die
- Direct statements or indirect comments about wanting to die. Indirect clues might arise through jokes or comments in school assignments.
- Previous attempts of suicide
- Depression (helplessness/hopelessness)
- Risk-taking behaviors that are out of character for the student
- Giving away prized possessions
- Inability to concentrate or think clearly
- Changes in physical habits and appearance
- Sudden changes in personality, friends, or behaviors

Most important is to never take these warning signs lightly. Consult your school counselor, school nurse, or administrator immediately to determine the best way to intervene.

Self-Injury Behavior

Nonsuicidal self-injury (NSSI) behavior can be defined as any behavior performed intentionally that will result in some degree of physical injury to oneself. Self-injury is not a one-time event but a pattern of behavior to cope with unwanted and strong emotions. In some studies, children as young as 7 years of age are engaging in NSSI behavior. Children may self-injure by scratching, picking, biting, burning, head banging, pulling hair, or pulling out eyelashes. This behavior may also be noticed as scabs that will not heal, pockmarked skin, or fresh bruises. Injuries are most commonly inflicted on the wrists or forearms, although cuts to the face, genitals, thighs, legs, abdomen, and breasts have been observed.

Signs of self-injury might include the following:

- Changes in dress, such as a hat or long sleeves to hide marks
- Mood or personality changes
- Increased isolation
- Trouble managing stress
- Regressive behavior (e.g., soiling themselves at school, tantrums)
- A drop in grades
- Changes in friendships or new sets of friends
- Discipline problems at school
- Increased irritability, sullenness

Children who engage in self-injury are not suicidal, although they may be depressed. If children are taught to stuff their feelings because their emotions are not valued, NSSI can be one of the behaviors children exhibit. It would be wise for teachers and other school personnel to be trained in identifying NSSI behaviors so that they can then give outside referrals to an appropriate health care provider.

Eating Disorders

Eating disorders are serious, potentially life-threatening conditions that affect emotional and physical well-being. They tend to affect females disproportionally as compared to males. By age 6, girls may express concerns about their own weight or body shape. Research suggests that more than 40 percent of elementary school girls (ages 6-12) are concerned about their weight or about becoming fat (O'Dea & Caputi, 2001). **Eating disorders** are a category of diagnoses that include anorexia, bulimia, and binge eating. These disorders involve an extreme preoccupation with food, weight, and body shape.

Characteristics of anorexia nervosa include a preoccupation with food, fear of gaining weight, significant weight loss, or a failure to gain normal weight in a growing, elementary-age child. Children often see themselves as fat, when in reality they may be very thin. This distorted body image is also a feature of the disorder. Difficulty identifying and regulating feelings frequently accompanies an inability to regulate normal food intake. Bulimia nervosa and binge eating are less common in elementary-aged children. Loss of control over eating and bingeing combined with vomiting, excessive exercise, or dieting to prevent weight gain are characteristics of bulimia and binge eating.

Children at risk of an eating disorder share similar personality traits such as high anxiety, perfectionism, and obsessive-compulsive behaviors. Contributing factors may include depression, stress, and low self-esteem. Restricting or obsessing about food and body shape is a way for a child to feel in control of his or her life. Early intervention is essential to overcoming eating disorders, so identifying children at risk for developing eating disorders is key. A counselor with the appropriate training can work with any underlying social or emotional issues that may contribute to these eating patterns among this population.

Intellectual Dimension of Health

Intellectual wellness involves thinking skills, intellectual growth, and mental stimulation. It is the thought process applied to new ideas and experiences to develop understanding and discovery. To be healthy, students should seek challenges, use creativity, and have the desire to learn. They should engage in problem solving and conflict resolution. This dimension even includes travel and cultural activities.

The theory of multiple intelligences suggests that the traditional view of intelligence is far too limiting, especially when boiled down to a single intelligence quotient (IQ). Intelligence may be thought of in broader terms in these eight areas:

- Verbal-linguistic intelligence (word smart)
- Logical-mathematical intelligence (logic smart)
- Bodily-kinesthetic intelligence (body smart)
- Visual-spatial intelligence (picture smart)
- Auditory-musical intelligence (music smart)
- Naturalistic intelligence (nature smart)
- Interpersonal intelligence (people smart)
- Intrapersonal intelligence (self smart)

Teachers should be aware that student intelligence is more than an IQ number. Take care to stimulate all areas of intelligence in your classroom each day. See chapter 3 for more discussion on multiple intelligences and learning styles.

Teachers play an important role in developing their students' intellectual curiosity. Provide students time and opportunity for exploration, field trips, and sharing of personal interests through show-and-tell sessions or all-about-me posters. Take time for teachable moments to talk about the weather or something interesting in nature such as a leaf changing color or a cicada shell. Give students open access to a variety of measurement tools such as a measuring tape, plastic thermometers, scales, balances, levels, measuring cups, pedometers, measuring wheels, and stopwatches.

Invite parents, administrators, community leaders, or other guest speakers to share with your class about their hobbies, careers, travel experiences, and culture. Provide a variety of stimulating age-appropriate books, newspapers, magazines, and travel brochures for your students to read in class or borrow and take home. Your local library, travel agent, chamber of commerce, or students' parents may be willing to save these print materials for your classroom instead of tossing them in the recycling bin.

Be supportive of music, art, and drama programs at your school and in your district by providing performance information details to students and parents and attending performances yourself when you can. Better yet, have your students create and perform a play. Make a class art museum by taking pictures of student creations, and assemble them into a photo album or post online on your class website.

Elementary teachers are encouraged to offer enrichment or modifications to classroom assignments to satisfy the intellectual hunger of their students. A few students are remarkably intellectual and considered gifted. Common characteristics of gifted students include advanced vocabulary, outstanding memory, sensitivity, rapid learning, and asking lots of questions. Sometimes gifted children may even present behavior problems from frustration with boredom or daydreaming. Many elementary schools offer gifted and talented programs for exceptional students. Frequently, these programs require special testing or classroom accommodations. Check with the school counselor, administration, or special education teacher at your school to learn more.

Physical Dimension of Health

The physical dimension of health is characterized by behaviors that are incorporated into daily life that improve health and wellness. Typical behaviors in this category might include daily exercise, eating healthy foods, not using tobacco products, and covering your mouth when you sneeze or cough.

Preventing Disease Transmission

The viruses responsible for colds and flu cause the most common illnesses in schools. Even though children may be immunized, they can spread communicable diseases, which can cause stuffy noses, sore throats, coughing, vomiting, and diarrhea. Preventing the spread of common communicable disease is essential.

Hand Hygiene

Keeping hands clean is one of the best ways to reduce germ transmission and prevent illnesses. Practicing good hand hygiene gets rid of bacteria and viruses from contact with other people and from surfaces touched by human hands. Classrooms play an important role in supporting hand hygiene. This includes teach-

Digital Literacy and Internet Safety

No discussion about the intellectual dimension of wellness would be complete without addressing the vast wealth of information available through the Internet. Digital media defines modern life in extraordinary ways. The use of portable technologies, unfiltered access to information, and user-generated content profoundly impacts how children learn and their impressions of the world. **Digital literacy** is the ability to use technology competently; interpret and understand digital content and assess its credibility; and create, research, and communicate with appropriate tools (Common Sense Media, 2009). Teachers should create opportunities for students to explore what it means to be responsible and respectful online. Such explorations may include some or all of these topics:

- Authorship and plagiarism
- How to protect privacy online
- Common expectations of online behavior, including etiquette
- Importance of digital footprint
- How photos are digitally altered and how alteration affects perceptions of health and beauty

Although the Internet can be a fantastic learning tool, students must be taught how to use it safely and responsibly. Teach your students not to give out personal information, passwords, or send a picture to anyone online without parental permission. Train them to tell you or their parents if anyone or anything on the Internet or social media makes them uncomfortable. They should never reply to inappropriate messages or agree to physically meet someone who they have met online. When gaming, students should not provide their real names or locations and never provide actual pictures, voices, or use web cameras. By the same token, students need to be aware that people may not be who they seem in the virtual world. An adult with harmful intentions could be posing as a teenage girl.

Many resources are available to help educators, parents, and students cope with security in the ever-changing digital world. The National Center for Missing & Exploited Children challenges middle schoolers to test their "websmarts" with their online quiz about web safety at www.netsmartz.org. The National Cyber Security Alliance lists Gaming Safety Tips for Kids, Tweens, and Teens in pdf form here: www.aacc.edu/technology/file/GamingTips.pdf. Consider providing a link to parents at an open house or orientation, sending it home in a class newsletter, and posting it on your class or school website.

ing and using good hand-hygiene behaviors, and providing hand soap, paper towels, and hot water. These are the tools necessary to reduce the spread of infectious diseases in the school environment. Students should be encouraged to wash their hands several times a day. A general rule of thumb is to wash hands before and after preparing food, before eating, after changing diapers, after coughing or sneezing, after using the bathroom, before and after treating a cut or wound, after touching garbage, and after touching animals or anything in the animal's environment.

How should you wash your hands?

- Wet your hands with running water, and apply soap.
- Lather your hands by rubbing them together with the soap. Be sure to lather the backs of your hands, between your fingers, and under your nails.
- Scrub your hands for at least 20 seconds. Hum the "Happy Birthday" song from beginning to end twice.
- Rinse your hands well under clean, running water.

- Dry your hands using a clean towel or air-dry them.

Young children need you to demonstrate this handwashing technique repeatedly in order to do it correctly. Send home a copy of the directions, and have parents practice this with their children at home.

It is hard to imagine, but some teachers feel so pressed for time that they do not allow their students an opportunity to wash their hands before lunch. Soap and water are ideal, but if circumstances are limited, providing the students with hand-sanitizer is a viable option.

In addition to handwashing, take the opportunity to wipe down desks, tabletops, and doorknobs with a disinfectant a couple times a day. This action is especially beneficial during cold and flu season. Choose a couple of students to help, and supply them with disposable gloves. Disposable wipes with bleach are a convenient and easy way to accomplish this important task. Add disinfectant wipes to your classroom supply list to defray the cost.

Respiratory Etiquette

Respiratory infections spread from person to person in droplets of coughs and sneezes. Droplets from an infected person can be propelled through the air and land on people nearby or surfaces commonly touched. To prevent the spread of respiratory infections, the nose and mouth should be covered with a tissue when coughing or sneezing and the tissue should be thrown in the trash immediately. Teachers should teach and practice respiratory etiquette. This includes coughing or sneezing into the arm if no tissue is available. Practice fake sneezing and coughing into a tissue or arm. Send instructions home to parents and have them emphasize and practice proper respiratory etiquette at home with their children.

Be sure to request boxes of tissue on the class supply list at the beginning of the year. Do not be shy about requesting more if you run out halfway through cold and flu season. Most parents are happy to send donations of tissue when it comes to slowing down the transmission of germs in their child's classroom.

Standard Precautions

Standard precautions (also referred to as "universal precautions") are guidelines designed to prevent the transmission of infections that can be found in blood and other body fluids. The CDC recommends that if you come into contact with feces, nasal secretions, saliva, urine, or vomit, you should wear gloves. Standard precautions are designed to reduce the risk of spreading infections from both recognized and unrecognized sources. Germs spread through blood and body fluids can come at any time from anyone. For example, you may not know if someone is infected with hepatitis B; sometimes the infected person may not even know. Standard precautions dictate that you behave as if every individual could be infected with any germ in all situations that place you in contact with blood or body fluids. This keeps both you and the other person protected. Always use these categories of standard precautions whenever blood or body fluids are present:

- Handwashing before and after contact
- Use of disposable latex or vinyl gloves (which are bagged in plastic bags after use and disposed of in the garbage)
- Environmental sanitization of any areas that come in contact with blood or body fluids with bleach and water
- Proper disposal of any items that come in contact with blood or body fluids. This may require placing in plastic bags and disposing of in garbage red biohazard container. Items used for procedures on children with special conditions (such as lancets for finger sticks or syringes for injections) require a special container for safe disposal. A "sharps container" safely stores lancets or needles. Never put these items in the garbage.

Child Abuse and Neglect

Child abuse and neglect continue to be a serious public health issue that can have lasting harmful effects on children. Maltreatment can disrupt the development of the brain and compromise the immune system. It puts children at risk for health problems in adulthood, including depression, drug and alcohol abuse, and certain chronic diseases. By law teachers are required to report suspected child abuse and neglect. People legally required to do so are referred to as **mandated reporters**. You are protected from liability if your report is made in good faith. Teachers have daily contact with their students and are in a position to recognize indicators of child abuse and neglect. As a teacher, you will most likely be the first professional to notice that one of your students might be experiencing some form of maltreatment. If so, your action can make a difference. Four types of child abuse are commonly seen in children—physical abuse, sexual abuse, emotional abuse, and neglect. The following paragraphs define them and outline their characteristics.

Physical abuse is any act that, regardless of intent, results in a nonaccidental physical injury to a child. The types of physical abuse may include questionable bruises and welts, burns, cuts, scrapes, and fractures. Physical abuse is frequently accompanied by certain behaviors from the child. They may include the following:

- Being uncomfortable with physical contact
- Being wary of adult contact
- Being apprehensive when other children cry
- Showing behavioral extremes—aggression or withdrawal
- Being frightened of parents
- Being afraid to go home
- Arriving at school early or staying late, as if afraid to be at home
- Reporting being hurt by a parent
- Complaining of soreness or moving uncomfortably
- Wearing clothing inappropriate for the weather in order to cover the body
- Chronically running away from home
- Being reluctant to change clothes for gym (attempt to hide injuries, bruises)

Neglect is a caregiver's failure to provide for a child's developmental and related needs. Neglect may include a failure to provide a child with adequate food, clothing, shelter, or supervision. Neglect may be accompanied by several physical and behavioral indicators on the part of the child.

Physical Indicators

- Looks undernourished and is usually hungry
- Is often lethargic, as if the child hasn't slept well
- Has untreated injuries or maladies, such as a badly infected cut or a toothache

- Chronically has injuries that you can attribute to a lack of supervision, including being harmed by others

Behavioral Indicators

- Begging for or stealing food because of persistent hunger
- Noticeably poor hygiene
- Inappropriate dress for the weather
- Accidents and injuries
- Risky adolescent behavior (e.g., alcohol or drug use that is out of character)
- Poor ability to relate to others

Sexual abuse is defined as any sexual act upon a child and may include incest, rape, indecent exposure, fondling, child prostitution, and child pornography. Sexual abuse of a child is a devastating breach of trust for the child. Further, the adult may manipulate the child into silence with threats and intimidation. It is not surprising that the child may experience a range of emotional responses including shame, guilt, depression, anxiety, and mood swings. In the classroom you may see a wide range of behavioral indicators of child sexual abuse, including the following:

- Expressions of age-inappropriate knowledge of sex and sexual behaviors
- Sexually explicit drawings
- Highly sexualized play
- Avoiding or attempting to avoid a familiar adult
- Signs of posttraumatic stress disorder
- Signs of poor sleep or nightmares
- Withdrawal
- A child's statement

Emotional abuse is the most difficult form of abuse to define, yet its consequences can be devastating. Caregiver actions typically considered emotionally abusive include the following:

- Belittling or ridiculing of the child
- Intimidation
- Ignoring or rejection
- Withholding love
- Bizarre forms of discipline (e.g., locking a child in a dark room or closet)

Behavioral indicators of emotional abuse may include the following:

- Habit disorders (sucking, biting, rocking)
- Conduct disorders (antisocial, destructive)
- Neurotic traits (sleep disorders, inhibition of play)
- Behavioral extremes (compliant, passive, undemanding, aggressive, demanding, raging)
- Overly adaptive behavior (inappropriately adult, inappropriately infantile and needy)
- Self-destructive behavior and suicide attempts
- Cruelty; seemingly taking pleasure in hurting other people or animals
- Delinquent behavior

Disclosing to an adult that child abuse or neglect is taking place is extremely challenging for a child for a variety of reasons. Often shame is associated with the abuse. In addition, the child may have a sense of loyalty toward the abuser. The child may think they won't be believed if they disclose the abuse. The child may fear the consequences of telling someone. Often, the abuser will threaten the child. This fear of what might happen makes the disclosure difficult for the child. Children instead are likely to disclose in a more indirect way. For example, a student might say, "What would happen if a girl was being touched in a bad way and she told someone about it?" Another typical scenario is disclosing the issue but only if you promise not to tell anyone else.

Responding in the appropriate way is essential and has important consequences. Not responding may leave the child feeling more anxious, abandoned, or unprotected. However, being overly emotional may scare the child and hinder the disclosure. Here are some ideas about how to respond to a child's disclosure:

- Find a place that is private and where you will not be interrupted.
- Don't touch the child without permission. Touch may be associated with the abuse.
- Remain calm.
- Avoid technical words or words the child might find embarrassing.

- Honor the child's method of disclosure. If the child is making a disguised disclosure (for instance, claiming that the abuse happened to someone else), encourage the child to tell you about the situation on the child's terms. The child will often reveal that he or she is the actual victim after talking for a while.
- Reassure the child that she or he is not to blame for what is happening.
- Try to get enough information to determine the child's safety.
- Let the child know what you will do now that you know about the abuse or neglect.
- Reassure the child that you will not share the information with teachers or children but let them know you will need to tell an authority such as a counselor.

As a teacher, you are not responsible for proving that abuse or neglect has occurred; you must only have a suspicion that a child is being abused. It is essential that you know your school's reporting policies and procedures. Check with your principal to find out what the procedure is in your school. You may be asked to provide information in writing that documents the reasons for your concern. Your school may have a policy that governs who makes the report to Child Protective Services. People who are designated to receive reports from mandated reporters in schools must notify the personnel who made the initial report when the report is made to Child Protective Services, who received the report, and any communication resulting from the report.

Recognizing, Preventing, and Reporting Child Abuse

Helpguide.org (www.helpguide.org/articles/abuse/child-abuse-and-neglect.htm) is a nonprofit organization dedicated to providing mental health and well-being resources. You can find information on how to recognize and prevent child abuse and neglect, myths and facts about the issue, a free child abuse hotline, and other essential resources on this topic.

School Violence

School violence is youth violence that occurs on school property, on the way to or from school, or during a school-sponsored event. School violence can be prevented. Studies show that efforts from parents, school administrators, teachers, and students can reduce violence in the schools and improve the safety of everyone. Prevention efforts need to involve many stakeholders and include comprehensive strategies that are consistently implemented. Successful efforts at preventing violence in schools begin with a systematic and recurrent assessment of what is taking place in the schools. This might include data on the number of incidents or referrals, disciplinary procedures, and previous intervention efforts. Next, the development and implementation of a comprehensive plan to maintain a peaceful school campus should be a priority. This plan should include policies and practices for the building, in the classroom, and at the individual student level. Attention should also focus on reducing bullying as well as other forms of peer victimization.

There is no single reason why students become violent. Some are following patterns they've seen at home, in their neighborhoods, in video games, movies, or television. Sometimes, students who turn violent are victims of bullying. They may feel isolated and rejected by their peers. The following factors might put a student at greater risk of violent behavior:

- History of violent victimization
- Attention deficits, hyperactivity, or learning disorders
- Involvement with alcohol, tobacco, or other drugs
- Low IQ
- Poor behavioral control
- Deficits in social cognitive or information-processing abilities
- High emotional distress
- History of treatment for emotional problems
- Exposure to violence and conflict in the family

Bullying and Cyberbullying

Bullying represents a significant problem in U.S. schools. In a national study, nearly 30 per-

cent of the students surveyed reported being involved in bullying in the current term as either a perpetrator or a victim (Smokowski & Kopasz, 2005). One study suggests that more than one in five middle school students said they avoid restrooms at school out of fear of being bullied, and that at least 20 percent of all students are frightened during much of their school day (Smith & Brain, 2000). It is important to note that not every physical or verbal altercation between children is considered bullying. **Bullying** is characterized by repeated incidences of physical or emotional harm and a power imbalance between the people involved.

Both boys and girls engage in bullying, but some differences are evident. For example, boys typically engage in direct bullying behaviors, including physical assaults or verbal threats. Girls typically use more indirect, covert methods of bullying, such as intentionally excluding others from an activity or spreading rumors. Nevertheless, you may encounter cases that are not typical, too.

Common Characteristics of Bullies

- Overly aggressive, destructive, impulsive, low tolerance for frustration
- Family background; parents who are hostile, rejecting, and indifferent to their children
- Discipline at home that is usually inconsistent, very physical, and emotionally abusive

Common Characteristics of Victims

- Typically small in stature or weak compared with bullies
- Tend to be quiet, cautious, anxious, insecure, and sensitive
- Tend to have poor communication and problem-solving skills

Teachers and parents may not take bullying seriously; in fact, the misconception still exists that bullying is an unavoidable part of childhood. Unfortunately, victims of bullying report physical and mental health problems more often, and they may develop depression and low self-esteem and contemplate or complete suicide. Bullying can create a climate of anxiety, fear, and sadness, not only for the victims but for the bystanders as well. Check out www.stopbullying.gov/laws for specific information related to your state.

Help for Confronting Bullying

At stopbullying.gov you will find information on who is at risk and how to respond, and you will see featured videos. The site has a dedicated section for teachers, parents, teens, and kids. It also has information on cyberbullying, such as how to prevent it and best practices for reporting it.

Cyberbullying is a current form of bullying that makes use of the technology now available. It may include using email, texting, instant messaging, social networking sites, smartphone cameras, and websites to harass or bully others. Youth technology use is ever changing, so trends in cyberbullying are difficult to track. In 2007, 4 percent of high school students reported experiencing cyberbullying at some point in the school year (Dinkes, Kemp, & Baum, 2009). Female students are more likely to by cyberbullied than males, according to the data. Cyberbullying may have a far more significant impact than previous forms, because the technology can reach many more peers than ever before. In some ways, this form of bullying can be even more damaging, because it is more difficult to escape it. Cyberbullying can happen 24 hours a day, 7 days a week. Messages and images can be posted anonymously and distributed quickly to a wide audience.

Cyberbullying has various forms, which may include the following (Willard, 2007):

- **Flaming:** Online fights using electronic messages with angry and vulgar language
- **Harassment:** Repeatedly sending nasty, mean, and insulting messages
- **Denigration:** Sending or posting gossip or rumors about a person
- **Impersonation:** Pretending to be someone else and sending or posting material to get that person in trouble, endanger the person, or damage that person's reputation or friendships
- **Outing:** Sharing someone's secrets or embarrassing information or images online

- **Trickery:** Tricking someone into revealing secrets, and then sharing it online
- **Exclusion:** Intentionally and cruelly excluding someone from an online group
- **Cyberstalking:** Repeated, intense harassment that includes threats

Bullying and cyberbullying affect many of today's youth and deserve the attention of both educators and parents. The best strategy to address the problem is through creating and implementing schoolwide prevention programs and creating a comprehensive plan to impose strict policies against bullying. The first step is to interview or survey personnel in your school to determine how often bullying occurs, where it happens, how students and adults intervene, and whether your current strategies are effective. The next step is to adopt strict policies, codes of conduct, and a bullying reporting system, using feedback from parents, students, and teachers. Use school assemblies, parent–teacher conferences, newsletters, and school websites to educate and raise awareness of the issue. Consistent and regular communication is critical to maintaining an environment in which bullying is not acceptable behavior.

Back-to-School Supply List

As mentioned throughout the chapter, several supplies will help you promote student health. Classrooms operate on a limited budget, so if possible, ask parents to pitch in. Explain that health is a top priority in your classroom, and ask for these provisions on your back-to-school supply list:

- Family-size boxes of tissues
- Large containers of disinfectant wipes
- Reusable water bottles
- Hand sanitizer (individual bottles for students to keep at their desks and large pump bottles for classroom use)

Remind parents throughout the year that these items will make an impact in promoting health, decreasing the spread of illness, and reducing absenteeism in your class. Another strategy might be to host a class fundraiser early in the school year to help offset the costs associated with these needed supplies.

Unhealthy Teaching Practices

Just as teachers can build healthy components into daily classroom life, some practices are decidedly harmful to student health. These practices may lead to illness, dehydration, malnourishment, urinary tract infections, behavior problems, reduced socialization, and mental stress. Some of these practices are surprisingly common:

- Having students sit out from recess as a punishment for poor behavior
- Having students sit out from recess to finish homework or classwork
- Sitting silently or at an isolated place at lunchtime
- Skipping handwashing before lunch
- Rewarding students with food
- Punishing students by withholding food
- Skipping a water break after recess or physical education or allowing only a sip or two
- Punishing students by not allowing them to use the restroom
- Allowing students to purchase junk food or sugary drinks in school vending machines during school hours
- Allowing junk food or sugary drinks at class celebrations
- Eating junk food or sugary drinks in front of your students

Make the decision today that you will not succumb to any of these unhealthy teaching practices. Rise above, set an example, and make student health a top priority in your classroom every day.

Summary

Teachers are the gatekeepers to a healthy classroom. As a teacher you can initiate a variety of simple procedures and activities to bolster student health and improve the academic environment. Practices such as handwashing, maintaining food and drink standards, setting a good example, and even giving a warm smile or kind word can easily be administered every day throughout the year. You can incorporate monthly health-related themes into the school year. The six dimensions of health have a wide range of practical applications in the elementary classroom, such as respiratory etiquette and cyberbullying. Even items on the back-to-school supply list may promote health in the classroom. In addition, you should avoid ineffective and harmful practices such as using food as a reward and taking away recess as punishment.

Review Questions

1. What is the difference between intrinsic and extrinsic rewards? Provide examples of each.

2. What are some of the ways elementary teachers can give students recognition with little or no cost?

3. Why is it important for teachers to have rules concerning outside food brought in for class celebrations?

4. What types of safety issues are relevant to class field trips?

5. Describe some of the characteristics pertaining to eating disorders and how they are relevant to the elementary classroom environment.

6. What is digital literacy, and what can elementary teachers do to promote it?

Chapter 7

Creating an Active Classroom

Objectives

- Identify the need for activity breaks and brain breaks.
- List several ideas for activity breaks and brain breaks.
- Demonstrate how to make several homemade equipment items.
- Critique the Appropriate Instructional Practice Guidelines for Elementary Schools.
- Use safety assessment forms for playgrounds, gyms, and equipment.
- Create a class behavior management plan.

Lack of activity destroys the good condition of every human being, while movement and methodical physical exercise save it and preserve it.

Plato

Elementary classrooms are dynamic learning environments. The teacher has the choice to create an active or a sedentary classroom. With the growing health concerns of the current generation of children, small changes in the way that a teacher chooses to infuse activity into the classroom can make a big difference in the children they teach. Teachers should be purposeful about integrating movement activities into everyday learning. This chapter discusses the basics in creating an active classroom.

Having a healthy and active classroom starts with the teacher. If the teacher has a passion and enthusiasm for healthy, active living, that energy creates a positive atmosphere that is evident in the teaching environment. The teacher can encourage physical activity and a healthy lifestyle by simply displaying posters and bulletin boards that promote health and wellness. The teacher can design assignments to include class discussions, readings, journaling, and role playing ideas for healthy active living. Creating this healthy class climate will begin the transformation to an active classroom.

Activity Breaks and Brain Breaks

Research indicates "short activity breaks during the school day can improve students' concentration skills and classroom behavior" (Trost, 2007, p. 3). Physical activity breaks during the school day provide students an opportunity to be active, be social, and take a break from sedentary activities in the classroom. A classroom activity break is recommended after 50 minutes of continuous sitting or during transitions between subjects. The Centers for Disease Control and Prevention (CDC, 2010) states that physical activity breaks of about 5 to 20 minutes in the classroom can improve attention span, classroom behavior, and achievement test scores. These breaks can also increase daily physical activity levels of youth and help students return to their academic studies more focused and ready to learn. Here are a few examples of quick **activity breaks and brain breaks**:

- **Dance to music.** Students perform a set dance when you turn the music on (e.g., the hokey pokey), or they follow a video clip (e.g., the Sid shuffle).
- **Stretching/yoga poses/exercise.** You call out a stretch, pose, or exercise, then the students perform it at or near their desks.
- **Cross crawl.** Students touch the right elbow to the left knee, then the left elbow to the right knee while walking in place.
- **Lazy eights.** This exercise helps students reach across the midline of the body, which forces both sides of the brain to communicate with each other, strengthening the nerve cell pathways and energizing learning. Students trace the shape of a very large horizontal 8, first with one hand and then with both hands. Have them complete the movement three times with each hand and then three times with both hands together.

For more activity ideas, check out these websites:

- Search for "Cara Tidwell brain breaks" on YouTube to find a playlist of brain break videos.
- Search for the term "brain breaks" at teachtrainlove.com to find many short clips to play on your smartboard to quickly revive and energize kids. Clips are grouped by theme, such as "Fight the Fidgeting" and "Dance Like No One's Watching!"
- The Energizing Brain Breaks log (http://brainbreaks.blogspot.com) has videos, brain break ideas, and links.
- The website Minds in Bloom: Strategies and Activities to Promote Creativity and Critical Thinking has a page with 20 three-minute brain breaks (www.minds-in-bloom.com/2012/04/20-three-minute-brain-breaks.html).
- Gonoodle (www.gonoodle.com) is an excellent resource. This site is designed so teachers can personalize the activities for each class.

Integrating Movement Into Academic Lessons

Classroom teachers have the opportunity to add activity to academic lessons while in the classroom or by going to an outside space or gym. These opportunities can influence healthy behaviors of students by including physical activity into the total learning experience. The challenge is to change the classroom from mostly sedentary to active and learning through integrating meaningful activity during the school day. Physical activity in the classroom helps improve on-task behavior during academic instruction time and increases daily in-school physical activity levels (CDC, 2010). You can have worksheet stations in the classroom where students move around the room to complete the assignment. Instead of just raising a hand to answer a question from their desks, students can stand up or walk to the front of the class to give the answer. You can integrate movement into transitions or breaks between lessons. Students can march in place while you or designated students hand out materials in the classroom. Instead of sitting and waiting for the next activity, students can stand up and hold yoga poses or stretches. You can weave movement into mathematics (e.g., using body parts or equipment, clapping, or dribbling to count), social studies (e.g., providing role play to act out a historical event), science (e.g., demonstrating gravity by juggling), and language arts (e.g., tracing letters or words on the ground by walking the chalk lines). You will find out more about how to create integrated active academic lessons in chapter 9.

 See lab 7.1 for a brainstorming practice activity.

Equipment Needs for an Active Classroom

Most classroom teachers do not have the money to buy equipment for an active classroom. One way to address this issue is to make equipment. You can make balls out of paper or yarn and add tape to make them heavier. To make beanbags, put rice or beans in a sock or in other material that can be sewn together. To make

> ### DIY Equipment Resources
>
> For an excellent source of ideas about homemade equipment, visit this page on the PE Central website: www.pecentral. org/preschool/prekhomemadeequipmentmenu.html. This website is the home for great teacher created ideas. The section on homemade equipment includes 50 items that you can make for your classroom at little to no cost.

scoops, cut milk jugs or other bottles with handles. You can make rackets out of clothes hangers and hose. Use your creativity to create your own jump ropes, Frisbees, hoops, rhythm sticks, and bats. For athletic equipment that cannot be created out of recycled materials, try borrowing from physical educators or from people in the community. Table 7.1 lists basic equipment suggestions for an active classroom.

See lab 7.2 for information on your homemade equipment assignment.

Class Management and Organization

Active classrooms require the teacher to use different class management and organization skills. The following ideas will help you to have a successful and active physical environment in your classroom.

Start and Stop Signals

Establishing and using a clear and consistent signal for starting and stopping is critical in an active environment, particularly if the lesson includes equipment. Some examples of stop activity signals include using a verbal cue such as "freeze," holding a hand up with a finger and using your voice to count down from 5 to 1, clapping a certain rhythm and expecting the students to repeat the rhythm back, and playing music when the students are active and stopping the music when you want the students to freeze. According to Graham, Holt/Hale, and Parker (2012), regardless

Table 7.1 Basic Equipment Suggestions for an Active Classroom

Uses	Equipment
Tossing and throwing or striking	Beanbags, scarves, balloons, beach balls, yarn balls, foam balls, tennis balls, Frisbees, Wiffle balls, and soft playground balls
Catching objects	Scoops
Striking objects	Rackets, paddles, bats, clubs, sticks, noodles
Swinging, rotating, waving, pulling, shaking, or jumping	Jump ropes, elastic bands, hoops, wands, ribbons, rhythm shakers
Markers and space awareness	Cones, bases, dots, carpet squares

of the signal the students should know what to do when the signal is given. For example, when the teacher sends the signal of an index finger in the air while counting backward from 5 to 1, the students put equipment down on the floor and look at the teacher.

Grouping Students

Grouping students should not take a lot of time and should never include student captains who choose teams or groups. Teachers can divide students into groups by ability, gender, social compatibility, or size. The most important key to remember is the students need to be in a group size where all students in the group are physically active and not waiting to participate or just observing. Consider these examples of grouping: The students get back-to-back with a partner of similar height; the students connect elbows with two people who have a birthday in the same month; the students find three people with the same color shoes; you distribute color popsicle sticks to the students upon entering the class and group according to the color on the stick; and you group students together who work well together (separating students who often can distract others if they are on the same team). Another way to group students is to use apps that divide the class for you. For example, *Team Shake* is an excellent app that is easy to use in class with a tablet or smartphone (see Resources for more information).

Appropriate Spacing

Always use the space wisely, with safety as your main priority. One important safety concern is for students to move in similar directions. It

eliminates students crossing paths and reduces their risk of running into each other. Always be careful to give specific directions for the activity *before* sending students out in the space. Yelling the directions to a class while they are moving is not very effective. Bring students in close to give directions, then send them back out to participate in the activity. To change the activity directions, give a signal for all students to come back in to a central location, give the new directions, then send them back out again to practice.

Handling Equipment

Students should not handle equipment while you are talking. Directions at the beginning of an activity are easy to hear, because the students usually do not have equipment yet. However, during the activity when you need to talk, set a rule that equipment is out of the students' hands on your signal. For example, require that on your signal they stop, lower their equipment to the ground, and look at you. This rule will reduce the noise level and will enhance the ability for students to hear what you need to say.

Distributing equipment effectively is a learned class routine where the teacher uses an organized procedure that is not time consuming. Before distributing equipment, specifically state where students should go and what they will do. Place the equipment in several locations so that the students can retrieve the equipment safely and quickly. Another way to distribute equipment is for a group leader to pick up all equipment needed for everyone in the group and then help to distribute it around the perimeter of the activity space. It will allow students to begin participating in the activity as soon as they get to the equipment.

Classroom chairs can be removed and stability balls can be used as chairs instead. This simple change of furniture can help students engage core muscles while they do seat work.

Equipment of all sizes and weights can help students achieve success as well as challenge them. Ideally, students would each have their own equipment. If that is not possible, at least have equipment for every two students. At the end of class, students should have a manageable way of putting away equipment. If you are in stations, the equipment can be left in the stations. The best way to put away equipment after an activity is similar to the method used for distribution. Have partners or group leaders assist in bringing all equipment back to the proper area.

Effective Communication in an Active Setting

An effective communication skill used while teaching in an active environment is to tell the students when to perform the activity before giving the instructions on the activity. For example: "When I say go, I would like for you to . . . " This important communication technique will keep the students listening to the directions to hear the cue to start activity. It will enable you to clearly direct the students on the expectations of the activity before the students get started.

During the instruction time, make sure to position the class to reduce visual distractions (e.g., sun, other classes, disruptive students). As discussed earlier in the chapter, all equipment should be out of the hands of students during all instruction times.

Short instructional episodes help students to concentrate on fewer concepts that they need to practice. According to Pangrazi and Beighle (2013), teachers should refrain from lengthy skill descriptions. Use less than 30 seconds to give one or two instructional points, then send the students to practice those points.

Positive reinforcement and corrective skill feedback are the most important ways you can communicate with your students. Comments such as "Good job" or "Way to go" are general praise comments that are positive but are not specific enough to help a student with skill or behavior improvement. Statements that provide specific feedback are more beneficial. For example, "Good job; I like the way you stepped with opposition to throw the ball." Another example is "Way to go; you are staying on task and working well with your partner." Providing this communication during the activity helps the students know how they are doing and motivates them to hear more positive feedback. It also helps other students learn indirectly.

Other Best Practices for Teaching an Activity Lesson

Following are some other things you can do to make activity lessons run smoothly.

• Develop routines that you do every time you teach an activity lesson. Besides the routines listed earlier for equipment distribution and start and stop signals, other routines should include where to go at the beginning of the activity (always having an instructional zone), what to do if you get injured, what to do if there is a class emergency, and where to go at the end of the activity lesson.

• Design activity and practice time to be greater than instruction and management time. Use the short instructional episodes discussed earlier to minimize instruction time. Also use cues for instruction so that students are reminded how to perform the skills needed for the activity. To minimize management time,

follow the equipment distribution ideas listed earlier. Setting up fields and nets for games is best completed before the class begins. However, if it is not possible, use groups of students to divide the work for quick setup and takedown.

• Offer an initial instant activity that involves the class immediately and warms up the muscles. Warm-up is important especially for activities that require quickness, force, or endurance. Instant activities are quick to start and involve movements the students have practiced before, such as walking and jumping rope. Instant activities can also include practicing skills needed for the activities, such as throwing, catching, dribbling, or kicking. The key to successful instant activities is to have little to no instruction time. Students can see the board that lists the activity, and they move to start participating immediately.

• Use class time effectively by beginning and ending on time. Time is often wasted in long lines, moving equipment, and making transitions from one activity to the other. One way to help is to use small groups or teams to play the activities. It will get students playing faster, and they will get to participate more. Using an app to display the time remaining in the activity will help students to know when activity will start and stop. Following a detailed and organized lesson also helps.

• Move throughout the lesson so that you can see and help everyone during the activity. Students need to be seen by their teacher. In fact, student behavior will improve if you move around, giving feedback to all students during the activity. Catching a student doing something good is better than catching them off task. Teacher feedback is a critical component to help students improve on-task behavior and skill development.

Inappropriate Practices

Some games and activities should be avoided in the elementary classroom. Some of these **inappropriate practices** are elimination games or activities that remove students from playing during the game (where the students sit and watch the rest of the game/activity), activities that involve throwing objects at each other, activities where students push or shove each other, and activities that embarrass or demean each other. Games where the majority of students in the class stand and wait their turn often cause elevated student discipline problems. Using more teams where fewer students are on each team will reduce waiting and provide more opportunities for students to participate in the game. Several games specifically listed in the Physical Education Hall of Shame should not be played during class time. Some examples are dodgeball, duck–duck–goose, kickball, musical chairs, relay races, steal the bacon, line soccer, red rover, Simon says, tag, and tug-of-war (Williams, 1992; 1994).

Williams (1996) also addressed inappropriate teacher practices. Some of the practices that he suggested avoiding are putting students on display; using one line, one ball, one chance; using exercise as punishment; and allowing student captains to choose teams. The National Association for Sport and Physical Education (NASPE), which recently changed its name to SHAPE America – Society of Health and Physical Educators, published *Appropriate Instructional Practice Guidelines, K-12: A Side-by-Side Comparison* (NASPE, 2009) to address appropriate and inappropriate instructional practices in a K-12 grid to easily review and compare the three grade levels (elementary, middle, and high school). These practices reflect several of the Hall of Shame practices, but this document added the **appropriate practices** that teachers *should* do to replace the inappropriate ones. See table 7.2 for examples of appropriate and inap-

Physical Education Hall of Shame

For more information about the Hall of Shame, go to www.pecentral.org/professional/hos/index.html. This section of PE Central names all of the inducted Hall of Shame activities from the articles plus recent inducted activities and practices. This site also includes great resources, such as books and videos, and recommendations for modifying the shamed activities.

propriate instruction. The full grid is available at www.shapeamerica.org/standards/guidelines/upload/Appropriate-Instructional-Practices-Grid.pdf.

See lab 7.3 to complete your critique assignment of the Appropriate Practices grid.

Safety

Safety is a priority in schools. Having an active environment will increase the importance of following guidelines for having a safe environment. Safety precautions include making sure the activity space is safe and free of hazards. All equipment for the physical activity should be developmentally appropriate and in good repair. A first aid kit should be stocked and readily available to use for student injuries.

It is the responsibility of every teacher to provide a safe environment. Using a safety checklist is one way to insure a safe teaching environment. Providing a daily inspection of the activity space and equipment is important. If a "no" is checked on the list, you should not use the space and should submit the form to the administration of the school to report the safety issues. The assessment checklists will help you provide a safe environment as well as provide documentation that a safety hazard exists on school property and must be addressed by the administration.

See lab 7.4 for your assignment on playground, gym, and equipment safety assessment.

Class Behavior Management

Active classrooms can increase issues of managing class behavior, because students move more and use equipment items such as bats and balls. Thus, you need to develop a plan to address behavior issues.

Creating class rules is a good way to let the students know what behaviors are allowed and what behaviors are not allowed. The rules are specific statements for observable student behavior written in positive terms that are few in number. The rules and consequences are developed and agreed upon by the entire class.

Table 7.2 Examples of Appropriate and Inappropriate Instructional Practices

Categories	Appropriate practices	Inappropriate practices
1.0 Learning environment		
1.1 Establishing the learning environment	1.1.2 The environment is supportive of all children and promotes developing a positive self-concept. Children are allowed to try, to fail, and to try again, free of criticism or harassment from the teacher or other students.	1.1.2 Only highly skilled or physically fit children are viewed as successful learners. Teachers and peers overlook and/or ignore students who are not highly skilled or physically fit.
1.2 Exercise as punishment	1.2.1 Teachers promote exercise for its contribution to a healthy lifestyle. Children are encouraged to participate in physical activity and exercise outside of the physical education setting for enjoyment, skill development, and health reasons.	1.2.1 Teachers use activities/ exercises (e.g., running laps, performing push-ups) to punish misbehavior.
2.0 Instructional strategies		
2.5 Maximizing participation	2.5.1 Teachers organize their classes to maximize opportunities for all children to learn and be physically active. Enough equipment is provided so that children spend virtually no time waiting for turns or standing in lines. At least half of class time is spent in moderate-to-vigorous activity.	2.5.1 Lessons are organized poorly, so students spend much of the class time waiting for roll call, waiting in lines and/ or waiting for equipment to be distributed. The first few minutes of the class are always spent sitting, getting organized or simply waiting for the teacher to signal that the class is about to begin.
2.7 Teacher enthusiasm	2.7.1 The teacher shows enthusiasm for an active, healthy lifestyle.	2.7.1 The teacher appears not to enjoy physical activity (e.g., instructs from a chair or the bleachers).
3.0 Curriculum		
3.3 Regular participation	3.3.1 The teacher extends experiences from in-class activity lessons to community and family activities, promoting a physically active lifestyle.	3.3.1 No effort is made to connect physical education instruction to community offerings, recreation opportunities, or family involvement.
3.6 Valuing physical activity	3.6.1 Teachers encourage all children to experience the satisfaction and joy that can result from learning about and participating regularly in physical activity.	3.6.1 Negative experiences in physical education class (e.g., running as punishment) lead students to devalue the importance and enjoyment of physical activity.

Table 7.2 *(continued)*

4.0 Assessment		
4.4 Testing procedures	4.4.1 Teachers make every effort to create testing situations that are private, nonthreatening, educational, and encouraging (e.g., they explain what the test is designed to measure).	4.4.1 Testing is public (e.g., students observe others completing the test while they wait for their turn to take it), with no reason given for the test.
	4.4.2 Teachers encourage children to avoid comparisons with others and, instead, use the results as a catalyst for personal improvement.	4.4.2 Teachers overlook taunting or teasing based on test results. Results are interpreted based on comparison to norms, rather than how they apply to children's future health and well-being.
5.0 Professionalism		
5.1 Professional growth	5.1.1 The teacher continually seeks new information to stay current (e.g., reads journals, attends conferences and in-services).	5.1.1 The teacher makes no effort to stay current.
5.3 Advocacy	5.3.2 The teacher helps create a school culture of physical activity.	5.3.2 The teacher doesn't promote the physical education program; therefore, it's not a visible part of the school community.

Reprinted, by permission, from SHAPE America, 2009, *Appropriate instructional practice guidelines, K-12: A side-by-side comparison* (Reston, VA: NASPE).

The rules are displayed for everyone to see and understand expectations.

See lab 7.5 to complete your assignment on creating a behavior management plan.

Creating a positive, caring, and consistent environment is critical in behavior management. Rewarding good behavior with praise and encouragement is as important as handling disruptive behaviors. Having a plan for behavior management and following it consistently will help you run your active classroom more efficiently.

Summary

Active classrooms are created by the passion and enthusiasm of the teacher who is concerned with the health and wellness of the students. Creating a class environment that encourages activity is planned and purposeful. From posters on the wall to activity breaks between classwork to integrating movement into academic lessons, you choose the level of infusion of movement and activity. With active lessons, you must address various organization and management strategies to help enhance the teaching environment. The challenge of changing to an active classroom is rewarded with the benefits, which include improved attention span, classroom behavior, and achievement test scores.

Review Questions

1. Why should a classroom teacher offer activity breaks?

2. Name three activity or brain breaks.

3. Describe how to make two items that you can use as equipment in your classroom.

4. Name three practices that are listed in the Appropriate Practices grid and are important for you to use in your classroom. The full grid is available at www.shapeamerica.org/standards/guidelines/upload/Appropriate-Instructional-Practices-Grid.pdf.

5. Why should you use a safety assessment form for the activity space your class will use?

6. Why is a behavior management plan important?

Lab 7.1: Brainstorming Ideas for Activity Breaks

Brainstorm ideas for five 20-minute activities that could be used in the classroom for activity breaks. Ideas mentioned earlier in the chapter include the following:

- **Dance to music.** Students perform a set dance when you turn the music on (e.g., the hokey pokey), or they follow a video clip (e.g., the Sid shuffle).
- **Stretching/yoga poses/exercise.** You call out a stretch, pose, or exercise, then the students perform it at or near their desks.
- **Cross crawl.** Students touch the right elbow to the left knee, then the left elbow to the right knee while walking in place.
- **Lazy eights.** This exercise helps students reach across the midline of the body, which forces both sides of the brain to communicate with each other, strengthening the nerve cell pathways and energizing learning. Students trace the shape of a very large horizontal 8, first with one hand and then with both hands. Have them complete the movement three times with each hand and then three times with both hands together.

Your five activity ideas should be different than these, but you can use them for inspiration as you brainstorm.

Lab 7.2: Homemade Equipment

 Make the following equipment that could be used in an elementary physical education program: one yarn ball, one nylon paddle, one plastic scoop, and two equipment items of your choice. You can find directions for making the three required pieces of equipment on PE Central's website: www.pecentral.org/preschool/prekhomemadeequipmentmenu.html. There are videos on YouTube for making yarn pom-poms that are also helpful.

Lab 7.3: Appropriate Practices Critique

Review the *Appropriate Instructional Practice Guidelines, K-12* (www.shapeamerica.org/standards/guidelines/upload/Appropriate-Instructional-Practices-Grid.pdf), and critique the elementary level. Choose what you think is the most important appropriate practice, and explain why you think this practice is needed in elementary schools.

Table 7.3 Appropriate Practices Critique

AP sections	Grade level	My choice for most important practice (include the number and the practice)	Why this practice is needed
Learning environment	Elementary		
Instructional strategies	Elementary		
Curriculum	Elementary		
Assessments	Elementary		
Professionalism	Elementary		

Lab 7.4:   Using Safety Assessment Forms

 Complete the following assessment forms at one local elementary school for the playground, gymnasium, and the equipment.

Safety Assessment Form for an Outdoor Playground

YES	NO	N/A	Item	Comments:
			1. Can children with disabilities use playground equipment?	
			2. Is the playground equipment designed to be used by elementary students?	
			3. Is the playground equipment free of excessive rust and warped, cracked, and rotting wood?	
			4. Is the playground equipment free from protruding bolt ends, S-hooks, or other hardware that can entrap or entangle clothing or jewelry?	
			5. Is the playground equipment free from broken, missing, damaged, or loose parts?	
			6. Is the playground equipment free from sharp or jagged edges?	
			7. Is the fall zone beneath and 6 feet around playground equipment composed of soft surface (clean sand, wood, mulch, or manufactured material)?	
			8. Is the depth of fall zone material between 9 and 12 inches?	
			9. Are the grounds clean, well drained, and well maintained? (Field is mown. No trash, large rocks, tree stumps, broken glass, needles, nails, damaged safety signs, tripping obstacles, or standing water.)	
			10. Are the outdoor electrical appliances (air conditioners, switch boxes, transformers) inaccessible to children?	
			11. Do you have easy access to a first aid kit that is stocked and readily available to use for student injuries?	
			12. Other (write description):	

Modified from Geiger's 2005 Assessment of an Outdoor Elementary Playground.

Safety Assessment Form for an Indoor Activity Space

YES	NO	N/A	Item	Comments:
			1. Is the space for physical activity large enough to accommodate all students of a class moving at the same time?	
			2. Is the area clean without trash, debris, and spills?	
			3. If the space includes bleachers, are they safely pushed in to keep equipment (balls) from going in and under the bleachers?	
			4. Is the equipment for the physical education program developmentally appropriate and in good repair?	
			5. Is special equipment provided for students with disabilities?	
			6. Are the electrical appliances (air conditioners, power outlets, switch boxes, transformers) inaccessible to children?	
			7. Do you have easy access to a first aid kit that is stocked and readily available to use for student injuries?	
			8. Other (write description):	

Safety Assessment Form for Equipment

YES	NO	N/A	Item	Comments:
			1. Can children with disabilities use the equipment?	
			2. Is the equipment designed for use by elementary students?	
			3. Do the students have a choice of equipment size and weight according to their developmental strength level?	
			4. Is the equipment safe to use (no broken parts that could cause a safety risk)?	

Lab 7.5: Creating a Class Behavior Management Plan

Complete the following plan that could be used in an elementary classroom.

Behavior Management Plan

To create a safe and caring environment, as the teacher I will encourage positive behaviors and discourage inappropriate behaviors.

Positive Behaviors

Targeted positive behaviors	Specific praise to be given
Stays on task	
Follows rules	
Displays good sporting behavior	
Listens and follows instructions	
Other positive behaviors	

Inappropriate Behaviors

Demonstrated behavior	Consequence
Angry	
Bullying	
Constant complaining	
Disrespectful	
Interrupting instruction	
Inappropriate language	
Late to class	
Not dressing properly	
Nonparticipation	
Off task	
Overly aggressive	
Other disruptive behaviors?	

Chapter 8

Integrating Health Education Into the Classroom

Objectives

- List the four steps in integrating health education into the academic curriculum.
- List ideas for integrating health education into the classroom.
- Determine a link between the National Health Education Standards and academic standards.
- Develop grade-specific interdisciplinary activities.
- Develop a plan to implement the activity.

Health, learning and virtue will ensure your happiness; they will give you a quiet conscience, private esteem and public honour.

Thomas Jefferson

The U.S. classroom teacher is required to follow many courses of study, most notably the core subjects of mathematics, English language arts, science, and social studies. The health education course of study is required in most states but is often overlooked because of the lack of an accountability measure such as an exam. However, the content covered in the health education course of study is valuable for the health knowledge and application of that knowledge for students to live healthy lives. With the need to address student wellness, classroom teachers should find a way to add this important course of study to their daily lessons. One way to do so is to integrate the health content standards with core academic standards.

National Standards for Academic Performance

Classroom teachers are expected to teach specific academic subjects and are held accountable for ensuring that their students meet those academic expectations for each grade level. Some states have a course of study for each academic area, and they are the **minimal student expectations** for each grade level.

A national movement is occurring for states to adopt **Common Core State Standards** (National Governors Association Center for Best Practices & Council of Chief State School Officers, 2010). These standards provide consistent and clear academic expectations for all students across the nation. The Common Core State Standards were developed by state leaders in 48 states to establish guidelines for what every student should know and be able to do in kindergarten through grade 12. The main aim of the standards is to ensure that all students are prepared for success in entry-level careers, freshman-level college courses, and workforce training programs. The standards do not dictate how teachers should teach. In most states and local schools districts, teachers have the autonomy to design their own lessons in order to meet the individual needs of the students in their classrooms.

This chapter includes several examples that demonstrate how to enhance a curriculum by incorporating health education into the academic classroom. The Common Core State Standards for mathematics and English language arts were used for these examples along with state standards for science and social studies. If a school has adopted the Common Core standards, then teachers are expected to design their lessons to address these student expectations. You can find the Common Core standards at www.corestandards.org. If states have not adopted the Common Core standards, then state academic standards should be used.

National Health Education Standards (NHES)

The National Health Education Standards (NHES) were developed by American Association for Health Education, American School Health Association, American Public Health Association and the Society of State Directors of Health, Physical Education and Recreation in 2007. The NHES are as follows:

Standard 1 Students will comprehend concepts related to health promotion and disease prevention to enhance health.

Standard 2 Students will analyze the influence of family, peers, culture, media, technology, and other factors on health behaviors.

Standard 3 Students will demonstrate the ability to access valid information, products, and services to enhance health.

Standard 4 Students will demonstrate the ability to use interpersonal communication skills to enhance health and avoid or reduce health risks.

Standard 5 Students will demonstrate the ability to use decision-making skills to enhance health.

Standard 6 Students will demonstrate the ability to use goal-setting skills to enhance health.

Standard 7 Students will demonstrate the ability to practice health-enhancing behaviors and avoid or reduce health risks.

Standard 8 Students will demonstrate the ability to advocate for personal, family, and community health.

(Joint Committee on National Health Education Standards, 2007)

Integrating Nutrition Education Into Academic Subjects

MyPlate: A Yummy Curriculum (www.fns.usda.gov/tn/serving-myplate-yummy-curriculum) is an excellent collection of lesson ideas that are ready to use. The lessons are grouped into grade levels; 1 to 2, 3 to 4, and 5 to 6. The interdisciplinary plans make it easy for you to integrate this aspect of the health curriculum into the classroom with a click of the button.

Classroom teachers need to be able to connect the NHES with the four main academic areas of mathematics, English language arts, science, and social studies. One approach to integration is the focus of this chapter. The following sections outline four steps to help you create classroom activities that integrate health education into the academic curriculum. These steps will help you move from brainstorming general ideas to creating a plan to teach the activity in class.

Brainstorm Integration Ideas

The first step in this approach is to brainstorm ideas about how you can integrate health education into academic subjects. Consider mathematics. Your goal is to identify ways health education could support the acquisition of mathematics skills expected of your students according to the standards. This might include logs, graphs, charts, and polls of healthy practices. For example, you chart how often students wash their hands at school and display it on a poster in the room. Older elementary students graph the sugar content in drinks and determine the healthiest drink to consume.

Integrating science and health education in the elementary classroom is not very hard to imagine. Health education addresses the systems of the body, and you can integrate all of the systems easily through activities. For example, you can provide a class discussion on the relationship between unhealthy eating behaviors and diabetes. Another idea could be to discuss the effects of smoking on the respiratory system. You could also share information on the impact of the sun on the integumentary system (skin) and ways to prevent damage to this system. Another easy area of integration for health is the science curriculum. One example is to discuss the impact of pollution on environmental health. Another example is to address the importance of recycling.

Integrating health education with social studies involves more creativity on the part of the teacher. Some examples include service projects that involve the physical environment of the school; civics lessons that are focused on being a health advocate in the community; and healthy ways to solve conflicts instead of fighting.

Integrating health education into the English language arts curriculum in elementary school is one of the easiest connections. For the integration of reading, numerous books are centered on health issues that the teacher can read in class, such as *Germs Make Me Sick!* by Melvin Berger, *Dem Bones* by Bob Baner, *Eating the Alphabet* by Lois Ehlert, and *The Very Hungry Caterpillar* by Eric Carle. Also health issues are covered in the news, and students can read journal articles about current health topics. Integrating writing could include writing reflections about how they feel about bullying. Also, students could write reports about why it is important to eat properly. For the speaking and listening part of the curriculum, students could give oral reports on the importance of dental health and other hygiene topics. Class discussions could include how to encourage peers with positive health behaviors instead of using negative peer pressure. Integrating language skills into health education can be accomplished through using a healthy word wall.

See lab 8.1 to brainstorm ideas for how health education can be integrated into mathematics, English language arts, science, and social studies.

Link Health Education Standards With Academic Standards

When the brainstorming activities are completed, you will then move to more specific integration by using the NHES. This second step will connect a health education standard with an academic standard that the students are expected to meet. One way to get started is to brainstorm ideas of how an academic subject area could integrate with the National Standards. For example, National Standard 1 states that students will comprehend concepts related to health promotion and disease prevention to enhance health. A language arts lesson could have the students read the book *Germs Make Me Sick!* by Melvin Berger. After some discussion on the book, you introduce a handwashing activity. The children gather around a central area. Each child is given some lotion to spread on their hands, then you sprinkle glitter on their hands. The children then go around the room and shake hands with each other. You explain how easy it is to spread germs. Then, you give each student a paper towel and ask the students to try and wipe the germs off their hands. Of

course this won't work; germs don't just wipe off. You then explain that the best way to get rid of germs is to wash them off with soap. A student in social studies could research community services that are trusted and promote health as required by Standard 3. Table 8.1 provides examples of how NHES can be integrated with four academic subjects.

See lab 8.2 to practice integrating the NHES with the **core academic subjects** (mathematics, English language arts, science, and social studies).

Develop Grade-Specific Interdisciplinary Activities

Now that you have developed a lot of ideas about connecting the academic standards to

Table 8.1 Ideas for Integrating Core Academic Subjects With National Health Education Standards (NHES)

NHES	Mathematics	English language arts	Science	Social studies
1. Students will comprehend concepts related to health promotion and disease prevention to enhance health.	Display a class log of healthy hygiene practices used during the school day.	Read a book about germs, then demonstrate with a germ activity simulation (lotion and glitter).	Watch a CDC video on cigarettes and the lungs, then draw what the lungs look like (healthy and unhealthy).	Discuss how the environment affects people's health.
2. Students will analyze the influence of family, peers, culture, media, technology, and other factors on health behaviors.	Create a graph of popular influences on health behavior.	Present a news broadcast using different speakers to demonstrate the impact of the media on a story.	Discuss how weather impacts family health behaviors.	Review the history of technological advances in health awareness.
3. Students will demonstrate the ability to access valid information, products, and services to enhance health.	Track the opportunities that students have to access health information during the school day.	Research resources that provide valid health information.	Create a brochure that includes health products that protect the environment.	Discuss community services that are trusted and promote health.

Table 8.1 (continued)

NHES	Mathematics	English language arts	Science	Social studies
4. Students will demonstrate the ability to use interpersonal communication skills to enhance health and avoid or reduce health risks.	Take a class poll after seeing a scenario involving unhealthy practices and peer pressure.	Present skits using effective ways to tell someone you are being hurt.	Draw a class KWL* chart on information concerning impact of poor health choices on all of the body systems.	Discuss war and conflict resolution, and address positive ways to solve conflicts.
5. Students will demonstrate the ability to use decision-making skills to enhance health.	Compare sugar content in drinks by demonstrating the grams of sugar in each product.	Read a book on bullying, then discuss ways that students should respond to bullying.	Chart activities on how to reduce, reuse, and recycle.	Create a plan and mini emergency disaster kit for the classroom.
6. Students will demonstrate the ability to use goal-setting skills to enhance health.	Create a chart where students check off when they meet health goals discussed in class.	Create a class book on healthy snacks, and meet the goal of eating only healthy snacks in school.	Track sleeping hours during the week, and discuss how lack of sleep impacts different body systems. Set a sleep goal.	Review the CDC obesity charts for the United States; share how geographical factors affect this issue; discuss realistic solutions.
7. Students will demonstrate the ability to practice health-enhancing behaviors and avoid or reduce health risks.	Discuss percentage of class that practices good health behaviors.	Create a collage of personal pictures displaying positive health behaviors.	Identify the size, shape, color, and texture of certain foods, healthy and unhealthy.	Discuss littering, and complete a service project in the community to reduce trash.
8. Students will demonstrate the ability to advocate for personal, family, and community health.	Categorize foods into healthy and unhealthy choices.	Write a letter to a policymaker on a specific health topic that needs to be addressed.	Complete a MyPlate for a healthy family dinner, and discuss how to request healthier dinners at home.	Create a poster to encourage classmates to make healthy choices.

*KWL = Already **K**now, **W**ant to know, ultimately **L**earn
National Health Education Standards reprinted from Joint Committee on National Health Education Standards (2007).

the NHES, it is time to address grade-level expectations for each NHES. (See appendix A for all of the K-2 and 3-5 performance indicators.) The third step includes working on grade-specific interdisciplinary activities. When developing **interdisciplinary activities**, each activity should be detailed enough that anyone reading the activity can see clearly the integration of both the health education standard and the academic standard. In other words, the activity should detail what the students will be asked to do in order to meet the standards.

Here is an example of how an interdisciplinary activity can integrate a second grade math standard and a specific health education standard: Second graders need to be able to represent and interpret data. A second grader also needs to identify a short-term personal health goal and take action toward achieving the goal. What sort of interdisciplinary activity can a teacher develop to help the young student meet both standards? One idea could be to record the ounces of water consumed each day for 3 days, then determine a goal for the next 3 days. Another activity could be to keep a chart on how much candy is eaten in a week. The student will write a goal for reducing candy intake for the next week and report the results to the teacher.

Review the next examples in table 8.2 to see how interdisciplinary activities can be developed to integrate health education and academic standards for various subjects and grade levels. For states not using Common Core State Standards or for other academic standards, you can find state standards and courses of study by searching state websites for education standards.

See lab 8.3 to practice developing grade-specific interdisciplinary activities.

Table 8.2 Interdisciplinary Activities

NHES	Performance indicator for grade band K-2	Grade-specific interdisciplinary activities	State-specific academic standard
First grade science in Alabama			
7	7.2.2 Demonstrate behaviors that avoid or reduce health risks.	Divide into small groups with each group working with a bag of different food items. Students will identify the basic properties (e.g., size, shape, color, texture) of each food item. The group will discuss whether the foods have properties that help identify them as healthy or unhealthy.	Alabama science standard Identify basic properties of objects. Examples: size, shape, color, texture.
Third grade social sciences (history) in Oklahoma			
2	2.2.3 Describe how the media can influence health behaviors.	Discuss the history of the advertisement of cigarettes. The class will create a historic timeline to show the media impact on smoking.	Oklahoma social sciences standard Understand and describe the relationship between historic events and chronology through the creation of basic timelines.
Fifth grade English language arts for Common Core			
4	4.5.1 Demonstrate effective verbal and nonverbal communication skills to enhance health.	Create posters and flyers to be displayed around the school on health topics using persuasive language and images on health topics to encourage healthy eating habits; to expect zero tolerance for bullying; to promote active living; to say no to drugs; or to recommend that everyone recycle.	Common Core State Standard for English language arts Write opinion pieces on topics or texts, supporting a point of view with reasons and information.

Develop an Integrated Activity Plan

The final step in this integration process moves the activity idea to a plan to teach the activity. Choose one activity listed in the charts, and plan how to use the activity in a lesson. See the example of a fifth grade activity suggestion in the following chart.

The integrated lesson activity form is used for planning the activity. The activity form is similar to a class lesson plan, but it is shorter in duration because it only addresses one integrated activity that the classroom teacher can use to reinforce an academic lesson plan.

Teachers need to create a name for the activity, then list the objective and standards that are addressed in the activity. For the fifth grade example, the health education standard includes expressing opinions and giving accurate information about health issues. The math standard addresses converting like measurement units within a given measurement system. The specific lesson objectives are as follows: The students will use food labels to provide accurate information to determine healthy and unhealthy snacks. Students will use adding and multiplying skills to calculate total calories, fat calories, carbohydrate calories, and protein calories. The foods will then be ranked from healthiest snack to least healthy snack. The name of the activity might be The Label Tells Us Everything We Need to Know. The teacher will need 6 sets of handouts and 10 food labels from different snack packages, and there are no noted safety concerns for the activity. Finally, the teacher will plan how to explain the activity and organize the students and the event.

The following sample activity provides a model format for developing the activity plan that reflects this 15-minute lesson.

NHES	Performance indicator for grade band 3-5	Grade-specific interdisciplinary activities	State-specific academic standard
8	8.5.1 Express opinions and give accurate information about health issues.	Use food labels to determine total calories along with totals of fat calories, carbohydrate calories, and protein calories of popular snack foods. The foods will then be ranked from healthiest snack to least healthy snack.	Convert as measurement units within a given measurement system.

The Label Tells Us Everything We Need to Know

Grade

5

Target Objective

Students will use food labels to provide accurate information to determine healthy and unhealthy snacks. Students will use adding and multiplying skills to calculate total calories, fat calories, carbohydrate calories, and protein calories. The foods will then be ranked from healthiest snack to least healthy snack.

Content Standards Applied

NHES	Performance indicator for grade band 3-5	State-specific academic standard
Standard 8: Students will demonstrate the ability to advocate for personal, family, and community health.	8.5.1 Express opinions and give accurate information about health issues.	Mathematics—measurement and data Convert like measurement units within a given measurement system.

Equipment Needed

6 sets of handouts and 10 food labels from different snack packages

Activity explanation	Organization
What do you need to tell the students in order for them to perform the activity?	How many students will be in a group? Where will the students go to do the activity?
Introduction of Activity 2 minutes: Review how to read a food label. 1 minute: Review how to find calories using grams of fat, carbohydrates, and protein.	Students are in their seats listening to instructions.
Participation in the Activity 1 minute: The teacher will ask the students to get into groups of 5 students. 1 minute: The teacher will hand out 10 labels and handouts to each group. Each student will have 2 labels to calculate. 4 minutes: Students will follow the directions to calculate total calories, fat calories, carbohydrate calories, and protein calories. 1 minute: The group will rank the foods from most to least healthy snack.	Students will find their group members and move chairs to sit as a group to work on activity.
Closing 5 minutes: The teacher will ask each group to reveal their conclusions by displaying their worksheet using an Elmo projector. After all groups have presented, the teacher will ask for individual opinions on healthy snacks.	Students will turn their chairs to face the screen.

See lab 8.4 to develop an integrated lesson activity.

Summary

Classroom teachers are expected to teach so that their students meet the student expectations for each grade level. These minimal expectations are often driven by national standards. The standards mentioned in the chapter are the National Health Education Standards (NHES), the Common Core State Standards, and state-specific standards for academic subjects. Teachers interested in addressing the health needs of their students can do so through integrating the NHES with either the Common Core State Standards or state-specific standards for academic subjects.

One way to integrate the standards is to use the four-step approach discussed in this chapter. The four steps for integrating health education into the academic curriculum are (1) brainstorm integration ideas, (2) link NHES with academic standards, (3) develop grade-specific interdisciplinary activities, and (4) develop a plan to implement the activity. This process will help classroom teachers to create a classroom that integrates health literacy with academic standards. This process works. Teachers move from a simple idea to expanding that idea to a lesson activity that will meet more than one expected standard.

Review Questions

1. List the four steps for integrating health education into the academic curriculum.

2. Name three ways to integrate health education into the classroom.

3. Discuss the link between the National Health Education Standards and academic standards.

4. Identify one grade-specific interdisciplinary activity.

5. Discuss how to create a plan to implement the interdisciplinary activity.

Lab 8.1: Brainstorming Integration Ideas

Brainstorm ideas for how health education can be integrated into mathematics, English language arts, science, and social studies.

	Mathematics	English language arts	Science	Social studies
Ideas that you could do to integrate health education into the academic subjects				

Lab 8.2: Integrating the NHES With Core Subjects

After brainstorming about how you could integrate the four core subject areas, the next step is to expand those initial thoughts by connecting those ideas plus other ideas with the eight National Health Education Standards (NHES). For this lab, do not focus on a specific grade level; just think about K-5 in general. Complete the following chart for all subjects and all standards.

NHES	Mathematics	English language arts	Science	Social studies
1. Students will comprehend concepts related to health promotion and disease prevention to enhance health.				
2. Students will analyze the influence of family, peers, culture, media, technology, and other factors on health behaviors.				
3. Students will demonstrate the ability to access valid information, products, and services to enhance health.				
4. Students will demonstrate the ability to use interpersonal communication skills to enhance health and avoid or reduce health risks.				
5. Students will demonstrate the ability to use decision-making skills to enhance health.				
6. Students will demonstrate the ability to use goal-setting skills to enhance health.				
7. Students will demonstrate the ability to practice health-enhancing behaviors and avoid or reduce health risks.				
8. Students will demonstrate the ability to advocate for personal, family, and community health.				

National Health Education Standards from Joint Committee on National Health Education Standards (2007).

Lab 8.3: Developing Grade-Specific Interdisciplinary Activities

In this lab, each NHES is presented for grades K-5. The student expectations are grade band (K-2 and 3-5) performance indicators. You have access to all standards and performance indicators in the appendix. You will need to choose one of the indicators listed in the chart and apply that indicator to create a grade-appropriate activity to address it. Complete the charts by identifying interdisciplinary activities to integrate health education across all grades. Don't duplicate the examples that were displayed in previous sample charts. The National Health Education Standards and performance indicators are reprinted from Joint Committee on National Health Education Standards (2007).

K-2 Health Education Curriculum

National Standard 1: Students will comprehend concepts related to health promotion and disease prevention to enhance health.

NHES	Performance indicators for grade band K-2	Grade-specific interdisciplinary activities	State-specific academic standard
K-2: 1	1.2.1 Identify that healthy behaviors that affect personal health. 1.2.2 Recognize that there are multiple dimensions of health. 1.2.3 Describe ways to prevent communicable diseases. 1.2.4 List ways to prevent common childhood injuries. 1.2.5 Describe why it is important to seek health care.	Kindergarten: First grade: Second grade:	

(continued)

Lab 8.3: *(continued)*

3-5 Health Education Curriculum

National Standard 1: Students will comprehend concepts related to health promotion and disease prevention to enhance health.

NHES	Performance indicators for grade band 3-5	Grade-specific interdisciplinary activities	State-specific academic standard
3-5: 1	1.5.1 Describe the relationship between healthy behaviors and personal health. 1.5.2 Identify examples of emotional, intellectual, physical, and social health. 1.5.3 Describe ways in which safe and healthy school and community environments can promote personal health. 1.5.4 Describe ways to prevent common childhood injuries and health problems. 1.5.5 Describe when it is important to seek health care.	Third grade:	
		Fourth grade:	
		Fifth grade:	

K-2 Health Education Curriculum

National Standard 2: Students will analyze the influence of family, peers, culture, media, technology, and other factors on health behaviors.

NHES	Performance indicators for grade band K-2	Grade-specific interdisciplinary activities	State-specific academic standard
K-2: 2	2.2.1 Identify how the family influences personal health practices and behaviors. 2.2.2 Identify what the school can do to support personal health practices and behaviors. 2.2.3 Describe how the media can influence health behaviors.	Kindergarten:	
		First grade:	
		Second grade:	

(continued)

Lab 8.3: *(continued)*

3-5 Health Education Curriculum

National Standard 2: Students will analyze the influence of family, peers, culture, media, technology, and other factors on health behaviors.

NHES	Performance indicators for grade band 3-5	Grade-specific interdisciplinary activities	State-specific academic standard
3-5: 2	2.5.1 Describe how the family influences personal health practices and behaviors. 2.5.2 Identify the influence of culture on health practices and behaviors. 2.5.3 Identify how peers can influence healthy and unhealthy behaviors. 2.5.4 Describe how the school and community can support personal health practices and behaviors. 2.5.5 Explain how media influences thoughts, feelings, and health behaviors. 2.5.6 Describe ways that technology can influence personal health.	Third grade: Fourth grade: Fifth grade:	

K-2 Health Education Curriculum

National Standard 3: Students will demonstrate the ability to access valid information and products and services to enhance health.

NHES	Performance indicators for grade band K-2	Grade-specific interdisciplinary activities	State-specific academic standard
K-2: 3	3.2.1 Identify trusted adults and professionals who can help promote health. 3.2.2 Identify ways to locate school and community health helpers.	Kindergarten:	
		First grade:	
		Second grade:	

(continued)

Lab 8.3: *(continued)*

3-5 Health Education Curriculum

National Standard 3: Students will demonstrate the ability to access valid information and products and services to enhance health.

NHES	Performance indicators for grade band 3-5	Grade-specific interdisciplinary activities	State-specific academic standard
3-5: 3	3.5.1 Identify characteristics of valid health information, products, and services. 3.5.2 Locate resources from home, school, and community that provide valid health information.	Third grade:	
		Fourth grade:	
		Fifth grade:	

K-2 Health Education Curriculum

National Standard 4: Students will demonstrate the ability to use interpersonal communication skills to enhance health and avoid or reduce health risks.

NHES	Performance indicators for grade band K-2	Grade-specific interdisciplinary activities	State-specific academic standard
K-2: 4	4.2.1 Demonstrate healthy ways to express needs, wants, and feelings. 4.2.2 Demonstrate listening skills to enhance health. 4.2.3 Demonstrate ways to respond when in an unwanted, threatening, or dangerous situation. 4.2.4 Demonstrate ways to tell a trusted adult if threatened or harmed.	Kindergarten:	
		First grade:	
		Second grade:	

(continued)

Lab 8.3: *(continued)*

3-5 Health Education Curriculum

National Standard 4: Students will demonstrate the ability to use interpersonal communication skills to enhance health and avoid or reduce health risks.

NHES	Performance indicators for grade band 3-5	Grade-specific interdisciplinary activities	State-specific academic standard
3-5: 4	4.5.1 Demonstrate effective verbal and nonverbal communication skills to enhance health. 4.5.2 Demonstrate refusal skills that avoid or reduce health risks. 4.5.3 Demonstrate nonviolent strategies to manage or resolve conflict. 4.5.4 Demonstrate how to ask for assistance to enhance personal health.	Third grade:	
		Fourth grade:	
		Fifth grade:	

K-2 Health Education Curriculum

National Standard 5: Students will demonstrate the ability to use decision-making skills to enhance health.

NHES	Performance indicators for grade band K-2	Grade-specific interdisciplinary activities	State-specific academic standard
K-2: 5	5.2.1 Identify situations when a health-related decision is needed. 5.2.2 Differentiate between situations when a health-related decision can be made individually or when assistance is needed.	Kindergarten:	
		First grade:	
		Second grade:	

(continued)

Lab 8.3: *(continued)*

3-5 Health Education Curriculum

National Standard 5: Students will demonstrate the ability to use decision-making skills to enhance health.

NHES	Performance indicators for grade band 3-5	Grade-specific interdisciplinary activities	State-specific academic standard
3-5: 5	5.5.1 Identify health-related situations that might require a thoughtful decision. 5.5.2 Analyze when assistance is needed in making a health-related decision. 5.5.3 List healthy options to health-related issues or problems. 5.5.4 Predict the potential outcomes of each option when making a health-related decision. 5.5.5 Choose a healthy option when making a decision. 5.5.6 Describe the outcomes of a health-related decision.	Third grade: Fourth grade: Fifth grade:	

K-2 Health Education Curriculum

National Standard 6: Students will demonstrate the ability to use goal-setting skills to enhance health.

NHES	Performance indicators for grade band K-2	Grade-specific interdisciplinary activities	State-specific academic standard
K-2: 6	6.2.1 Identify a short-term personal health goal and take action toward achieving the goal. 6.2.2 Identify who can help when assistance is needed to achieve a personal health goal.	Kindergarten:	
		First grade:	
		Second grade:	

(continued)

Lab 8.3: *(continued)*

3-5 Health Education Curriculum

National Standard 6: Students will demonstrate the ability to use goal-setting skills to enhance health.

NHES	Performance indicators for grade band 3-5	Grade-specific interdisciplinary activities	State-specific academic standard
3-5: 6	6.5.1 Set a personal health goal and track progress toward its achievement. 6.5.2 Identify resources to assist in achieving a personal health goal.	Third grade:	
		Fourth grade:	
		Fifth grade:	

K-2 Health Education Curriculum

National Standard 7: Students will demonstrate the ability to practice health-enhancing behaviors and avoid or reduce health risks.

NHES	Performance indicators for grade band K-2	Grade-specific interdisciplinary activities	State-specific academic standard
K-2: 7	7.2.1 Demonstrate healthy practices and behaviors to maintain or improve personal health. 7.2.2 Demonstrate behaviors that avoid or reduce health risks.	Kindergarten:	
		First grade:	
		Second grade:	

(continued)

Lab 8.3: *(continued)*

3-5 Health Education Curriculum

National Standard 7: Students will demonstrate the ability to practice health-enhancing behaviors and avoid or reduce health risks.

NHES	Performance indicators for grade band 3-5	Grade-specific interdisciplinary activities	State-specific academic standard
3-5: 7	7.5.1 Identify responsible personal health behaviors. 7.5.2 Demonstrate a variety of healthy practices and behaviors to maintain or improve personal health. 7.5.3 Demonstrate a variety of behaviors that avoid or reduce health risks.	Third grade:	
		Fourth grade:	
		Fifth grade:	

K-2 Health Education Curriculum

National Standard 8: Students will demonstrate the ability to advocate for personal, family, and community health.

NHES	Performance indicators for grade band K-2	Grade-specific interdisciplinary activities	State-specific academic standard
K-2: 8	8.2.1 Make requests to promote personal health. 8.2.2 Encourage peers to make positive health choices.	Kindergarten:	
		First grade:	
		Second grade:	

(continued)

Lab 8.3: *(continued)*

3-5 Health Education Curriculum

National Standard 8: Students will demonstrate the ability to advocate for personal, family, and community health.

NHES	Performance indicators for grade band 3-5	Grade-specific interdisciplinary activities	State-specific academic standard
3-5: 8	8.5.1 Express opinions and give accurate information about health issues. 8.5.2 Encourage others to make positive health choices.	Third grade:	
		Fourth grade:	
		Fifth grade:	

Lab 8.4: Develop an Integrated Activity Plan

The last step in this integration process moves the activity idea to a lesson activity. Choose one activity idea listed in lab 8.3, and plan how to use the activity in a lesson. Start by using the following form to name the activity, the grade level, and the target objective. Then list the standards that you are integrating (NHES, performance indicators for the grade band [K-2 or 3-5], and the state-specific academic standards). List all of the equipment you will need to perform the activity in the class, and state safety concerns for the activity. Each activity lesson should include an introduction section, participation section, and a closing section. List the time that you think it will take to complete each section. Give specific directions for the activity explanation so that anyone who reads this could teach the activity. To complete the Organization column, list the number of students needed to start the activity (number of groups or lines and the number of students in each) as well as the direction of movement for the students to other lines. An example of a completed form is displayed earlier in the chapter in the sample activity The Label Tells Us Everything We Need to Know.

Health Education Integrated Activity

Activity name:

Grade:

Target objective:

Content standards applied:

NHES	Performance indicators for grade band K-2 or 3-5	State-specific academic standard

(continued)

Lab 8.4: *(continued)*

Equipment needed:

Safety concerns:

Activity explanation	Organization
What do you need to tell the students for them to perform the activity?	How many students will be in a group? Where will the students go to do the activity?
Introduction of Activity	
Participation in the Activity	
Closing	

Chapter 9

Integrating Physical Education Into the Classroom

Objectives

- List the four steps in integrating physical education into the academic curriculum.
- List ideas for integrating physical education into the classroom.
- Determine a link between the National Standards for K-12 Physical Education and academic standards.
- Develop grade-specific interdisciplinary activities.
- Develop a plan to implement the activity.

Intelligence and skill can only function at the peak of their capacity when the body is healthy and strong.

John F. Kennedy

In many U.S. states, the classroom teacher is also designated as the physical education teacher for that class. For this reason, university courses that prepare these teachers must also provide basic information on teaching physical education. If you are in this situation, one strategy for teaching physical education to your class is to focus on integrating physical education into the required classroom expectations. To build an integrated curriculum, you must recognize and address the state and national standards for each discipline.

National Standards for Academic Performance

Classroom teachers are expected to teach specific academic subjects and are held accountable for ensuring that their students meet those academic expectations for each grade level. Some states have a course of study for each academic area, and they are the minimal student expectations for each grade level.

A national movement is occurring for states to adopt Common Core State Standards (National Governors Association Center for Best Practices & Council of Chief State School Officers, 2010). These standards provide consistent and clear academic expectations for all students across the nation. The Common Core State Standards were developed by state leaders in 48 states to establish guidelines for what every student should know and be able to do in kindergarten through grade 12. The main aim of the standards is to ensure that all students are prepared for success in entry-level careers, freshman-level college courses, and workforce training programs. The standards do not dictate how teachers should teach. In most states and local schools districts, teachers have the autonomy to design their own lessons in order to meet the individual needs of the students in their classrooms.

This chapter includes several examples that demonstrate how to enhance a curriculum by incorporating physical education into the academic classroom. The Common Core State Standards for mathematics and English language arts were used for these examples along with state standards for science and social studies. If a school has adopted the Common Core standards, then teachers are expected to design their lessons to address these student expectations. You can find the Common Core standards at www.corestandards.org. If states have not adopted the Common Core standards, then state academic standards should be used.

National Standards for K-12 Physical Education

In 2013, the American Alliance for Health, Physical Education, Recreation and Dance—now named SHAPE America – Society of Health and Physical Educators—revised the National Standards for K-12 Physical Education. The standards now specifically address the concern for physical literacy across the nation by adding "The physically literate individual . . ." to the beginning of each standard. The National Standards for K-12 Physical Education are as follows:

Standard 1 The physically literate individual demonstrates competency in a variety of motor skills and movement patterns.

Standard 2 The physically literate individual applies knowledge of concepts, principles, strategies and tactics related to movement and performance.

Standard 3 The physically literate individual demonstrates the knowledge and skills to achieve and maintain a health-enhancing level of physical activity and fitness.

Standard 4 The physically literate individual exhibits responsible personal and social behavior that respects self and others.

Standard 5 The physically literate individual recognizes the value of physical activity for health, enjoyment, challenge, self-expression and/or social interaction.

Reprinted from SHAPE America, 2014, *National standards & grade-level outcomes for K-12 physical education* (Champaign, IL: Human Kinetics), 12.

The National Standards are broad statements that are to be used across K-12 programs. To understand grade-level expectations, teachers should use *National Standards & Grade-Level Outcomes for K-12 Physical Education* (SHAPE America, 2014), which documents grade-specific outcomes to help teachers sequence their curricula and address specific expectations and goals for students at each grade level.

The Grade-Level Outcomes outline these expectations for each physically literate student ending the elementary years:

> By the end of Grade 5, the learner will demonstrate competence in fundamental motor skills and selected combinations of skills; use basic movement concepts in dance, gymnastics, and small-sided practice tasks; identify basic health-related fitness concepts; exhibit acceptance of self and others in physical activities; and identify the benefits of a physically active lifestyle. (SHAPE America, 2014, p. 26)

For all of the K-5 outcomes, see appendix B.

The concept of integrating physical education into the academic curriculum may seem a daunting task for classroom teachers. However, it is necessary, especially given that many students are kinesthetic learners (Hannaford, 1995). This chapter outlines these four steps for integrating physical education activities into the academic curriculum: (1) brainstorm integration ideas, (2) link physical education standards with academic standards, (3) develop grade-specific interdisciplinary activities, and (4) develop a plan to implement the activity. These steps will help you move from brainstorming general ideas to creating a plan to teach the activity in class.

Integrated Physical Education Lesson Ideas

PE Central has a section devoted to the classroom teacher and integrated lesson ideas (www.pecentral.org/lessonideas/classroom/classroom.asp). With over 250 lesson ideas, this section is a great place for classroom teachers to go for ready-made integrated lessons.

Brainstorm Integration Ideas

The first step in this approach is to brainstorm ideas for how physical education can be integrated into academic subjects. Consider mathematics. Your goal is to identify ways physical education could support the acquisition of mathematics skills expected of your students according to the standards. This might include outlining shapes with a rope or with the body, tossing balls or beanbags at specific geometric shapes, or traveling in a specific pathway. Elementary students need to be able to count in sequence, skip count, add, subtract, multiply, and divide. You can use several physical activities in a mathematics lesson to help students with these skills. For example, the student could move to the number of claps or beats, count the number of times a target is hit, or use movement to answer math flash cards. Older elementary students can measure time spent on a particular activity or tasks, construct graphs showing changes in heart rate during activity, or use pedometer data to show movement counts of different activities as ways to meet the standards for measuring, graphing, and so on.

Integrating science and physical education in the elementary classroom is not hard to imagine. Physical activity addresses the systems of the body, and you can integrate the muscular and skeletal system easily through identifying muscles and bones used for activities. Involving other systems may require more setup. For example, you might do a physical demonstration of the cardiovascular system in which you use physical education equipment to create a course; students travel through the course like a drop of blood through the heart and lungs out to the body then back to the heart again. Another idea could be to illustrate the movement of the solar system by having the students physically moving like the planets would around the sun. You could also demonstrate Newton's laws of motion, bringing the laws off the pages of a book into real-life view with physical movement.

Integrating physical education with social studies involves more creativity. Some examples include performing historical dances or reenacting historical events. Memorizing states or capitals may be easier for students in an activity setting (e.g., naming the states in alphabetical order while jumping rope), and using pedometers in the classroom can help students walk across the United States without leaving the community.

The elementary English language arts curriculum offers an array of areas that can be integrated with physical education. Reading ideas include performing the instructions written on station cards, reading about famous athletes or favorite sports, reading and assessing partners using a checklist of cue words for skill performance, and acting out the content of a book while reading it. Integrating writing could include writing reflections or journals about physical activity experiences. Also, students could write reports about how to make healthy choices in nutrition and physical activities. For the speaking and listening part of the curriculum, students could give oral reports on various sport-related topics. Class discussions could include students sharing experiences with others in groups or in front of the class. You can integrate language skills into physical education through activities involving spelling words, sounding out syllables while dribbling a basketball, and acting out verbs.

See lab 9.1 to brainstorm ideas for how physical education can be integrated into mathematics, English language arts, science, and social studies.

Link Physical Education Standards With Academic Standards

When the brainstorming activities are completed, teachers will then move to more specific integration by using the National Standards for K-12 Physical Education. This second step will connect a physical education standard with an academic standard that the students are expected to meet. One way to get started is to brainstorm ideas of how an academic subject area could integrate with the National Standards. For example, National Standard 1 states that a physically literate individual will demonstrate competency in a variety of motor skills and movement patterns. A language arts lesson could have the student spell words using large movements of the arms. A student in social studies could discuss the history and importance of fitness levels of men and women serving in the armed forces, demonstrating the knowledge and skills needed to achieve and maintain a health-enhancing level of physical activity and fitness, as required by Standard 3. Table 9.1 provides examples of how National Standards for K-12 Physical Education can be integrated with four academic subjects.

See lab 9.2 to integrate the National Standards for K-12 Physical Education with the core academic subjects (mathematics, English language arts, science, and social studies). For states not using Common Core State Standards or for other academic standards, you can find state standards and courses of study by searching state websites for education standards.

Develop Grade-Specific Interdisciplinary Activities

Now that you have developed a lot of ideas about connecting the academic standards to the National Standards for K-12 Physical Education, it is time to address the **Grade-Level Outcomes**. The third step includes working on grade-specific interdisciplinary activities. When developing interdisciplinary activities, each activity should be detailed enough that anyone reading the activity can see clearly the integration of both the physical education standard and the academic standard. In other words, the activity should detail what the students will be asked to do in order to meet the outcome.

Here is an example of how an interdisciplinary activity can integrate a kindergarten math standard and a specific physical education grade-level outcome: Kindergartners need to be able to know number names and the count sequence to meet Common Core math standards for that grade level. A kindergartner also needs to be able to hop, gallop, run, slide, and skip while maintaining balance to meet the standard for locomotor skills. What sort of in-

Table 9.1 Ideas for Integrating Core Subjects With National Standards for K-12 Physical Education

National Standards for K-12 Physical Education	Mathematics	English language arts	Science	Social studies
1. The physically literate individual demonstrates competency in a variety of motor skills and movement patterns.	Use motor skills as you count, multiply, or divide numbers.	Use movement patterns to spell words.	Demonstrate various movement patterns used by animals.	Reenact a historical event using a variety of movement patterns.
2. The physically literate individual applies knowledge of concepts, principles, strategies and tactics related to movement and performance.	Construct a chart of successful scoring strategies (e.g., a shooting chart), and discuss strengths and weaknesses of percentages.	Act out the scenes of a literature book.	Relate the strategies needed to juggle to the laws of physics.	Perform multicultural dances from the past.
3. The physically literate individual demonstrates the knowledge and skills to achieve and maintain a health-enhancing level of physical activity and fitness.	Graph heart rate intensity for several types of physical activity.	Journal nutrition intake, and reflect on making healthy food choices.	Understand the function of burning calories by discussing the amount of activity needed to expend the calories consumed of favorite food items.	Discuss the history and importance of fitness levels of men and women serving in the armed forces.
4. The physically literate individual exhibits responsible personal and social behavior that respects self and others.	Create a chart for acts of kindness that students perform during school, and keep a running total.	Write class rules that demonstrate good sporting behavior.	Discuss the emotional impact of bullying and how to eliminate it in class activities.	Work together in a group to answer historical questions in a small-sided relay game.
5. The physically literate individual recognizes the value of physical activity for health, enjoyment, challenge, self-expression and/or social interaction.	Collect pedometer data for enjoyable activities that the class chooses to do after school for a week.	Journal specific physical activities and games that are participated in for enjoyment by oneself and those enjoyed with others.	Share the health benefits that the body receives from physical activity.	Research the history of women's athletics since 1972 to recognize the opportunities that women now have to enjoy physical activities.

National Standards for K-12 Physical Education reprinted from SHAPE America (2014).

terdisciplinary activity can a teacher develop to help the young student meet both expectations? One idea could be to have the student count the number of hops it took to get from one spot to another. Another activity could be to draw the numbers from 1 to 10 on the floor and have the student say the number names as students skip over them.

Table 9.2 shows examples of how to develop interdisciplinary activities to integrate physical education and academic standards for various subjects and grade levels. For states not using Common Core standards or for other academic standards, you can find state standards and courses of study by searching each state's website for education standards. Another way to find state physical education standards is at www.shapeamerica.org/standards/pe/state-standards.cfm. From there, you can search for academic standards for the state.

See lab 9.3 to develop grade-specific interdisciplinary activities.

Table 9.2 Interdisciplinary Activities

National Standard (S#) for K-12 Physical Education and Elementary (E) Outcome Specific Area	Grade-Level Outcome	Grade-specific interdisciplinary activities	State-specific academic standard
First grade science in Alabama			
S3.E3 Fitness knowledge	Identifies the heart as a muscle that grows stronger with exercise/play and physical activity. (S3.E3.1)	Students will discuss the parts of the body used to participate in healthy physical activities. Students will name the bones and muscles needed to play those activities.	Alabama—science standard Identify parts of the human body, including the head, neck, shoulders, arms, spine, and legs. Discuss the relationship of muscles and bones to locomotion.
Second grade social sciences (history) in Oregon			
S4.E4 Working with others	Works independently with others in partner environments. (S4.E4.2)	Students will participate in an orienteering activity where partners will use a GPS app and a map of the school community to complete a scavenger hunt that includes information about the community. A follow-up lesson will be a GPS cache hunt (geocaching).	Oregon—social sciences standard Use basic information on maps and other geographic tools to locate and identify physical and human features of the community.
Fifth grade English language arts for Common Core			
S5.E3 Self-expression/enjoyment	Analyzes different physical activities for enjoyment and challenge, identifying reasons for positive or negative response. (S5.E3.5)	Students will list their most enjoyable and least enjoyable physical activities. They will discuss these lists in partners and share the reasons for each choice. The teacher will then move to a class discussion to address the levels of enjoyment and the reasons for these levels.	Common Core State Standard for English language arts Engage effectively in a range of collaborative discussions (one-on-one, in groups, and teacher-led) with diverse partners on grade 5 topics and texts, building on others' ideas, and expressing their own clearly.

Develop an Integrated Activity Plan

The final step in this integration process moves the activity idea to a lesson activity. Choose one activity listed in the charts, and plan how to use the activity in a lesson. See the example of a kindergarten activity suggestion in the following chart.

The integrated lesson activity form is used for planning the activity. The activity form is similar to a class lesson plan, but it is shorter in duration because it only addresses one integrated activity that the classroom teacher can use to reinforce an academic lesson plan or to provide a specific brain break activity to help classroom performance. This lesson activity can take place in the classroom, or the teacher can take the students to an open space area outside the classroom.

Teachers need to create a name for the activity, then list the objective and standards that are addressed in the activity. For the kindergarten example, the physical education grade-level outcome addressed is related to locomotor skills, and the math standard is counting and cardinality. The specific lesson objectives are to practice locomotor skills while counting in a sequence and to practice locomotor skills on the letters of the names of numbers drawn on the floor. The name of the activity might be Locomotion Numbers. The teacher will need chalk or tape for numbers, and everyone will need to be aware of personal space so that students can move safely without running into each other. Finally, the teacher will plan how to explain the activity and organize the students and the event.

The following sample activity provides a model format for developing the activity plan that reflects this 15-minute lesson.

National Standard (S#) for K-12 Physical Education and Elementary (E) Outcome Specific Area	Grade-Level Outcome	Grade-specific interdisciplinary activities	State-specific academic standard
S1.E1 Locomotor	Performs locomotor skills (hopping, galloping, running, sliding, skipping) while maintaining balance. (S1.E1.K)	Students will practice locomotor skills while counting in a sequence. Also, students will practice locomotor skills on the letters of the names of numbers drawn on the floor.	Counting and cardinality Know number names and the count sequence.

Locomotion Numbers

Grade

K

Target Objective

Practice locomotor skills while counting in a sequence. Also, practice locomotor skills on the letters of the names of numbers drawn on the floor.

Content Standards Applied

National Standards for K-12 Physical Education	Grade-Level Outcome	State-specific academic standard
Standard 1: The physically literate individual demonstrates competency in a variety of motor skills and movement patterns.	S1.E1: Locomotor Performs locomotor skills (hopping, galloping, running, sliding, skipping) while maintaining balance. (S1.E1.K)	Mathematics—counting and cardinality Know number names and the count sequence.

Equipment Needed

Chalk or tape for numbers

Safety Concerns

Awareness of personal space so that students do not run into other students

Activity explanation	Organization
What do you need to tell the students in order for them to perform the activity?	How many students will be in a group? Where will the students go to do the activity?
Introduction of Activity 2 minutes: Review the following locomotor skills with the students: hopping, galloping, running, sliding, and skipping. Remind students of the importance of doing the skill correctly. 1 minute: Review counting sequence with the students.	Students stand side by side, facing the teacher. The students will practice the locomotor skills at the command of the teacher and in the direction stated.
Participation in the Activity 2 minutes: The teacher will combine a counting sequence with one locomotor skill at a time. The class will perform the skill, counting in unison with other classmates. 2 minutes: The teacher will combine a counting sequence with one locomotor skill at a time. The class will perform the skill by counting individually, and the teacher will move through the class while helping the students with counting as well as locomotor skills. 5 minutes: After completing the previous two sets, the teacher will ask each student to move to the chalk area where a number is written on the ground. The students will choose one locomotor skill to perform while following the lines of the word written on the ground. During this movement activity, the students call out the letter that they see; at the end of the word, the students call out the name of the word (which is the name of one number). Before leaving that word, each student will perform a locomotor skill equal to the number represented by the word. The students will rotate to a new word at the direction of the teacher.	Students will complete activities in their personal space while respecting each other's personal space. Students will rotate to a new word at the direction of the teacher.
Closing 3 minutes: The teacher will review all locomotor skills used in this activity as well as review the chalk number words.	Students will sit in a semicircle in front of the teacher.

See lab 9.4 to develop an integrated lesson activity.

Summary

Classroom teachers are expected to teach in such a way that students meet minimal expectations for each grade level. The minimal expectations are often driven by national standards. The standards mentioned in the chapter are the National Standards for K-12 Physical Education, the Common Core State Standards, and state-specific standards for academic subjects. Teachers interested in addressing the needs of kinesthetic learners can do so through integrating the National Standards for K-12 Physical Education with either the Common Core State Standards or state-specific standards for academic subjects.

One way to integrate the standards is to use the four-step approach discussed in this chapter. The four steps for integrating physical education into the academic curriculum are (1) brainstorm integration ideas, (2) link National Standards for K-12 Physical Education with academic standards, (3) develop grade-specific interdisciplinary instructional activities, and (4) develop a plan to implement the activity. This four-step process will help classroom teachers to create a fun and exciting classroom that integrates physical education with academic standards. This process works. Teachers move from a simple idea to expanding that idea to a lesson activity that will meet more than one expected standard. Beyond meeting the standards, another great benefit is that the students will enjoy the instruction provided in an active classroom environment.

Review Questions

1. List the four steps for integrating physical education into the academic curriculum.

2. Name three ways to integrate physical education into the classroom.

3. Discuss the link between the National Standards for K-12 Physical Education and academic standards.

4. Identify one grade-specific interdisciplinary activity.

5. Discuss how to create a plan to implement the interdisciplinary activity.

Lab 9.1: Brainstorming Integration Ideas

Brainstorm ideas for how physical education can be integrated into academic subjects.

	Mathematics	English language arts	Science	Social studies
Ideas that you could do to integrate physical education into the academic subjects				

Lab 9.2: Integrating the National Standards for K-12 Physical Education With Core Subjects

 After brainstorming about how you could integrate the four core subject areas, the next step is to expand those initial thoughts by connecting those ideas plus other ideas with the five National Standards for K-12 Physical Education. For this lab, do not focus on a specific grade level; just think about K-5 in general. Complete the following chart for all subjects and all standards.

National Standards for K-12 Physical Education	Mathematics	English language arts	Science	Social studies
Standard 1: The physically literate individual demonstrates competency in a variety of motor skills and movement patterns.				
Standard 2: The physically literate individual applies knowledge of concepts, principles, strategies and tactics related to movement and performance.				
Standard 3: The physically literate individual demonstrates the knowledge and skills to achieve and maintain a health-enhancing level of physical activity and fitness.				
Standard 4: The physically literate individual exhibits responsible personal and social behavior that respects self and others.				
Standard 5: The physically literate individual recognizes the value of physical activity for health, enjoyment, challenge, self-expression and/or social interaction.				

National Standards for K-12 Physical Education reprinted from SHAPE America (2014).

Lab 9.3: Developing Grade-Specific Interdisciplinary Activities

In this lab, each National Standard is presented for grades K-5. Complete the charts by identifying interdisciplinary activities to integrate physical education across all grades. Don't duplicate the examples that were displayed in the previous sample charts. The National Standards and Grade-Level Outcomes are reprinted from SHAPE America (2014).

K-5 Physical Education Curriculum

National Standard 1: The physically literate individual demonstrates competency in a variety of motor skills and movement patterns.

National Standard (S#) for K-12 Physical Education and Elementary (E) Outcome Specific Area	Grade-Level Outcome	Grade-specific interdisciplinary activities	State-specific academic standard
S1.E1 Locomotor	Kindergarten: Performs locomotor skills (hopping, galloping, running, sliding, skipping) while maintaining balance. (S1.E1.K)	Kindergarten:	
	First grade: Hops, gallops, jogs, and slides using a mature pattern. (S1.E1.1)	First grade:	
	Second grade: Skips using a mature pattern. (S1.E1.2)	Second grade:	
	Third grade: Leaps using a mature pattern. (S1.E1.3)	Third grade:	
	Fourth grade: Uses various locomotor skills in a variety of small-sided practice tasks, dance, and educational gymnastics experiences. (S1.E1.4)	Fourth grade:	
	Fifth grade: Combines traveling with manipulative skills for execution to a target (e.g., scoring in soccer, hockey, and basketball). (S1.E1.5c)	Fifth grade:	

(continued)

Lab 9.3: *(continued)*

K-5 Physical Education Curriculum

National Standard 2: The physically literate individual applies knowledge of concepts, principles, strategies and tactics related to movement and performance.

National Standard (S#) for K-12 Physical Education and Elementary (E) Outcome Specific Area	Grade-Level Outcome	Grade-specific interdisciplinary activities	State-specific academic standard
S2.E2 Pathways, Shapes, Levels	Kindergarten: Travels in three different pathways. (S2.E2.K)	Kindergarten:	
	First grade: Travels demonstrating a variety of relationships with objects (e.g., over, under, around, through). (S2.E2.1b)	First grade:	
	Second grade: Combines shapes, levels, and pathways into simple travel, dance, and gymnastics sequences. (S2.E2.2)	Second grade:	
	Third grade: Recognizes locomotor skills specific to a wide variety of physical activities. (S2.E2.3)	Third grade:	
	Fourth grade: Combines movement concepts with skills in small-sided practice tasks, gymnastics, and dance environments. (S2.E2.4)	Fourth grade:	
	Fifth grade: Combines movement concepts with skills in small-sided practice tasks, games environments, gymnastics, and dance with self-direction. (S2.E2.5)	Fifth grade:	

K-5 Physical Education Curriculum

National Standard 3: The physically literate individual demonstrates the knowledge and skills to achieve and maintain a health-enhancing level of physical activity and fitness.

National Standard (S#) for K-12 Physical Education and Elementary (E) Outcome Specific Area	Grade-Level Outcome	Grade-specific interdisciplinary activities	State-specific academic standard
S3.E3 Fitness knowledge	Kindergarten: Recognizes that when you move fast, your heart beats faster and you breathe faster. (S3.E3.K)	Kindergarten:	
	First grade: Identifies the heart as a muscle that grows stronger with exercise/play and physical activity. (S3.E3.1)	First grade:	
	Second grade: Identifies physical activities that contribute to fitness. (S3.E3.2b)	Second grade:	
	Third grade: Describes the concept of fitness and provides examples of physical activity to enhance fitness. (S3.E3.3)	Third grade:	
	Fourth grade: Identifies the components of health-related fitness. (S3.E3.4)	Fourth grade:	
	Fifth grade: Differentiates between skill-related and health-related fitness. (S3.E3.5)	Fifth grade:	

(continued)

Lab 9.3: *(continued)*

K-5 Physical Education Curriculum

National Standard 4: The physically literate individual exhibits responsible personal and social behavior that respects self and others.

National Standard (S#) for K-12 Physical Education and Elementary (E) Outcome Specific Area	Grade-Level Outcome	Grade-specific interdisciplinary activities	State-specific academic standard
S4.E4 Working with others	Kindergarten: Shares equipment and space with others. (S4.E4.K)	Kindergarten:	
	First grade: Works independently with others in a variety of class environments (e.g., small and large groups). (S4.E4.1)	First grade:	
	Second grade: Works independently with others in partner environments. (S4.E4.2)	Second grade:	
	Third grade: Praises others for their success in movement performance. (S4.E4.3b)	Third grade:	
	Fourth grade: Accepts players of all skill levels into the physical activity. (S4.E4.4b)	Fourth grade:	
	Fifth grade: Accepts, recognizes, and actively involves others with both higher and lower skill abilities into physical activities and group projects. (S4.E4.5)	Fifth grade:	

K-5 Physical Education Curriculum

National Standard 5: The physically literate individual recognizes the value of physical activity for health, enjoyment, challenge, self-expression and/or social interaction.

National Standard (S#) for K-12 Physical Education and Elementary (E) Outcome Specific Area	Grade-Level Outcome	Grade-specific interdisciplinary activities	State-specific academic standard
S5.E3 Self-expression/enjoyment	Kindergarten: Identifies physical activities that are enjoyable. (S5.E3.Ka)	Kindergarten:	
	First grade: Discusses personal reasons for enjoying physical activities. (S5.E3.1b)	First grade:	
	Second grade: Identifies physical activities that provide self-expression (e.g., dance, gymnastics routines, practice tasks in games environment). (S5.E3.2)	Second grade:	
	Third grade: Reflects on the reasons for enjoying selected physical activities. (S5.E3.3)	Third grade:	
	Fourth grade: Ranks the enjoyment of participating in different physical activities. (S5.E3.4)	Fourth grade:	
	Fifth grade: Analyzes different physical activities for enjoyment and challenge, identifying reasons for a positive or negative response. (S5.E3.5)	Fifth grade:	

Lab 9.4:   Developing an Integrated Activity Plan

 The last step in this integration process moves the activity idea to a lesson activity. Choose one strategy listed in lab 9.3, and plan how to use that strategy in a lesson. Start by using the following form to name the activity, the grade level, and the target objective. Then list the National Standards that you are integrating along with the state-specific academic standards. List all of the equipment you will need in order to perform the activity in the class, and state safety concerns for the activity. Each activity lesson should include an introduction section, a participation section, and a closing section. List the time that you think it will take to complete each section. Give specific directions for the activity explanation so that anyone who reads it could teach the activity. Complete the organization column by listing the number of students needed to start the activity (number of groups or lines and the number of students in each) as well as the direction of movement for the students to other lines. An example of a completed form is displayed earlier in the chapter in the sample activity Locomotion Numbers.

Physical Education Integrated Activity

Activity name:

Grade:

Target objective:

Content standards applied:

National Standards for K-12 Physical Education	Grade-Level Outcome	State-specific academic standard

Equipment needed:

Safety concerns:

Activity explanation	Organization
What do you need to tell the students in order for them to perform the activity?	How many students will be in a group? Where will the students go to do the activity?
Introduction of Activity	
Participation in the Activity	
Closing	

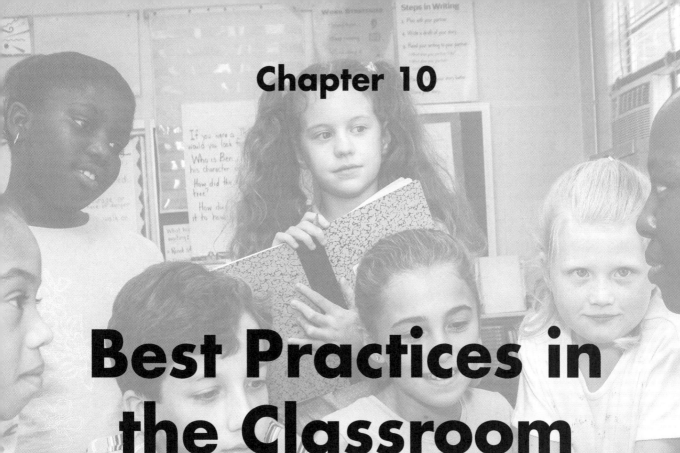

Chapter 10

Best Practices in the Classroom and Beyond

Objectives

- Describe steps to organizing your yearly curriculum to include health and physical education.
- Define scaffolding, and apply it to teaching a health or physical education topic.
- Identify three effective teaching methods commonly used in health education.
- Describe the difference between formative and summative assessment.
- List one assessment strategy used to gauge understanding of material taught in class.
- Identify policies that support wellness.

You can't educate a child who isn't healthy and you can't keep a child healthy who isn't educated.

Jocelyn Elders, former U.S. Surgeon General

Effective health and physical education must be comprehensive, sequential, standards-based, and student focused. How does this idea translate into best practices in your elementary classroom and school? In this chapter you will learn six important practices to keep in mind when designing your healthy classroom and beyond. These include but are not limited to the following: planning ahead, using effective teaching methods, creating effective assessment, providing the best learning environment, increasing professional knowledge and competence, and supporting policies that encourage wellness.

Planning Ahead

Meaningful planning begins with a look at the big picture and deciding on what knowledge your students need to possess and what skills they need to have by the end of the school year. This approach is called **backward design planning**. Backward design planning encourages educators to first determine what outcomes they desire, then plan the curriculum based on those outcomes. A solid health education curriculum should address the 10 content areas discussed in chapter 3; those areas are shown in table 10.1.

In addition, the curriculum must be aligned with the National Health Education Standards (NHES), as discussed earlier and shown here in figure 10.1.

Next, does your district provide a curriculum for elementary health education and physical education? Download a copy of your state's curriculum guide for health education and physical education. Finally, using these documents, develop a yearly plan. One approach is to focus each month on a particular content area. See table 10.2 for a 3-month sample of what a yearly plan may look like.

Teaching Methods That Work

Effective classroom teachers understand the importance of their lesson design and the learning

Table 10.1 Ten Content Areas of Health Education

Content area	Potential topics for grades K-3	Potential topics for grades 4-6
Mental and emotional health	Expressing feelings Managing feelings Respect Positive self-image Role models Making friends Listening to others Resisting peer pressure Conflict resolution Being a responsible family member	Effective communication Conflict resolution Developing good character Responsible decision making How to listen Role models Being a responsible family member Family communication Listening in families Problems in families Positive self-image Caring for self Caring for others
Promoting health and preventing disease	Covering coughs and sneezes Washing hands Immunizations Checkups Brushing and flossing teeth Skin care Sun safety Lice Eye care Ear care	Personal hygiene Dental hygiene Preventing infectious diseases Preventing/managing diabetes Preventing/managing asthma Sun safety Reducing health risks Health care services

Table 10.1 *(continued)*

Content area	Potential topics for grades K-3	Potential topics for grades 4-6
Promoting physical activity	Safety Movement Physical fitness Heart rate Injury prevention	Promoting health through movement Benefits of physical activity Influences on activity level Developing fitness Safety Flexibility Cardiovascular and respiratory fitness Warming up Cooling down Healthy body composition Injury prevention
Promoting healthy eating	Food safety Washing hands Nutrition Food groups Nutrients Meals and snacks Shopping for food Storing food Drinking water Digestive system	The digestive process Following dietary guidelines Healthy snacks Food labels Food packaging Food choices Storing food Meal planning Nutrients Importance of water Disease prevention through food Improving eating through behavior change Preventing foodborne illness Maintaining a healthy weight Recognizing eating disorders
Growth and sexual development	Growth and development Circulatory system Nervous system Respiratory system Muscular system Skeletal system Respect for self and others Family roles Owner's manual to body care Puberty 101: mood swings, developmental changes	Growth and development Owner's manual to body care Puberty Changing bodies Changing minds Respect for self and others Family roles Responsibility HIV/AIDS Pregnancy and childbirth Male and female reproduction
Community and consumer health	Looking at medicine labels Our community Doctors Pharmacists Nurses Paramedics Firefighters Police officers	Being an informed consumer Spending time and money wisely Reading medicine labels Using medications correctly Prescription medications Over-the-counter medications Health services in our community Health career development Evaluating health information Developing health literacy

(continued)

Table 10.1 *(continued)*

Content area	Potential topics for grades K-3	Potential topics for grades 4-6
Environmental health	Reducing waste Recycling Sanitation workers Clean water Clean air	Connections between the environment and personal health Reducing waste Recycling Preventing pollution of air, water, and soil Conserving resources Reducing, reusing, and recycling Conserving water Conserving energy Advocating for a healthy environment
Alcohol and drug prevention	Safely using medicine Being safe around medicine Difference between over-the-counter and prescription medicines Dangerous substances Choosing friends Problem solving and goal setting	Responsible drug use: prescription drugs, over-the-counter drug use/abuse and dependency Inhalants Protective factors to resist alcohol, tobacco, and drugs Evaluating how alcohol and tobacco are harmful Evaluating the media's promotion of tobacco and alcohol Alcohol, tobacco, and drugs in the news Resisting peer pressure to use alcohol, tobacco, and drugs
Preventing intentional injury and violence	Conflict resolution Expressing feelings Managing feelings Respect Listening to others Positive self-image Role models Making friends Avoiding weapons Dealing with bullies Emergency preparedness	Risk and protective factors associated with youth violence Preventing school violence Violence and maltreatment at home Protecting yourself from gangs and weapons Bullying, cyberbullying Effective communication Conflict resolution How to listen Role models Positive self-image
Injury prevention and safety	Wearing seatbelts Riding in the backseat Getting help in emergencies Staying safe at home Pedestrian safety Using a buddy system Wearing helmets Water safety Fire safety Electrical safety Staying away from poison Preventing dog bites Basic first aid	Emergency preparedness Universal precautions Fire safety Preventing accidents in the water Motor vehicle safety Being home alone Pedestrian and bike safety Calling someone in an emergency Staying safe during severe weather and natural disasters Preventing illness during hot/cold weather

Figure 10.1 National Health Education Standards (NHES)

Standard 1 Students will comprehend concepts related to health promotion and disease prevention to enhance health.

Standard 2 Students will analyze the influence of family, peers, culture, media, technology, and other factors on health behaviors.

Standard 3 Students will demonstrate the ability to access valid information, products, and services to enhance health.

Standard 4 Students will demonstrate the ability to use interpersonal communication skills to enhance health and avoid or reduce health risks.

Standard 5 Students will demonstrate the ability to use decision-making skills to enhance health.

Standard 6 Students will demonstrate the ability to use goal-setting skills to enhance health.

Standard 7 Students will demonstrate the ability to practice health-enhancing behaviors and avoid or reduce health risks.

Standard 8 Students will demonstrate the ability to advocate for personal, family, and community health.

Reprinted from Joint Committee on National Health Education Standards, 2007, *National Health Education Standards: Achieving Excellence.* (Washington, DC: American Cancer Society).

Table 10.2 Three-Month Sample Health Curriculum Plan

Month	Time needed for content	Content area/topics for study (K-3)	NHES	State standard
September	Five 1-hour lessons (You develop lessons on the topics listed in the next column.)	Mental and emotional health ▪ Expressing and managing feelings ▪ Positive self-image ▪ Role models ▪ Making friends ▪ Resisting peer pressure	Standards 1, 3, 4, and 5	See your state standards.
October	Seven 30-minute lessons (You develop lessons on topics listed in the next column.)	Promoting health and preventing disease ▪ Covering coughs and sneezes ▪ Washing hands ▪ Immunizations ▪ Checkups ▪ Brushing and flossing teeth ▪ Skin care ▪ Sun safety	Standards 1, 2, 4, 5, 6, and 8	See your state standards.
November	Five 1-hour lessons (You develop lessons on topics listed in the next column.)	Promoting physical activity ▪ Safety ▪ Movement ▪ Physical fitness ▪ Heart rate ▪ Injury prevention	Standards 1, 2, 3, 5, 7, and 8	See your state standards.

environment of their classroom. A well-organized lesson and an environment conducive to learning will contribute to greater achievement of established goals. Good lesson design is a result of purposeful planning and thoughtful use of a variety of teaching methods. Teaching methods should offer a way to teach the content in the most appropriate way for enhancing student learning and skill development. A good practice to use is **scaffolding**. When using scaffolding as an instructional technique, the teacher provides tasks that enable the learner to build on prior knowledge and internalize new concepts. Scaffolding simply directs the teacher to do the following:

- Teach the content in a developmentally appropriate way.
- Model the use of the new information.
- Practice the use of the new information.
- Apply the new information in a different way.

For example, when teaching about healthy decision making to your students, you would first clearly identify the decision-making steps: (1) identify the decision, (2) consider the choices, (3) think about the consequences of each decision, (4) make a decision, and (5) evaluate the decision. Next, you model the behavior by providing a health-related decision-making example (e.g., choosing a healthy snack) and demonstrate the decision-making process by thinking aloud. Then, provide an opportunity for students to practice with various health-related decisions (e.g., case studies with prepared options for students to complete in small groups, and then discuss as a class). Finally, provide each student with a scenario that requires them to use the decision-making model in order to come to a decision. Students would have to justify (in writing) their decision and how they came to that decision. Also keep in mind that in order for new information to be learned, it should be interactive, engaging, and personalized to the student. Use a variety of developmentally appropriate teaching methods, as shown in table 10.3.

Table 10.3 Developmentally Appropriate Teaching Methods

Teaching method	Description	Benefit
Decision mapping	Drawing a map of the thinking involved in a deliberative decision based on a range of options.	Great tool to help students understand the consequences for health-related decisions.
Class discussion	The class examines a problem or topic with the goal of better understanding an issue or skill, reaching the best solution, or developing new ideas.	Provides opportunities for students to learn from one another and solve problems as a group. Students gain a deeper understanding of the topic. Helps develop listening and assertiveness skills.
Brainstorming	Students generate a variety of ideas about a topic or question in a given amount of time. Quantity of ideas is the main objective.	Allows students to generate ideas quickly and spontaneously. Helps students use their imagination. Good discussion starter because the class can be creative.
Role playing	An informal dramatization in which students act out a situation.	Provides an excellent method to practice skills and advocacy, think critically, and gain exposure to others' point of view.
Think–pair–share	Ask a question, and have students individually answer on paper. Next, have them turn to a neighbor and exchange their answers in pairs. Finally, have the pairs share to the entire class.	Maximizes student input. Allows students to hear and learn from their peers.

Table 10.3 *(continued)*

Teaching method	Description	Benefit
Teachable moment	Sometimes opportunities pop up during the day for impromptu health lessons. For instance, a student may return from a dentist appointment with dental floss, which might be a good time to briefly reiterate oral hygiene with your class.	Provides relevant here-and-now topics that students can readily relate to. Requires flexibility and sensitivity.
Online simulations and games	Students play games that can be used for critical thinking, problem solving, and decision making. Simulations are activities structured to feel like the real experience.	They require the combined use of knowledge, attitudes, and skills and allow students to test out assumptions and abilities in a safe online environment.
Case studies	Real-life stories that describe a health-related problem or topic.	Forces students to think about their own behaviors and decision-making skills. Case studies can be tied to specific activities to help students practice healthy responses before they are confronted with a health risk.
Learning centers	Typically a table set up in a classroom or hallway containing a collection of activities and materials to teach, raise awareness about, or reinforce a health concept.	Requires students to work together to build a solid knowledge base on a particular health topic.
Graphic organizer, T-chart, Know/Wonder/Learn chart, Venn diagram, or word web	Visual representations of health-related blank areas for the student to fill in with related ideas and information on a chosen health topic.	Allows students to organize their thoughts about a health-related topic and draw connections to related concepts.
Modeling	Share your own appropriate health and physical activity journey nutrition journal, water consumption, hours of sleep, or daily pedometer count for inspiration.	Children naturally imitate those around them. Students are strongly influenced by their teachers and are likely to pick up on the health behaviors you exhibit.

Assessment of Learning

When you assess your students, you gather information about their level of performance or achievement. You can also define **assessment** as all activities teachers use to help students learn and gauge progress.

Formative and Summative Assessment

Formative assessment is used to measure learning during the unit and to provide feed-

back to students on their progress; it is often thought of as a form of "process" assessment. It includes all activities undertaken by teachers and students that provide vital information to be used as feedback in order to modify the teaching and learning strategies used during a unit of learning. Various formative assessment tools are available. Table 10.4 provides a short list of formative assessment strategies that are popular to use with elementary students. They help to quickly and easily gauge student learning during a lesson or at the conclusion of a lesson.

Table 10.4 Formative Assessment Strategies

Strategy	Description
Stoplights	Give each student a set of three colored circles (red, yellow, green). After a lesson, have students hold up the appropriate color corresponding to understanding (stop, wait, go on) of the lesson material.
1-minute essays	At the end of class, ask students to write a 1-minute essay summarizing their understanding of the key ideas presented in class. Use their essays to plan the next lesson's material based on gaps in understanding.
Index card questions	Distribute one blank index card per student before the lesson. At the end of the lesson instruct students to summarize three key points they learned from the lesson on one side, and on the other side write any questions they had about the lesson. Use the cards to plan the next lesson and answer questions.
Give me five	Ask students to show hand signals after a lesson, based on their understanding of the lesson. For example, say, "Show me five fingers if you understand all of what we just learned," and "Show me one finger if you do not understand what we just learned."

Summative assessment occurs at the end of an instructional unit, grading period, or year. Summative assessments are used to evaluate student learning, skill acquisition, and academic achievement at the conclusion of a defined instructional period. This type of assessment is typically used to determine to what degree students have learned the material they have been taught. Summative assessment is more "product" oriented. Following are a few examples of summative assessment.

Portfolios

A **portfolio** is a collection of student work that represents progress through a unit of learning. It should include a variety of completed assignments that reflect students' knowledge, critical-thinking skills, capability to access accurate health and fitness information for research, and the ability to reflect on what they have learned. The criteria for assessing portfolios should be established in collaboration with the student.

Rubrics

A **rubric** is a scoring chart that clearly and succinctly defines assignment expectations based on a predetermined standard. Rubrics can be used as formative or summative assessments. Rubrics are helpful in determining what the student must do in order to achieve the highest grade possible. Be sure to provide a copy of the rubric before students begin to work on the assignment so that they know your expectations well in advance.

Performances or Skits

Skits are good tools to assess learning of specific behaviors (anti-bullying, anti-smoking, choosing healthy foods). Students can choose the content and the characters, write the script, and be involved in making the costumes.

Health Fairs

Health fairs can be organized around a particular topic (cancer prevention, heart health, dental hygiene) at the end of a health unit and in collaboration with a national health awareness month. Students can research the topic; create banners, handouts, and other media materials; create a booth or other space for the health fair; and organize the event.

Authentic Assessment

Authentic assessment has become more popular in recent years. **Authentic assessment** is a form of assessment in which students are asked to perform real-world tasks that demonstrate the application of knowledge or skills. To use authentic assessment, a teacher must first determine the specific tasks a student would need to perform in order to demonstrate mastery. A rubric is designed around those tasks to determine whether they had been mastered. Lessons are developed to enable students to perform those tasks well, including the acquisition of related knowledge or skills.

Learning Environment

Adapting learning activities and the learning environment to students' physical, cognitive, and medical needs is beneficial to student learning. Before the start of each school year, familiarize yourself with student records and talk to the school nurse about any health concerns related to your students. Frequently, if health issues exist, students' parents or guardians will schedule a conference to discuss how to best meet possible health needs at school. You should expect to come across students with common conditions such as asthma, peanut allergies, and broken bones, but also be aware that students may enter your classroom with epilepsy, diabetes, ulcerative colitis, and other concerns. Be sure to document health-related incidents or accidents that occur during the school day, and report them to the proper authority. Always consult school district policy to determine how best to proceed.

If a student's medical issues significantly limit one or more major life activities, including school, then he or she may be eligible for a 504 plan. A 504 plan provides accommodations that allow the student the same opportunities as peers. 504b plans are for students who need environmental accommodations so their physical disability won't hinder their education. Students with disabilities requiring 504b plans may need help with a physical disability or condition, such as extra room for a child in a wheelchair, insulin shots for students with diabetes, or help with a colostomy bag for a student with spina bifida. Some examples of possible 504 disabilities include attention deficit/hyperactivity disorder, arthritis, asthma, cancer, and HIV.

General considerations for the learning environment include the following:

Guidance for Implementing Best Practices

SHAPE America developed a guidance document titled *Appropriate Practices in School-Based Health Education,* located at www.shapeamerica.org/publications/ products/upload/AppropriatePractic-esSchoolBasedHealthEducation.pdf. It includes best practices on the learning environment, the curriculum, instructional strategies, assessment, advocacy, and professionalism. The document provides examples within each category and is an excellent resource for those teaching health education in the elementary classroom.

- Use proper curriculum materials and visual aids in your classroom and around the school.
- Use age- and developmentally-appropriate information, materials, and teaching strategies.
- Provide visuals that are empowering and are free from gender bias and stereotypes.
- Determine whether materials are culturally sensitive and culturally inclusive in order to meet needs of an increasingly diverse classroom environment.
- Consider students with limited English proficiency or English as a second language and modify materials and visuals as needed.

Following these guidelines will enhance the learning experience for all of your students and offer an inclusive environment.

Resources for Children and Parents

Many student-friendly resources are available that can supplement what is being taught in the classroom. Magazine subscriptions, kid-friendly health-related websites, and dozens of books can offer supportive information about what you are teaching in your classroom. A great first step in finding these resources is to seek the advice of the school librarian or technology specialist. Many of these same resources offer valuable information for parents and families as well. Next, develop an ongoing resource list you can use to plan your health and physical education units of learning. Attach this list of web resources and literature to a short wellness newsletter that is sent home at the beginning of a new unit of learning. Use these resources during some of your lessons to supplement the material; give short **family homework** that requires the use of these materials so that parents and students become more familiar with accurate sources of health and wellness information.

Classroom Rewards

Schools should teach children how to make healthy choices and to eat to fulfill nutritional needs. Providing food based on performance or behavior connects food to mood. This practice can encourage children to eat when they are not hungry and can instill lifelong habits of emotional eating, which can increase the risks of overweight and obesity in adulthood. The best policy is not to use food to reward children for good behavior or academic performance in the classroom. Instead, use nonfood options such as school supplies, extra time at recess, or listening or dancing to music during class. Other examples might include paddle balls, Frisbees, stickers, or puzzles. See chapter 6 for more ideas.

Build Activity Into the Day

For good health, children need at least 60 minutes of physical activity each day. Physical activity helps children learn better and improves overall health and well-being. There are dozens of ways to get children up and moving around during the school day. Terms used to describe these initiatives include "brain breaks," "energizers," and "instant recess." The idea is to select various times during the school day to infuse short bouts of physical activity. They can be as short as 1 to 3 minutes or as long as 10 minutes (not including recess and physical education class). See chapter 7 for more information on this best practice.

Professional Development

One of the most commonly cited barriers for teachers in teaching health or physical education in the classroom is lack of knowledge or professional development. Teaching the content requires a level of understanding of the content as well as self-efficacy for the ability to competently teach the content to students. Ongoing professional development is critical for teachers to gain the knowledge and competence to develop lesson plans and teach developmentally appropriate content. Ask your school administration about workshops and professional development opportunities for teachers in the areas of health education and physical education. Attending local or state health education and physical education conferences is an important step in professional development and networking. You will find many experts in the field who are committed to the profession and eager to share their knowledge. Get to know those in the profession, and encourage your school or district administration to offer a series of workshops that can assist in training teachers about these important content areas. **SHAPE America – Society of Health and Physical Educators** is an organization dedicated to enhancing the professional practice and research related to health and physical education, physical activity, dance, and sport. This organization supports national, district, and state professional development and is a valuable resource for education for teachers. The **American School Health Association (ASHA)** is dedicated to supporting healthy students who learn and achieve in a safe and healthy environment. This organization hosts national and regional professional development opportunities for anyone teaching health education.

Collaborating with fellow teachers, school nursing staff, school nutrition personnel, and health professionals in the community (hospitals, health departments, dentist offices, health-related nonprofit organizations) is also key to gathering content specialists who can help with vital ongoing professional development in the schools.

Supporting Policies That Encourage Wellness

Teachers have a responsibility to encourage and promote policies and practices that support health and wellness in the classroom and across the school campus. Following are a few important topics related to policies that may be required of your school or district, or could be developed to ensure health and wellness are being addressed.

Local School Wellness Policies

School wellness policies are regulations that can help establish a healthy school environment, promote student health, and reduce childhood obesity. Because they are required for all school districts participating in the federal child nutrition programs including the National School Lunch Program and the School Breakfast Program, millions of children can be reached through implementation of these policies. Get informed about your district's wellness policies, and share them at a faculty meeting. Next, get involved with the committee charged with implementing and updating the local school wellness policy. If no committee exists, form one and begin strategically

planning initiatives that promote better health, physical activity, and nutrition in the schools.

Fundraising and School Vending

Many schools rely on fundraising to supplement school budgets and pay for equipment, supplies, and special events. Unfortunately, many school fundraisers also involve the sale of unhealthy foods. School fundraising has traditionally been littered with junk food. Work with your school administration and parents to make school fundraising both healthy and profitable. See table 10.5 for a few fundraising alternatives.

Starting in school year 2014-15, all foods sold at school during the school day must meet common nutrition standards. These standards are also known as **Smart Snacks in School regulations**. They apply to foods sold a la carte, in the school store, and vending machines. **School vending sales** are often used to supplement existing programs or services. Trading unhealthy options for more nutritious options is one way to keep the revenue while also keeping a healthy school environment. Work with vending machine suppliers to develop a list of healthy options that can increase the diversity of choices for students. Some distributors will work with schools to price healthy items

Table 10.5 Fundraising Alternatives

Traditional fundraising that does not support health and physical activity	Fundraising that supports health and physical activity
Bake sales Pizza sales Cookie dough sales Candy and doughnut sales Fundraisers at fast food restaurants	Sales of bottled water with school name printed on the bottle Fruit sales Sale of calendars, stationery, or greeting cards Sales of first aid kits Sale of weather preparedness kits Plant and flower sales Spices and cookbook sales Car washes Fun runs Sporting events Bowling or golf tournaments Raffles

Adapted from The Center for Science in the Public Interest, *Sweet deals: School funding can be healthy and profitable.* Available: www.cspinet.org/new/pdf/schoolfundraising.pdf

cheaper than less healthy choices. Following are a few examples of healthy vending options.

- 100-percent fruit or vegetable juice, low-fat plain milk, water
- Low-fat string cheese, yogurt
- Granola, natural snack bars, hummus
- Baked chips, nuts, trail mix, jerky
- Popcorn, whole-wheat crackers, peanut butter
- Fig Newtons, dried fruit
- Apples, celery sticks

Marketing and Advertising

Schools should be healthy places where kids aren't bombarded with ads for junk food. When parents teach their kids healthy habits at home, their work shouldn't be undone by unhealthy messages at school. Many schools still advertise sugary drinks and other junk foods on vending machines, on scoreboards, in gymnasiums, and in student newspapers. The Centers for Disease Control and Prevention, Institute of Medicine, and American Academy of Pediatrics recommend that school districts implement policies and practices to promote foods and beverages that support healthful diets. Work with your school to review and revise the school wellness policy to address the marketing and promotion of unhealthy foods and beverages in the school. In addition, be supportive of school efforts to develop policies that prohibit the use of food (including candy) in the classroom setting. Consider collaborating with parents and colleagues to develop policies and initiatives that support using physical activity and brain breaks during the day (such as including movement during morning announcements) to get both teachers and children up and moving.

Summary

Teachers who provide effective health and physical education for their students exemplify several practices in their classrooms and schools. They help to ensure that classroom, school, and district policies encourage wellness through committee involvement and strategic planning initiatives. Meaningful planning includes the use of the 10 health content areas and the National Health Education Standards (NHES). They use a variety of teaching methods and types of assessment to enhance learning. Best practices include attending workshops and ongoing professional development to keep content knowledge and competency skills sharp. Collaboration with colleagues, as well as health and physical activity professionals in the community, is key to enhancing the health and physical education initiatives in the classroom. Effective teachers provide appropriate health resources such as magazines, newsletters, and websites to parents and students. Teachers should build wellness into the day with brain breaks or instant recess. Teachers should ensure that all materials and visuals are developmentally appropriate, culturally sensitive, and free from gender bias. Accomplished teachers adapt the classroom environment to students' physical, cognitive, and medical needs. In combination, these practices can increase student engagement, health content knowledge, and physical activity levels and positively impact student health behaviors.

Review Questions

1. What are 4 of the 10 content areas of health education?

2. What is scaffolding, and how can it be helpful in teaching health and physical education content in the classroom?

3. What is formative assessment? Describe three formative assessment strategies.

4. What is summative assessment? List and describe one form of summative assessment.

Appendix A:
National Health Education Standards

The performance indicators articulate specifically what students should *know or be able to do* in support of each standard by the conclusion of each of the following grade spans: Pre-K-Grade 2; Grade 3-Grade 5; Grade 6-Grade 8; and Grade 9-Grade 12. The performance indicators serve as a blueprint for organizing student assessment.

Standard 1

Students will comprehend concepts related to health promotion and disease prevention to enhance health.

Rationale: The acquisition of basic health concepts and functional health knowledge provides a foundation for promoting health-enhancing behaviors among youth. This standard includes essential concepts that are based on established health behavior theories and models. Concepts that focus on both health promotion and risk reduction are included in the performance indicators.

Performance Indicators

Pre-K-Grade 2

1.2.1 Identify that healthy behaviors impact personal health.

1.2.2 Recognize that there are multiple dimensions of health.

1.2.3 Describe ways to prevent communicable diseases.

1.2.4 List ways to prevent common childhood injuries.

1.2.5 Describe why it is important to seek health care.

Grades 3-5

1.5.1 Describe the relationship between healthy behaviors and personal health.

1.5.2 Identify examples of emotional, intellectual, physical, and social health.

1.5.3 Describe ways in which safe and healthy school and community environments can promote personal health.

1.5.4 Describe ways to prevent common childhood injuries and health problems.

1.5.5 Describe when it is important to seek health care.

Standard 2

Students will analyze the influence of family, peers, culture, media, technology, and other factors on health behaviors.

Rationale: Health is affected by a variety of positive and negative influences within society. This standard focuses on identifying and understanding the diverse internal and external factors that influence health practices and behaviors among youth, including personal values, beliefs, and perceived norms.

Performance Indicators

Pre-K-Grade 2

2.2.1 Identify how the family influences personal health practices and behaviors.

2.2.2 Identify what the school can do to support personal health practices and behaviors.

2.2.3 Describe how the media can influence health behaviors.

Grades 3-5

2.5.1 Describe how family influences personal health practices and behaviors.

2.5.2 Identify the influence of culture on health practices and behaviors.

2.5.3 Identify how peers can influence healthy and unhealthy behaviors.

2.5.4 Describe how the school and community can support personal health practices and behaviors.

2.5.5 Explain how media influences thoughts, feelings, and health behaviors.

2.5.6 Describe ways that technology can influence personal health.

Standard 3

Students will demonstrate the ability to access valid information, products, and services to enhance health.

Rationale: Access to valid health information and health-promoting products and services is critical in the prevention, early detection, and treatment of health problems. This standard focuses on how to identify and access valid health resources and to reject unproven sources. Application of the skills of analysis, comparison, and evaluation of health resources empowers students to achieve health literacy.

Performance Indicators

Pre-K-Grade 2

3.2.1 Identify trusted adults and professionals who can help promote health.

3.2.2 Identify ways to locate school and community health helpers.

Grades 3-5

3.5.1 Identify characteristics of valid health information, products, and services.

3.5.2 Locate resources from home, school, and community that provide valid health information.

Standard 4

Students will demonstrate the ability to use interpersonal communication skills to enhance health and avoid or reduce health risks.

Rationale: Effective communication enhances personal, family, and community health. This standard focuses on how responsible individuals use verbal and nonverbal skills to develop and maintain healthy personal relationships. The ability to organize and to convey information and feelings is the basis for strengthening interpersonal interactions and reducing or avoiding conflict.

Performance Indicators

Pre-K-Grade 2

4.2.1 Demonstrate healthy ways to express needs, wants, and feelings.

4.2.2 Demonstrate listening skills to enhance health.

4.2.3 Demonstrate ways to respond in an unwanted, threatening, or dangerous situation.

4.2.4 Demonstrate ways to tell a trusted adult if threatened or harmed.

Grades 3-5

4.5.1 Demonstrate effective verbal and nonverbal communication skills to enhance health.

4.5.2 Demonstrate refusal skills that avoid or reduce health risks.

4.5.3 Demonstrate nonviolent strategies to manage or resolve conflict.

4.5.4 Demonstrate how to ask for assistance to enhance personal health.

Standard 5

Students will demonstrate the ability to use decision-making skills to enhance health.

Rationale: Decision-making skills are needed to identify, implement, and sustain health-enhancing behaviors. This standard includes the essential steps that are needed to make healthy decisions as prescribed in the performance indicators. When applied to health issues, the decision-making process enables individuals to collaborate with others to improve their quality of life.

Performance Indicators

Pre-K-Grade 2

5.2.1 Identify situations when a health-related decision is needed.

5.2.2 Differentiate between situations when a health-related decision can be made individually or when assistance is needed.

Grades 3-5

5.5.1 Identify health-related situations that might require a thoughtful decision.

5.5.2 Analyze when assistance is needed in making a health-related decision.

5.5.3 List healthy options to health-related issues or problems.

5.5.4 Predict the potential outcomes of each option when making a health-related decision.

5.5.5 Choose a healthy option when making a decision.

5.5.6 Describe the outcomes of a health-related decision.

Standard 6

Students will demonstrate the ability to use goal-setting skills to enhance health.

Rationale: Goal-setting skills are essential to help students identify, adopt, and maintain healthy behaviors. This standard includes the critical steps that are needed to achieve both short-term and long-term health goals. These skills make it possible for individuals to have aspirations and plans for the future.

Performance Indicators

Pre-K-Grade 2

6.2.1 Identify a short-term personal health goal and take action toward achieving the goal.

6.2.2 Identify who can help when assistance is needed to achieve a personal health goal.

Grades 3-5

6.5.1 Set a personal health goal and track progress toward its achievement.

6.5.2 Identify resources to assist in achieving a personal health goal.

Standard 7

Students will demonstrate the ability to practice health-enhancing behaviors and avoid or reduce health risks.

Rationale: Research confirms that practicing health-enhancing behaviors can contribute to a positive quality of life. In addition, many diseases and injuries can be prevented by reducing harmful and risk-taking behaviors. This standard promotes the acceptance of personal responsibility for health and encourages the practice of healthy behaviors.

Performance Indicators

Pre-K-Grade 2

7.2.1 Demonstrate healthy practices and behaviors to maintain or improve personal health.

7.2.2 Demonstrate behaviors that avoid or reduce health risks.

Grades 3-5

7.5.1 Identify responsible personal health behaviors.

7.5.2 Demonstrate a variety of healthy practices and behaviors to maintain or improve personal health.

7.5.3 Demonstrate a variety of behaviors to avoid or reduce health risks.

Standard 8

Students will demonstrate the ability to advocate for personal, family, and community health.

Rationale: Advocacy skills help students promote healthy norms and healthy behaviors. This standard helps students develop important skills to target their health-enhancing messages and to encourage others to adopt healthy behaviors.

Performance Indicators

Pre-K-Grade 2

8.2.1 Make requests to promote personal health.

8.2.2 Encourage peers to make positive health choices.

Grades 3-5

8.5.1 Express opinions and give accurate information about health issues.

8.5.2 Encourage others to make positive health choices.

Reprinted from Joint Committee on National Health Education Standards, 2007, *National Health Education Standards: Achieving Excellence*. (Washington, DC: American Cancer Society).

Appendix B:
National Standards and Grade-Level Outcomes for K-12 Physical Education

All material in appendix B is reprinted, by permission, from SHAPE America, 2014, *National standards & grade-level outcomes for K-12 physical education* (Champaign, IL: Human Kinetics), 26-37. The Grade-Level Outcomes displayed here are for grades K-5 only.

Standard 1: Demonstrates competency in a variety of motor skills and movement patterns.

Standard 1	Kindergarten	Grade 1	Grade 2	Grade 3	Grade 4	Grade 5
Locomotor						
S1.E1 Hopping, galloping, running, sliding, skipping, leaping	Performs locomotor skills (hopping, galloping, running, sliding, skipping) while maintaining balance. (S1.E1.K)	Hops, gallops, jogs and slides using a mature pattern. (S1.E1.1)	Skips using a mature pattern. (S1.E1.2)	Leaps using a mature pattern. (S1.E1.3)	Uses various locomotor skills in a variety of small-sided practice tasks, dance and educational gymnastics experiences. (S1.E1.4)	Demonstrates mature patterns of locomotor skills in dynamic small-sided practice tasks, gymnastics and dance. (S1.E1.5a) Combines locomotor and manipulative skills in a variety of small-sided practice tasks in game environments. (S1.E1.5b) Combines traveling with manipulative skills for execution to a target (e.g., scoring in soccer, hockey and basketball). (S1.E1.5c)
S1.E2 Jogging, running	Developmentally appropriate/emerging outcomes first appear in Grade 2.	Developmentally appropriate/emerging outcomes first appear in Grade 2.	Runs with a mature pattern. (S1.E2.2a) Travels showing differentiation between jogging and sprinting. (S1.E2.2b)	Travels showing differentiation between sprinting and running. (S1.E2.3)	Runs for distance using a mature pattern. (S1.E2.4)	Uses appropriate pacing for a variety of running distances. (S1.E2.5)

(continued)

Standard 1	Kindergarten	Grade 1	Grade 2	Grade 3	Grade 4	Grade 5
Locomotor (continued)						
S1.E3 Jumping & landing, horizontal	Performs jumping & landing actions with balance. (S1.E3.K)	Demonstrates 2 of the 5 critical elements for jumping & landing in a horizontal plane using 2-foot take-offs and landings. (S1.E3.1)	Demonstrates 4 of the 5 critical elements for jumping & landing in a horizontal plane using a variety of 1- and 2-foot take-offs and landings. (S1.E3.2)	Jumps and lands in the horizontal plane using a mature pattern. (S1.E3.3)	Uses spring-and-step take-offs and landings specific to gymnastics. (S1.E3.4)	Combines jumping and landing patterns with locomotor and manipulative skills in dance, gymnastics and small-sided practice tasks in game environments. (S1.E3.5)
S1.E4 Jumping & landing, vertical	*Refer to S1.E3.K.*	Demonstrates 2 of the 5 critical elements for jumping & landing in a vertical plane. (S1.E4.1)	Demonstrates 4 of the 5 critical elements for jumping & landing in a vertical plane. (S1.E4.2)	Jumps and lands in the vertical plane using a mature pattern. (S1.E4.3)	*Refer to S1.E3.4.*	*Refer to S1.E3.5.*
S1.E5 Dance	Performs locomotor skills in response to teacher-led creative dance. (S1.E5.K)	Combines locomotor and nonlocomotor skills in a teacher-designed dance. (S1.E5.1)	Performs a teacher- and/or student-designed rhythmic activity with correct response to simple rhythms. (S1.E5.2)	Performs teacher-selected and developmentally appropriate dance steps and movement patterns. (S1.E5.3)	Combines locomotor movement patterns and dance steps to create and perform an original dance. (S1.E5.4)	Combines locomotor skills in cultural as well as creative dances (self and group) with correct rhythm and pattern. (S1.E5.5)
S1.E6 Combinations	Developmentally appropriate/ emerging outcomes first appear in Grade 3.	Developmentally appropriate/emerging outcomes first appear in Grade 3.	Developmentally appropriate/emerging outcomes first appear in Grade 3.	Performs a sequence of locomotor skills, transitioning from one skill to another smoothly and without hesitation. (S1.E6.3)	Combines traveling with manipulative skills of dribbling, throwing, catching and striking in teacher- and/or student-designed small-sided practice tasks. (S1.E6.4)	Applies skill.

Standard 1	Kindergarten	Grade 1	Grade 2	Grade 3	Grade 4	Grade 5
Nonlocomotor (stability)[1]						
S1.E7 Balance	Maintains momentary stillness on different bases of support. (S1.E7.Ka) Forms wide, narrow, curled, and twisted body shapes. (S1.E7.Kb)	Maintains stillness on different bases of support with different body shapes. (S1.E7.1)	Balances on different bases of support, combining levels and shapes. (S1.E7.2a) Balances in an inverted position[1] with stillness and supportive base. (S1.E7.2b)	Balances on different bases of support, demonstrating muscular tension and extensions of free body parts. (S1.E7.3)	Balances on different bases of support on apparatus, demonstrating levels and shapes. (S1.E7.4)	Combines balance and transferring weight in a gymnastics sequence or dance with a partner. (S1.E7.5)
S1.E8 Weight transfer	Developmentally appropriate/ emerging outcomes first appear in Grade 1.	Transfers weight from one body part to another in self-space in dance and gymnastics environments. (S1.E8.1)	Transfers weight from feet to different body parts/bases of support for balance and/ or travel.[1] (S1.E8.2)	Transfers weight from feet to hands for momentary weight support. (S1.E8.3)	Transfers weight from feet to hands, varying speed and using large extensions (e.g., mule kick, handstand, cartwheel).[1] (S1.E8.4)	Transfers weight in gymnastics and dance environments. (S1.E8.5)
S1.E9 Weight transfer, rolling	Rolls sideways in a narrow body shape. (S1.E9.K)	Rolls with either a narrow or curled body shape. (S1.E9.1)	Rolls in different directions with either a narrow or curled body shape. (S1.E9.2)	Applies skill.	Applies skill.	Applies skill.
S1.E10 Curling & stretching; twisting & bending	Contrasts the actions of curling & stretching. (S1.E10.K)	Demonstrates twisting, curling, bending & stretching actions. (S1.E10.1)	Differentiates among twisting, curling, bending & stretching actions. (S1.E10.2)	Moves into and out of gymnastics balances with curling, twisting & stretching actions. (S1.E10.3)	Moves into and out of balances on apparatus with curling, twisting & stretching actions. (S1.E10.4)	Performs curling, twisting & stretching actions with correct application in dance, gymnastics and small-sided practice tasks in game environments. (S1.E10.5)

[1]Teachers must use differentiated instruction and developmentally appropriate practice tasks for individual learners when presenting transfers of weight from feet to other body parts.

NASPE, 1992, *Outcomes of Quality Physical Education Programs* (Reston, VA: Author), p. 12.

(continued)

Standard 1	Kindergarten	Grade 1	Grade 2	Grade 3	Grade 4	Grade 5
Nonlocomotor (stability)¹ *(continued)*						
S1.E11 Combinations	*Developmentally appropriate/ emerging outcomes first appear in Grade 2.*	*Developmentally appropriate/emerging outcomes first appear in Grade 2.*	Combines balances and transfers into a 3-part sequence (i.e., dance, gymnastics). (S1.E11.2)	Combines locomotor skills and movement concepts (levels, shapes, extensions, pathways, force, time, flow) to create and perform a dance. (S1.E11.3)	Combines locomotor skills and movement concepts (levels, shapes, extensions, pathways, force, time, flow) to create and perform a dance with a partner. (S1.E11.4)	Combines locomotor skills and movement concepts (levels, shapes, extensions, pathways, force, time, flow) to create and perform a dance with a group. (S1.E11.5)
S1.E12 Balance & weight transfers	*Developmentally appropriate/ emerging outcomes first appear in Grade 3.*	*Developmentally appropriate/emerging outcomes first appear in Grade 3.*	*Developmentally appropriate/emerging outcomes first appear in Grade 3.*	Combines balance and weight transfers with movement concepts to create and perform a dance. (S1.E12.3)	Combines traveling with balance and weight transfers to create a gymnastics sequence with and without equipment or apparatus. (S1.E12.4)	Combines actions, balances and weight transfers to create a gymnastics sequence with a partner on equipment or apparatus. (S1.E12.5)
Manipulative						
S1.E13 Underhand throw	Throws underhand with opposite foot forward. (S1.E13.K)	Throws underhand, demonstrating 2 of the 5 critical elements of a mature pattern. (S1.E13.1)	Throws underhand using a mature pattern. (S1.E13.2)	Throws underhand to a partner or target with reasonable accuracy. (S1.E13.3)	Applies skill.	Throws underhand using a mature pattern in nondynamic environments (closed skills), with different sizes and types of objects. (S1.E13.5a) Throws underhand to a large target with accuracy. (S1.E13.5b)

Standard 1	Kindergarten	Grade 1	Grade 2	Grade 3	Grade 4	Grade 5
Manipulative						
S1.E14 Overhand throw	*Developmentally appropriate/ emerging outcomes first appear in Grade 2.*	*Developmentally appropriate/emerging outcomes first appear in Grade 2.*	Throws overhand demonstrating 2 of the 5 critical elements of a mature pattern. (S1.E14.2)	Throws overhand, demonstrating 3 of the 5 critical elements of a mature pattern, in nondynamic environments (closed skills), for distance and/or force. (S1.E14.3)	Throws overhand using a mature pattern in nondynamic environments (closed skills). (S1.E14.4a) Throws overhand to a partner or at a target with accuracy at a reasonable distance. (S1.E14.4b)	Throws overhand using a mature pattern in nondynamic environments (closed skills), with different sizes and types of balls. (S1.E14.5a) Throws overhand to large target with accuracy. (S1.E14.5b)
S1.E15 Passing with hands	*Developmentally appropriate/ emerging outcomes first appear in Grade 4.*	*Developmentally appropriate/emerging outcomes first appear in Grade 4.*	*Developmentally appropriate/emerging outcomes first appear in Grade 4.*	*Developmentally appropriate/emerging outcomes first appear in Grade 4.*	Throws to a moving partner with reasonable accuracy in a nondynamic environment (closed skills). (S1.E15.4)	Throws with accuracy, both partners moving. (S1.E15.5a) Throws with reasonable accuracy in dynamic, small-sided practice tasks. (S1.E15.5b)

(continued)

Standard 1	Kindergarten	Grade 1	Grade 2	Grade 3	Grade 4	Grade 5
Manipulative *(continued)*						
S1.E16 Catching	Drops a ball and catches it before it bounces twice. (S1.E16.Ka) Catches a large ball tossed by a skilled thrower. (S1.E16.Kb)	Catches a soft object from a self-toss before it bounces. (S1.E16.1a) Catches various sizes of balls self-tossed or tossed by a skilled thrower. (S1.E16.1b)	Catches a self-tossed or well-thrown large ball with hands, not trapping or cradling against the body. (S1.E16.2)	Catches a gently tossed hand-size ball from a partner, demonstrating 4 of the 5 critical elements of a mature pattern. (S1.E16.3)	Catches a thrown ball above the head, at chest or waist level, and below the waist using a mature pattern in a nondynamic environment (closed skills). (S1.E16.4)	Catches a batted ball above the head, at chest or waist level, and along the ground using a mature pattern in a nondynamic environment (closed skills). (S1.E16.5a) Catches with accuracy, both partners moving. (S1.E16.5b) Catches with reasonable accuracy in dynamic, small-sided practice tasks. (S1.E16.5c)
S1.E17 Dribbling/ ball control with hands	Dribbles a ball with 1 hand, attempting the second contact. (S1.E17.K)	Dribbles continuously in self-space using the preferred hand. (S1.E17.1)	Dribbles in self-space with preferred hand demonstrating a mature pattern. (S1.E17.2a) Dribbles using the preferred hand while walking in general space. (S1.E17.2b)	Dribbles and travels in general space at slow to moderate jogging speed with control of ball and body. (S1.E17.3)	Dribbles in self-space with both the preferred and the nonpreferred hands using a mature pattern. (S1.E17.4a) Dribbles in general space with control of ball and body while increasing and decreasing speed. (S1.E17.4b)	Combines hand dribbling with other skills during 1v1 practice tasks. (S1.E17.5)

Standard 1	Kindergarten	Grade 1	Grade 2	Grade 3	Grade 4	Grade 5
Manipulative						
S1.E18 Dribbling/ball control with feet	Taps a ball using the inside of the foot, sending it forward. (S1.E18.K)	Taps or dribbles a ball using the inside of the foot while walking in general space. (S1.E18.1)	Dribbles with the feet in general space with control of ball and body. (S1.E18.2)	Dribbles with the feet in general space at slow to moderate jogging speed with control of ball and body. (S1.E18.3)	Dribbles with the feet in general space with control of ball and body while increasing and decreasing speed. (S1.E18.4)	Combines foot dribbling with other skills in 1v1 practice tasks. (S1.E18.5)
S1.E19 Passing & receiving with feet	*Developmentally appropriate/ emerging outcomes first appear in Grade 3.*	*Developmentally appropriate/emerging outcomes first appear in Grade 3.*	*Developmentally appropriate/emerging outcomes first appear in Grade 3.*	Passes & receives ball with the insides of the feet to a stationary partner, "giving" on reception before returning the pass. (S1.E19.3)	Passes & receives ball with the insides of the feet to a moving partner in a nondynamic environment (closed skills). (S1.E19.4a) Receives and passes a ball with the outsides and insides of the feet to a stationary partner, "giving" on reception before returning the pass. (S1.E19.4b)	Passes with the feet using a mature pattern as both partners travel. (S1.E19.5a) Receives a pass with the feet using a mature pattern as both partners travel. (S1.E19.5b)
S1.E20 Dribbling in combination	*Developmentally appropriate/ emerging outcomes first appear in Grade 4.*	*Developmentally appropriate/emerging outcomes first appear in Grade 4.*	*Developmentally appropriate/emerging outcomes first appear in Grade 4.*	*Developmentally appropriate/emerging outcomes first appear in Grade 4.*	Dribbles with hands or feet in combination with other skills (e.g., passing, receiving, shooting). (S1.E20.4)	Dribbles with hands or feet with mature patterns in a variety of small-sided game forms. (S1.E20.5)

(continued)

Standard 1	Kindergarten	Grade 1	Grade 2	Grade 3	Grade 4	Grade 5
Manipulative *(continued)*						
S1.E21 Kicking	Kicks a stationary ball from a stationary position, demonstrating 2 of the 5 elements of a mature kicking pattern. (S1.E21.K)	Approaches a stationary ball and kicks it forward, demonstrating 2 of the 5 critical elements of a mature pattern. (S1.E21.1)	Uses a continuous running approach and kicks a moving ball, demonstrating 3 of the 5 critical elements of a mature pattern. (S1.E21.2)	Uses a continuous running approach and intentionally performs a kick along the ground and a kick in the air, demonstrating 4 of the 5 critical elements of a mature pattern for each. (S1.E21.3a) Uses a continuous running approach and kicks a stationary ball for accuracy. (S1.E21.3b)	Kicks along the ground and in the air, and punts using mature patterns. (S1.E21.4)	Demonstrates mature patterns of kicking and punting in small-sided practice task environments. (S1.E21.5)
S1.E22 Volley, underhand	Volleys a lightweight object (balloon), sending it upward. (S1.E22.K)	Volleys an object with an open palm, sending it upward. (S1.E22.1)	Volleys an object upward with consecutive hits. (S1.E22.2)	Volleys an object with an underhand or sidearm striking pattern, sending it forward over a net, to the wall or over a line to a partner, while demonstrating 4 of the 5 critical elements of a mature pattern. (S1.E22.3)	Volleys underhand using a mature pattern in a dynamic environment (e.g., 2 square, 4 square, handball). (S1.E22.4)	Applies skill.

Standard 1	Kindergarten	Grade 1	Grade 2	Grade 3	Grade 4	Grade 5
Manipulative						
S1.E23 Volley, over-head	*Developmentally appropriate/ emerging outcomes first appear in Grade 4.*	*Developmentally appropriate/emerging outcomes first appear in Grade 4.*	*Developmentally appropriate/emerging outcomes first appear in Grade 4.*	*Developmentally appropriate/emerging outcomes first appear in Grade 4.*	Volleys a ball with a two-hand overhead pattern, sending it upward, demonstrating 4 of the 5 critical elements of a mature pattern. (S1.E23.4)	Volleys a ball using a two-hand pattern, sending it upward to a target. (S1.E23.5)
S1.E24 Striking, short implement	Strikes a lightweight object with a paddle or short-handled racket. (S1.E24.K)	Strikes a ball with a short-handled implement, sending it upward. (S1.E24.1)	Strikes an object upward with a short-handled implement, using consecutive hits. (S1.E24.2)	Strikes an object with a short-handled implement, sending it forward over a low net or to a wall. (S1.E24.3a) Strikes an object with a short-handled implement while demonstrating 3 of the 5 critical elements of a mature pattern. (S1.E24.3b)	Strikes an object with a short-handled implement while demonstrating a mature pattern. (S1.E24.4a) Strikes an object with a short-handled implement, alternating hits with a partner over a low net or against a wall. (S1.E24.4b)	Strikes an object consecutively, with a partner, using a short-handled implement, over a net or against a wall, in either a competitive or cooperative game environment. (S1.E24.5)

(continued)

Standard 1	Kindergarten	Grade 1	Grade 2	Grade 3	Grade 4	Grade 5
Manipulative (continued)						
S1.E25 Striking, long implement	*Developmentally appropriate/ emerging outcomes first appear in Grade 2.*	*Developmentally appropriate/emerging outcomes first appear in Grade 2.*	Strikes a ball off a tee or cone with a bat using correct grip and side orientation/ proper body orientation. (S1.E25.2)	Strikes a ball with a long-handled implement (e.g., hockey stick, bat, golf club), sending it forward, while using proper grip for the implement. Note: Use batting tee or ball tossed by teacher for batting. (S1.E25.3)	Strikes an object with a long-handled implement (e.g., hockey stick, golf club, bat, tennis or badminton racket) while demonstrating 3 of the 5 critical elements of a mature pattern for the implement (grip, stance, body orientation, swing plane, and follow-through). (S1.E25.4)	Strikes a pitched ball with a bat using a mature pattern. (S1.E25.5a) Combines striking with a long implement (e.g., bat, hockey stick) with receiving and traveling skills in a small-sided game. (S1.E25.5b)
S1.E26 In combination with locomotor	*Developmentally appropriate/ emerging outcomes first appear in Grade 4.*	*Developmentally appropriate/emerging outcomes first appear in Grade 4.*	*Developmentally appropriate/emerging outcomes first appear in Grade 4.*	*Developmentally appropriate/emerging outcomes first appear in Grade 4.*	Combines traveling with the manipulative skills of dribbling, throwing, catching and striking in teacher- and/ or student-designed small-sided practice-task environments. (S1.E26.4)	Combines manipulative skills and traveling for execution to a target (e.g., scoring in soccer, hockey, and basketball). (S1.E26.5)

Standard 1	Kindergarten	Grade 1	Grade 2	Grade 3	Grade 4	Grade 5
Manipulative						
S1.E27 Jumping rope	Executes a single jump with self-turned rope. (S1.E27.Ka) Jumps a long rope with teacher-assisted turning. (S1.E27.Kb)	Jumps forward or backward consecutively using a self-turned rope. (S1.E27.1a) Jumps a long rope up to 5 times consecutively with teacher-assisted turning. (S1.E27.1b)	Jumps a self-turned rope consecutively forward and backward with a mature pattern. (S1.E27.2a) Jumps a long rope 5 times consecutively with student turners. (S1.E27.2b)	Performs intermediate jump-rope skills (e.g., a variety of tricks, running in & out of long rope) for both long and short ropes. (S1.E27.3)	Creates a jump-rope routine with either a short or long rope. (S1.E27.4)	Creates a jump-rope routine with a partner using either a short or long rope. (S1.E27.5)

Standard 2: Applies knowledge of concepts, principles, strategies and tactics related to movement and performance.

Standard 2	Kindergarten	Grade 1	Grade 2	Grade 3	Grade 4	Grade 5
Movement concepts						
S2.E1 Space	Differentiates between movement in personal (self-space) and general space. (S2.E1.Ka) Moves in personal space to a rhythm. (S2.E1.Kb)	Moves in self-space and general space in response to designated beats/rhythms. (S2.E1.1)	Combines locomotor skills in general space to a rhythm. (S2.E1.2)	Recognizes the concept of open spaces in a movement context. (S2.E1.3)	Applies the concept of open spaces to combination skills involving traveling (e.g., dribbling and traveling). (S2.E1.4a) Applies the concept of closing spaces in small-sided practice tasks. (S2.E1.4b) Dribbles in general space with changes in direction and speed. (S2.E1.4c)	Combines spatial concepts with locomotor and non-locomotor movements for small groups in gymnastics, dance and games environments. (S2.E1.5)
S2.E2 Pathways, shapes, levels	Travels in 3 different pathways. (S2.E2.K)	Travels demonstrating low, middle and high levels. (S2.E2.1a) Travels demonstrating a variety of relationships with objects (e.g., over, under, around, through). (S2.E2.1b)	Combines shapes, levels and pathways into simple travel, dance and gymnastics sequences.[ii] (S2.E2.2)	Recognizes locomotor skills specific to a wide variety of physical activities. (S2.E2.3)	Combines movement concepts with skills in small-sided practice tasks, gymnastics and dance environments. (S2.E2.4)	Combines movement concepts with skills in small-sided practice tasks in game environments, gymnastics and dance with self-direction. (S2.E2.5)

[ii]NASPE, 1992, *Outcomes of Quality Physical Education Programs* (Reston, VA: Author), p. 11.

Standard 2	Kindergarten	Grade 1	Grade 2	Grade 3	Grade 4	Grade 5
Movement concepts						
S2.E3 Speed, direction, force	Travels in general space with different speeds. (S2.E3.K)	Differentiates between fast and slow speeds. (S2.E3.1a) Differentiates between strong and light force. (S2.E3.1b)	Varies time and force with gradual increases and decreases. (S2.E3.2)	Combines movement concepts (direction, levels, force, time) with skills as directed by the teacher. (S2.E3.3)	Applies the movement concepts of speed, endurance and pacing for running. (S2.E3.4a) Applies the concepts of direction and force when striking an object with a short-handled implement, sending it toward a designated target. (S2.E3.4b)	Applies movement concepts to strategy in game situations. (S2.E3.5a) Applies the concepts of direction and force to strike an object with a long-handled implement. (S2.E3.5b) Analyzes movement situations and applies movement concepts (e.g., force, direction, speed, pathways, extensions) in small-sided practice tasks in game environments, dance and gymnastics. (S2.E3.5c)

(continued)

Standard 2	Kindergarten	Grade 1	Grade 2	Grade 3	Grade 4	Grade 5
Movement concepts *(continued)*						
S2.E4 Alignment & muscular tension	*Developmentally appropriate/emerging outcomes first appear in Grade 3.*	*Developmentally appropriate/emerging outcomes first appear in Grade 3.*	*Developmentally appropriate/emerging outcomes first appear in Grade 3.*	Employs the concept of alignment in gymnastics and dance. (S2.E4.3a) Employs the concept of muscular tension with balance in gymnastics and dance. (S2.E4.3b)	Applies skill.	Applies skill.

Standard 2	Kindergarten	Grade 1	Grade 2	Grade 3	Grade 4	Grade 5
Movement concepts						
S2.E5 Strategies & tactics	*Developmentally appropriate/emerging outcomes first appear in Grade 3.*	*Developmentally appropriate/emerging outcomes first appear in Grade 3.*	*Developmentally appropriate/emerging outcomes first appear in Grade 3.*	Applies simple strategies & tactics in chasing activities. (S2.E5.3a) Applies simple strategies in fleeing activities. (S2.E5.3b)	Applies simple offensive strategies & tactics in chasing & fleeing activities. (S2.E5.4a) Applies simple defensive strategies & tactics in chasing and fleeing activities. (S2.E5.4b) Recognizes the types of kicks needed for different games & sports situations. (S2.E5.4c)	Applies basic offensive and defensive strategies & tactics in invasion small-sided practice tasks. (S2.E5.5a) Applies basic offensive and defensive strategies & tactics in net/wall small-sided practice tasks. (S2.E5.5b) Recognizes the type of throw, volley or striking action needed for different games & sports situations. (S2.E5.5c)

Standard 3: Demonstrates the knowledge and skills to achieve and maintain a health-enhancing level of physical activity and fitness.

Standard 3	Kindergarten	Grade 1	Grade 2	Grade 3	Grade 4	Grade 5
Physical activity knowledge						
S3.E1	Identifies active-play opportunities outside physical education class. (S3.E1.K)	Discusses the benefits of being active and exercising and/or playing. (S3.E1.1)	Describes large-motor and/or manipulative physical activities for participation outside physical education class (e.g., before and after school, at home, at the park, with friends, with the family). (S3.E1.2)	Charts participation in physical activities outside physical education class. (S3.E1.3a) Identifies physical activity benefits as a way to become healthier. (S3.E1.3b)	Analyzes opportunities for participating in physical activity outside physical education class. (S3.E1.4)	Charts and analyzes physical activity outside physical education class for fitness benefits of activities. (S3.E1.5)
Engages in physical activity						
S3.E2	Actively participates in physical education class. (S3.E2.K)	Actively engages in physical education class. (S3.E2.1)	Actively engages in physical education class in response to instruction and practice. (S3.E2.2)	Engages in the activities of physical education class without teacher prompting. (S3.E2.3)	Actively engages in the activities of physical education class, both teacher-directed and independent. (S3.E2.4)	Actively engages in all the activities of physical education. (S3.E2.5)

Standard 3	Kindergarten	Grade 1	Grade 2	Grade 3	Grade 4	Grade 5
Fitness knowledge						
S3.E3	Recognizes that when you move fast, your heart beats faster and you breathe faster.[iii] (S3.E3.K)	Identifies the heart as a muscle that grows stronger with exercise, play, and physical activity. (S3.E3.1)	Recognizes the use of the body as resistance (e.g., holds body in plank position, animal walks)[iv] for developing strength. (S3.E3.2a) Identifies physical activities that contribute to fitness. (S3.E3.2b)	Describes the concept of fitness and provides examples of physical activity to enhance fitness. (S3.E3.3)	Identifies the components of health-related fitness.[v] (S3.E3.4)	Differentiates between skill-related and health-related fitness.[vi] (S3.E3.5)
S3.E4	*Developmentally appropriate/ emerging outcomes first appear in Grade 3.*	*Developmentally appropriate/emerging outcomes first appear in Grade 3.*	*Developmentally appropriate/emerging outcomes first appear in Grade 3.*	Recognizes the importance of warm-up & cool-down relative to vigorous physical activity. (S3.E4.3)	Demonstrates warm-up & cool-down relative to the cardiorespiratory fitness assessment. (S3.E4.4)	Identifies the need for warm-up & cool-down relative to various physical activities. (S3.E4.5)

[iii]NASPE, 2012, *Instructional Framework for Fitness Education* (Reston, VA: Author), p. 14.
[iv]NASPE, 2012, *Instructional Framework for Fitness Education* (Reston, VA: Author), p. 6.
[v]NASPE, 2012, *Instructional Framework for Fitness Education* (Reston, VA: Author), p. 16.
[vi]NASPE, 2012, *Instructional Framework for Fitness Education* (Reston, VA: Author), p. 17.

(continued)

Standard 3	Kindergarten	Grade 1	Grade 2	Grade 3	Grade 4	Grade 5
Assessment & program planning						
S3.E5	*Developmentally appropriate/ emerging outcomes first appear in Grade 3.*	*Developmentally appropriate/emerging outcomes first appear in Grade 3.*	*Developmentally appropriate/emerging outcomes first appear in Grade 3.*	Demonstrates, with teacher direction, the health-related fitness components. (S3.E5.3)	Completes fitness assessments (pre- & post-). (S3.E5.4a) Identifies areas of needed remediation from personal test and, with teacher assistance, identifies strategies for progress in those areas. (S3.E5.4b)	Analyzes results of fitness assessment (pre- & post-), comparing results with fitness components for good health. (S3.E5.5a) Designs a fitness plan to address ways to use physical activity to enhance fitness. (S3.E5.5b)
S3.E6 Nutrition	Recognizes that food provides energy for physical activity. (S3.E6.K)	Differentiates between healthy and unhealthy foods. (S3.E6.1)	Recognizes the "good health balance" of nutrition and physical activity. (S3.E6.2)	Identifies foods that are beneficial for before and after physical activity. (S3.E6.3)	Discusses the importance of hydration and hydration choices relative to physical activities. (S3.E6.4)	Analyzes the impact of food choices relative to physical activity, youth sports & personal health. (S3.E6.5)

Standard 4: Exhibits responsible personal and social behavior that respects self and others.

Standard 4	Kindergarten	Grade 1	Grade 2	Grade 3	Grade 4	Grade 5
Personal responsibility						
S4.E1	Follows directions in group settings (e.g., safe behaviors, following rules, taking turns). (S4.E1.K)	Accepts personal responsibility by using equipment and space appropriately. (S4.E1.1)	Practices skills with minimal teacher prompting. (S4.E1.2)	Exhibits personal responsibility in teacher-directed activities. (S4.E1.3)	Exhibits responsible behavior in independent group situations. (S4.E1.4)	Engages in physical activity with responsible interpersonal behavior (e.g., peer to peer, student to teacher, student to referee). (S4.E1.5)
S4.E2	Acknowledges responsibility for behavior when prompted. (S4.E2.K)	Follows the rules & parameters of the learning environment. (S4.E2.1)	Accepts responsibility for class protocols with behavior and performance actions. (S4.E2.2)	Works independently for extended periods of time. (S4.E2.3)	Reflects on personal social behavior in physical activity. (S4.E2.4)	Participates with responsible personal behavior in a variety of physical activity contexts, environments, and facilities. (S4.E2.5a) Exhibits respect for self with appropriate behavior while engaging in physical activity. (S4.E2.5b)
Accepting feedback						
S4.E3	Follows instruction/directions when prompted. (S4.E3.K)	Responds appropriately to general feedback from the teacher. (S4.E3.1)	Accepts specific corrective feedback from the teacher. (S4.E3.2)	Accepts and implements specific corrective feedback from the teacher. (S4.E3.3)	Listens respectfully to corrective feedback from others (e.g., peers, adults). (S4.E3.4)	Gives corrective feedback respectfully to peers. (S4.E3.5)

(continued)

Standard 4	Kindergarten	Grade 1	Grade 2	Grade 3	Grade 4	Grade 5
Working with others						
S4.E4	Shares equipment and space with others. (S4.E4.K)	Works independently with others in a variety of class environments (e.g., small & large groups). (S4.E4.1)	Works independently with others in partner environments. (S4.E4.2)	Works cooperatively with others. (S4.E4.3a) Praises others for their success in movement performance. (S4.E4.3b)	Praises the movement performance of others both more- and less-skilled. (S4.E4.4a) Accepts players of all skill levels into the physical activity. (S4.E4.4b)	Accepts, recognizes, and actively involves others with both higher and lower skill abilities into physical activities and group projects. (S4.E4.5)
Rules & etiquette						
S4.E5	Recognizes the established protocols for class activities. (S4.E5.K)	Exhibits the established protocols for class activities. (S4.E5.1)	Recognizes the role of rules and etiquette in teacher-designed physical activities. (S4.E5.2)	Recognizes the role of rules and etiquette in physical activity with peers. (S4.E5.3)	Exhibits etiquette and adherence to rules in a variety of physical activities. (S4.E5.4)	Critiques the etiquette involved in rules of various game activities. (S4.E5.5)
Safety						
S4.E6	Follows teacher directions for safe participation and proper use of equipment with minimal reminders. (S4.E6.K)	Follows teacher directions for safe participation and proper use of equipment without teacher reminders. (S4.E6.1)	Works independently and safely in physical education. (S4.E6.2a) Works safely with physical education equipment. (S4.E6.2b)	Works independently and safely in physical activity settings. (S4.E6.3)	Works safely with peers and equipment in physical activity settings. (S4.E6.4)	Applies safety principles with age-appropriate physical activities. (S4.E6.5)

Standard 5: Recognizes the value of physical activity for health, enjoyment, challenge, self-expression and/or social interaction.

Standard 5	Kindergarten	Grade 1	Grade 2	Grade 3	Grade 4	Grade 5
Health						
S5.E1	Recognizes that physical activity is important for good health. (S5.E1.K)	Identifies physical activity as a component of good health. (S5.E1.1)	Recognizes the value of "good health balance." (Refer to S3.E6.2)	Discusses the relationship between physical activity and good health. (S5.E1.3)	Examines the health benefits of participating in physical activity. (S5.E1.4)	Compares the health benefits of participating in selected physical activities. (S5.E1.5)
Challenge						
S5.E2	Acknowledges that some physical activities are challenging/ difficult. (S5.E2.K)	Recognizes that challenge in physical activities can lead to success. (S5.E2.1)	Compares physical activities that bring confidence and challenge. (S5.E2.2)	Discusses the challenge that comes from learning a new physical activity. (S5.E2.3)	Rates the enjoyment of participating in challenging and mastered physical activities. (S5.E2.4)	Expresses (via written essay, visual art, creative dance) the enjoyment and/or challenge of participating in a favorite physical activity. (S5.E2.5)
Self-expression & enjoyment						
S5.E3	Identifies physical activities that are enjoyable.vii (S5.E3.Ka) Discusses the enjoyment of playing with friends. (S5.E3.Kb)	Describes positive feelings that result from participating in physical activities. (S5.E3.1a) Discusses personal reasons (i.e., the "why") for enjoying physical activities. (S5.E3.1b)	Identifies physical activities that provide self-expression (e.g., dance, gymnastics routines, practice tasks in game environments). (S5.E3.2)	Reflects on the reasons for enjoying selected physical activities. (S5.E3.3)	Ranks the enjoyment of participating in different physical activities. (S5.E3.4)	Analyzes different physical activities for enjoyment and challenge, identifying reasons for a positive or negative response. (S5.E3.5)

viiNASPE, 2012, *Instructional Framework for Fitness Education* (Reston, VA: Author), p. 19.   (continued)

Standard 5	Kindergarten	Grade 1	Grade 2	Grade 3	Grade 4	Grade 5
Self-expression & enjoyment *(continued)*						
S5.E4 Social inter-action	*Developmentally appropriate/ emerging outcomes first appear in Grade 3.*	*Developmentally appropriate/ emerging outcomes first appear in Grade 3.*	*Developmentally appropriate/ emerging outcomes first appear in Grade 3.*	Describes the positive social interactions that come when engaged with others in physical activity. (S5.E4.3)	Describes & compares the positive social interactions when engaged in partner, small-group and large-group physical activities. (S5.E4.4)	Describes the social benefits gained from participating in physical activity (e.g., recess, youth sport). (S5.E4.5)

Glossary

activity breaks and brain breaks—Short bouts of physical activity infused throughout the school day to help children improve learning, attention span, and health; also known as "energizers" or "instant recess." These are recommended after 50 minutes of continuous sitting or during transitions between subjects.

advocacy—A powerful set of action-based strategies through which people are engaged in the decision-making processes that affect their lives and the lives of others.

American School Health Association (ASHA)—A professional organization dedicated to supporting professionals teaching health to children and adolescents.

appropriate practices—Practices that recognize students' development and changing movement abilities as well as their individual differences. Appropriate practices reflect the best-known practices into a pattern of instruction that maximizes opportunities for learning and success for all students.

assessment—The process of documenting skill or knowledge level in a certain subject.

authentic assessment—A form of assessment in which students are asked to perform real-world tasks that demonstrate the application of knowledge or skills.

backward design planning—A method of designing educational curriculum by setting goals before choosing instructional methods and forms of assessment.

bullying—Repeated incidences of physical or emotional harm involving a power imbalance.

Child Nutrition and WIC Reauthorization Act of 2004—A law that extended existing guidelines regarding physical activity and nutritious foods to schools. It required school districts participating in National School Lunch Programs to write wellness policies.

Common Core State Standards—National standards for English language arts and mathematics that provide consistent and clear academic expectations for all students across the nation. English language arts and mathematics were the only subjects chosen for the CCSS because these are the areas in which students build skill sets that are used in other subject areas.

comprehensive school health education (CSHE)—A planned, sequential health education curriculum with appropriate scope and sequence, which addresses the mental, emotional, physical, and social dimensions of health and enables students to become healthy, productive citizens.

coordinated school health (CSH)—A collaborative effort to use existing resources to ensure the health and safety of school children.

core academic subjects—The core academic subjects are mathematics, English language arts, science, and social studies.

critical elements—The key observable components of a motor skill.

cyberbullying—A form of harassment that makes use of technology.

determinants of health—Factors involved in influencing people's health.

digital literacy—Ability to competently use, communicate, and interpret digital technology and content.

eating disorders—A category of diagnoses that include anorexia, bulimia, and binge eating.

effort—This movement concept category defines how the body moves: time or speed—fast/slow; force—strong/light; and flow—bound/free.

emotional abuse—A form of abuse characterized by the infliction of mental or emotional distress by using threats, humiliation, or other verbal and nonverbal conduct.

emotional health—Involves a person's feelings and how they are expressed.

environmental health—Consists of preventing or controlling disease and injury related to the interactions between people and their environments.

extrinsic reward—Something external and tangible given for an accomplishment, such as a trophy.

family homework—Assignment that involves parents and students with the use of accurate sources of health information.

formative assessment—Measurement of learning during an instructional unit to provide feedback to students on their progress.

grade band—In the NHES, the student expectations are written to be completed by the end of a group of grades (band). The bands are K-2 and 3-5. Therefore, the expectations are written to be met by grade 2 and by grade 5.

Grade-Level Outcomes—The specific developmental expectations for most children for meeting each of the National Standards for K-12 Physical Education (SHAPE America, 2013).

health—A state of complete physical, mental, and social well-being.

health behavior—The choices people make that influence health status; may include negative or positive behaviors.

health belief model—A model that seeks to explain and predict health behaviors by focusing on people's attitudes and beliefs.

health disparities—Preventable differences in the burden of disease, injury, violence, or opportunities to achieve optimal health that are experienced by socially disadvantaged populations.

health education—Planned and sequential learning experiences based on appropriate theories and research that provide learners the opportunity to acquire the information, skills, and practice necessary to make good health decisions.

Healthy People—A document that confirmed the shift from infectious to chronic disease within the U.S. population and recognized the importance of personal health behaviors and lifestyle in relation to health outcomes.

Healthy, Hunger-Free Kids Act of 2010—A law that expanded wellness policies to include additional stakeholders for support, public updates, and new guidelines for school nutrition services.

inappropriate practices—Practices that include games or activities that belittle, demean, or embarrass students. Games or activities that eliminate students from play where the students must sit out and watch others participate are inappropriate to play in schools.

incentive—Anything that motivates someone to do something; a form of extrinsic reward.

intellectual health—A state of well-being in which a person realizes his or her own abilities, can cope with the normal stresses of life, can work productively and fruitfully, and is able to make a contribution to his or her community.

interdisciplinary activities—Activities that connect at least one physical education standard to at least one academic standard.

intrinsic reward—Internal payoff for accomplishing a goal, such as a feeling of pride.

key informant interviews—In-depth interviews of key people in the community who have knowledge about the topic of interest.

learning styles—The ways in which information is processed in order for people to understand and remember new information as a response to social, environment, emotional, and physical stimuli.

Let's Move! Active School—A comprehensive program used by school champions (teachers, administrators, and parents) to create an active environment in the school.

life skills—A set of psychosocial competencies and interpersonal skills that help in decision making, problem solving, critical thinking, communicating effectively, and managing lives in a healthy and productive way.

literacy—A general term used to represent basic knowledge, understanding, and application of reading and writing.

locomotor/transport skills—Skills that move the body from one place to another, including walking, jogging, running, hopping (one foot), jumping (two feet),

skipping galloping, sliding, leaping, chasing, fleeing, and dodging.

mandated reporters—People who, as a result of their profession, are required by law to report cases of suspected abuse or neglect.

manipulative skills—Skills that mostly involve using the hands or feet (however, other body parts can also be used), including throwing, catching, kicking, punting, dribbling, volleying, and striking.

minimal student expectations—The expectations students should meet by the end of the school year. *Minimal* is added to reflect that teachers must teach to meet these standards but could add other expectations for those students as well.

National Health Education Standards (NHES)—Written indicators to establish, promote, and support healthy behaviors for students in pre-kindergarten through grade 12. They provide a standardized framework and expectations for health education.

National School Lunch Program—A federally funded program to provide nutritious meals at a free or reduced price to qualified students.

National Standards for K-12 Physical Education—A set of standardized outcomes established by the Society of Health and Physical Educators (SHAPE America). These outcomes aim at providing K-12 students with the knowledge, skills, and confidence for a lifetime of physical activity.

neglect—A caregiver's failure to provide for a child's developmental and related needs.

nonlocomotor/nonmanipulative skills—Skills that don't move from one place to another and don't use the hands and fingers, including twisting, turning (in place), leaning, stretching, curling, bending, swinging, balancing, and weight transfer.

nonsuicidal self-injury (NSSI) behavior—Any behavior performed intentionally that results in physical injury to oneself.

physical abuse—Any act that, regardless of intent, results in a nonaccidental physical injury to a child.

physical activity—Any body movement that results in energy expenditure.

physical education—An academic subject that provides a planned, sequential, K-12 standards-based program of curricula and instruction designed to develop motor skills, knowledge, and behaviors for healthy, active living, physical fitness, good sporting behavior, self-efficacy, and emotional intelligence.

physical environment—Factors of the school setting that impact student health and achievement, including safety, security, aesthetics, lighting, air quality, cleanliness, noise, and overcrowding.

physical health—The most visible dimension of health. It can be influenced by multiple variables such as genetic makeup; exposure to infectious agents; access to medical care; and personal health-related behaviors such as tobacco use, levels of physical activity, and nutritional habits.

physical literacy—The ability to move with competence and confidence in a wide variety of physical activities in multiple environments that benefit the healthy development of the whole person.

physically literate person—Someone who has learned the skills necessary to participate in a variety of physical activities, knows the implications and the benefits of involvement in the various types of physical activities, participates regularly in physical activity, is physically fit, and values physical activity and its contributions to a healthful lifestyle.

portfolio—A collection of student work that represents progress through a unit of learning.

relationship—This movement concept category defines with whom and/or what the body relates. This involves relationship of the body (curved, narrow, wide, twisted, and symmetrical/asymmetrical), relationships with objects and/or others (over/under, on/off, near/far, along/though, in front/behind, meeting/parting, surrounding, around, and alongside), and relationships with people (leading/following, mirroring/matching, unison/contrast, solo, partners, between groups, groups, and alone in a mass).

rubric—Scoring chart that clearly and succinctly defines assignment expectations based on a predetermined standard.

scaffolding—Teaching practice in which a teacher provides, models, practices, and applies new health content information.

school vending sales—Revenue from school vending machines used to supplement existing programs or services. Food and beverages sold are traditionally unhealthy.

school violence—Violence that occurs on school property, on the way to or from school, or during a school-sponsored event.

school wellness policies—Regulations that help establish a healthy school environment; required for all school districts participating in federal child nutrition programs.

self-efficacy—Extent of one's belief in one's own ability to complete tasks and reach goals.

sexual abuse—Any sexual act on a child (e.g., rape, incest, indecent exposure, child pornography).

SHAPE America – Society of Health and Physical Educators—An organization dedicated to enhancing professional practice and research related to health and physical education, physical activity, dance, and sport. It is a valuable professional development resource.

Smart Snacks in School regulations—Science-based national standards developed by the USDA for snack foods and beverages sold to children at school during the school day.

social and emotional climate—The physical, emotional, and social conditions that affect the well-being of students and staff and impact student health and achievement, including collective attitudes, values, beliefs, behaviors, expectations, and connectedness.

social cognitive theory—A theory that focuses on the idea that learning occurs in a social setting and that much of what is learned is gained through observation.

social health—Ability to navigate social environments while maintaining healthy relationships with others.

space awareness—This movement concept category defines where the body can move. Space is explained using the following terms: direction (forward/backward, left/ right, up/down, clockwise/counterclockwise), level (low, medium, high), pathways (straight, curved, zigzag), and extension (small/large, far/near).

spiritual health—State of being in which a person can deal with daily life in a manner that leads to the realization of one's full potential, finding meaning and purpose of life, and experiencing happiness from within.

standard precautions—Guidelines designed to prevent the transmission of infections found in blood and other body fluids; formerly known as "universal precautions."

subjective norms—Social pressures to perform or not perform a particular health behavior.

summative assessment—Measurement of learning occurring at the end of an instructional unit, grading period, or year to evaluate learning, skill acquisition, and academic achievement.

theory of planned behavior—A theory used to predict how a person's attitudes about a behavior may affect the intention to engage in that behavior.

transtheoretical model of behavior change—A model that categorizes a person's readiness to change a particular behavior.

U.S. Dietary Guidelines for Americans—A set of recommendations to help Americans make healthy food and beverage choices. These guidelines are used to set nutritional polices and develop programs across the United States.

wellness policies—Written guidelines produced by schools addressing healthful eating and physical activity required for all school districts participating in the national free or reduced lunch program.

Whole School, Whole Community, Whole Child (WSCC) model—A collaborative model that builds on elements of the traditional coordinated school health approach, which provides a framework for enhancing and protecting the health of children, faculty, and staff in schools.

windshield tour—An observation method conducted by driving through a community and recording important observations about the school, neighborhood, and physical environment.

References

Chapter 1

Centers for Disease Control and Prevention. (1999). Ten great public health achievements—United States, 1990-1999. *Morbidity and Mortality Weekly Report, 48*(12), 241-243.

Centers for Disease Control and Prevention. (2010). Injury prevention and control. www.cdc.gov/injury/overview/leading_cod.html.

Centers for Disease Control and Prevention. (2011a). Adolescent and school health: Health and academics. www.cdc.gov/HealthyYouth/health_and_academics.

Centers for Disease Control and Prevention. (2011b). Adolescent and school health: YRBSS I brief. www.cdc.gov/healthyyouth/yrbs/brief.htm.

Centers for Disease Control and Prevention. (2011c). National Health and Nutrition Examination Survey: NHANES. www.cdc.gov/healthyyouth/yrbs/brief.htm.

Grøntved, A., & Hu, F.B. (2011). Television viewing and risk of type 2 diabetes, cardiovascular disease, and all-cause mortality: A meta-analysis. *Journal of American Medical Association, 305*(23), 2448-2455.

Healthy People 2020. (2011). Determinants of health. www.healthypeople.gov/2020/about/DOHAbout.aspx.

Marks, J.S. (2009). Communities taking charge of their health. *Health Promotion Practice, 10*(2) [Supplement], 88S-90S.

Murphy, S.L., Xu, J.Q., & Kochanek, K.D. (2012). Deaths: Preliminary data for 2010. *National Vital Statistics Reports, 60*(4). Hyattsville, MD: National Center for Health Statistics. www.cdc.gov/nchs/data/nvsr/nvsr60/nvsr60_04.pdf.

National Health and Nutrition Examination Survey. (2011). Overweight and obesity. www.cdc.gov/obesity/data/childhood.html.

Rew, L., & Wong, Y.J. (2006). A systematic review of associations among religiosity/spirituality and adolescent health attitudes and behaviors. *Journal of Adolescent Health, 38*(4), 433-442.

Robert Wood Johnson Foundation. (2008). Overcoming obstacles to health: Report from the Robert Wood Johnson Foundation to the Commission to Build a Healthier America. www.commissiononhealth.org/PDF/ObstaclesToHealth-Report.pdf.

Rosen, G. (1993). *A history of public health.* Baltimore: Johns Hopkins University Press.

United States Department of Health and Human Services. (2008). Physical activity guidelines for Americans. www.health.gov/paguidelines/guidelines.

United States Department of Health and Human Services and United States Department of Agriculture. (2015). 2015-2020 Dietary guidelines for Americans. 8th ed. http://health.gov/dietaryguidelines/2015/guidelines/.

World Health Organization. (2012). Arsenic. www.who.int/mediacentre/factsheets/fs372/en/index.html.

World Health Organization. (2013). IARC press release: Outdoor air pollution a leading environmental cause of cancer deaths. www.iarc.fr/en/media-centre/iarc-news/pdf/pr221_E.pdf.

World Health Organization. (2014a). Ambient (outdoor) air quality and health. www.who.int/mediacentre/factsheets/fs313/en/index.html.

World Health Organization. (2014b). Lead poisoning and health. www.who.int/mediacentre/factsheets/fs379/en/index.html.

Chapter 2

Birch, D.A., & Videto, D.M. (2015). *Promoting health and academic success.* Champaign, IL: Human Kinetics.

Centers for Disease Control and Prevention. (2012). Components of coordinated school health. www.cdc.gov/healthyyouth/cshp/components.htm.

National Center for Education Statistics. (2013). Student reports of bullying and cyber-bullying: Results from the 2011 School Crime Supplement to the National Crime Victimization Survey. http://nces.ed.gov/pubs2013/2013329.pdf.

Office of Disease Prevention and Health Promotion. (2015). Dietary guidelines. http://health.gov/dietaryguidelines/.

Office of Safe and Drug-Free Schools. (2004). Practical information on crisis planning: A guide for schools and communities. Washington, DC: Office of Safe and Drug-Free Schools, U.S. Department of Education. Available at: www.ed.gov/emergencyplan.

USDA Food and Nutrition Service. (2013). National School Lunch Programs. www.fns.usda.gov/sites/default/files/NSLPFactSheet.pdf.

U.S. Government Accountability Office. (2007). Report to congressional requesters. Emergency management: Most school districts have developed emergency medical plans but would benefit from additional federal guidance. Washington, DC: U.S. Government Accountability Office. Available at: www.gao.gov/cgi-bin/getrpt?GAO-07-609.

Vinciullo, F.M., & Bradley, B.J. (2009). A correlational study of the relationship between a coordinated school health program and school achievement: A case for school health. *The Journal of School Nursing, 25*(6), 453-465.

Chapter 3

Centers for Disease Control and Prevention. (2009). School health programs: Improving the health of our nation's youth. www.cdc.gov/nccdphp/publications/aag/pdf/dash.pdf.

Centers for Disease Control and Prevention. (2012). Youth risk behavior surveillance: United States, 2011. *Morbidity and Mortality Weekly Report, 61*(4), 1-168. Available at: www.cdc.gov/mmwr/pdf/ss/ss6104.pdf.

Clancy, M.E. (2006). *Active bodies, active brains: Building thinking skills through physical activity.* Champaign, IL: Human Kinetics.

U.S. Department of Health and Human Services. (2011). Child welfare outcomes 2008-2011: Report to congress. www.acf.hhs.gov/sites/default/files/cb/cwo08_11.pdf.

Chapter 4

Graham, G. (2008). *Teaching children physical education: Becoming a master teacher.* 3rd ed. Champaign, IL: Human Kinetics.

Graham, G., Holt/Hale, S., & Parker, M. (2012). *Children moving: A reflective approach to teaching physical education.* 9th ed. Boston: McGraw-Hill.

Mandigo, J., Francis, N., Lodewyk, K., & Lopez, R. (2012). Physical literacy for educators. *Physical Education and Health Journal, 75*(3), 27-30.

McKenzie, T.L., Rosengard, P., & Willison, B. (2006). *SPARK physical education program, grades 3-6.* San Diego: SDSU Foundation.

Mitchell, S.A., & Walton-Fisette, J.L. (2016). *The essentials of teaching physical education.* Champaign, IL: Human Kinetics.

Pangrazi, R.P., & Beighle, A. (2013). *Dynamic physical education for elementary school children.* 17th ed. Glenview, IL: Pearson Education.

Ratey, J. (2008). *Spark: The revolutionary new science of exercise and the brain.* Boston: Little, Brown & Company.

SHAPE America – Society of Health and Physical Educators. (2014). *National standards & grade-level outcomes for K-12 physical education.* Champaign, IL: Human Kinetics.

SHAPE America – Society of Health and Physical Educators. (2015). *The essential components of physical education.* Reston, VA: Author.

United States Department of Health and Human Services. (2008). Physical activity guidelines. www.health.gov/paguidelines/guidelines.

Whitehead, M. (2001). The concept of physical literacy. *European Journal of Physical Education, 6,* 127-138.

Chapter 5

None

Chapter 6

Centers for Disease Control and Prevention. (2013). Mental health surveillance among children—United States, 2005-2011. *MMWR 2013, 62*(Suppl; May 16), 1-35.

Common Sense Media. (2009). Digital literacy and citizenship in the 21st century: Educating, empowering, and protecting America's kids. A Common Sense Media White Paper. June 2009. www.itu.int/council/groups/wg-cop/second-meeting-june-2010/CommonSenseDigitalLiteracy-CitizenshipWhitePaper.pdf.

Dinkes, R., Kemp, J., & Baum, K. (2009). *Indicators of school crime and safety: 2009* (NCES 2010–012/NCJ 228478). Washington, DC: National Center for Education Statistics, Institute of Education Sciences, U.S. Department of Education, and Bureau of Justice Statistics, Office of Justice Programs, U.S. Department of Justice.

O'Dea, J.A., & Caputi, P. (2001). Association between socioeconomic status, weight, age and gender, and the body image and weight control practices of 6- to 19-year-old children and adolescents. *Health Education Research, 16*(5), 521-532.

Smith, P.K., & Brain, P. (2000). Bullying in schools: Lessons from two decades of research. *Aggressive Behavior, 26,* 1-9.

Smokowski, P.R., & Kopasz, K. (2005). Bullying in school: An overview of types, effects, family characteristics, and intervention strategies. *Children & Schools, 27*(2), 101-110.

Willard, N. (2007). Educator's guide to cyberbullying and cyberthreats. https://education.ohio.gov/getattachment/Topics/Other-Resources/School-Safety/Safe-and-Supportive-Learning/Anti-Harassment-Intimidation-and-Bullying-Resource/Educator-s-Guide-Cyber-Safety.pdf.aspx.

Chapter 7

Centers for Disease Control and Prevention. (2010). *The association between school based physical activity, including physical education, and academic performance.* Atlanta: U.S. Department of Health and Human Services.

Geiger, B. (2005). *Assessment of an outdoor elementary playground.* Birmingham, AL: University of Alabama at Birmingham.

Graham, G., Holt/Hale, S., & Parker, M. (2012). *Children moving: A reflective approach to teaching physical education.* 9th ed. Boston: McGraw-Hill.

National Association for Sport and Physical Education. (2009). *Appropriate instructional practice guidelines, K-12: A side-by-side comparison.* Reston, VA: Author.

Pangrazi, R.P., & Beighle, A. (2013). *Dynamic physical education for elementary school children.* 17th ed. Boston: Pearson.

Trost, G. (2007). *Active education: Physical education, physical activity and academic performance.* San Diego: Active Living Research. www.rwjf.org/childhoodobesity/product.jsp?id=23456.

Williams, N. (1992). The physical education hall of shame. *Journal of Physical Education, Recreation & Dance, 63*(6), 57-60.

Williams, N. (1994). The physical education hall of shame, part II. *Journal of Physical Education, Recreation & Dance, 65*(2), 17-20.

Williams, N. (1996). The physical education hall of shame, part III: Inappropriate teaching practices. *Journal of Physical Education, Recreation & Dance, 67*(8), 45-48.

Chapter 8

Joint Committee on National Health Education Standards. (2007). *National health education standards: Achieving excellence.* 2nd ed. Atlanta: American Cancer Society.

National Governors Association Center for Best Practices & Council of Chief State School Officers. (2010). *Common Core State Standards.* Washington, DC: National Governors Association Center for Best Practices & Council of Chief State School Officers.

Chapter 9

Hannaford, C. (1995). *Smart moves.* 2nd ed. Salt Lake City: Great River Books.

National Governors Association Center for Best Practices & Council of Chief State School Officers. (2010). *Common Core State Standards.* Washington, DC: National Governors Association Center for Best Practices & Council of Chief State School Officers.

SHAPE America – Society of Health and Physical Educators. (2014). *National standards & grade-level outcomes for K-12 physical education.* Champaign, IL: Human Kinetics.

Chapter 10

None

Resources

These resources are also listed in the web resource, and you can link directly to these web pages from there.

Chapter 1

www.healthypeople.gov

Healthy People is a governmental website that provides science-based, 10-year national objectives for improving the health of all Americans. Teachers and administrators should use this site to explore leading health indicators, health topics and objectives, up-to-date government data, and a variety of tools and resources.

www.cdc.gov/healthyyouth/index.htm

This information portal goes deeply into all things related to adolescents and school health. Educators should delve into this site for topics such as health and academics, asthma, health disparities, school health, policy, and school success stories.

www.cdc.gov/healthyyouth/data/yrbs/index.htm

Youth Risk Behavior Surveillance System (YRBSS) is a CDC website that monitors six types of health-risk behaviors that contribute to the leading causes of death and disability among youth and adults. Educators should use this site to examine specific health-risk behaviors for which students in their city or state are at risk. Examples include alcohol and drug use, tobacco use, unhealthy dietary behaviors, inadequate physical activity, sexual behaviors, and behaviors that contribute to injuries and violence.

www.cdc.gov/mmwr/pdf/rr/rr6005.pdf

The CDC's School Health Guidelines to Promote Healthy Eating and Physical Activity provides background for, an introduction to, outcomes of, and epidemiologic aspects of healthy eating and physical activity. In addition, this document details guidelines for implementation in schools and partnering with families and the community.

Chapter 2

www.actionforhealthykids.org

Action for Healthy Kids is dedicated to making healthy kids a national priority by developing effective plans to implement direct wellness policies, health programs and practices, and school–family–community partnerships.

www.healthinschools.org

The Center for Health and Health Care in Schools (CHHCS) is a nonpartisan policy, resource, and technical assistance center dedicated to developing school-connected strategies for better health and education outcomes for children.

www.ashaweb.org

The American School Health Association (ASHA) is a multidisciplinary professional organization dedicated to healthy students.

Chapter 3

www.healthychildren.org

A nonprofit website backed by pediatricians committed to the attainment of optimal physical, mental, and social health and well-being for all infants, children, adolescents, and young adults.

www.cancer.org/acs/groups/content/@nho/documents/document/healthedstatementpdf.pdf

Health Education in Schools—The Importance of Establishing Healthy Behaviors in our Nation's Youth. A Position Statement from the American Cancer Society, the American Diabetes Association, and the American Heart Association.

Chapter 4

www.fitness.gov

The President's Council on Fitness, Sports & Nutrition is an excellent resource for information on being active and eating healthy.

www.health.gov/paguidelines/default.aspx

This website includes information on the physical activity guidelines and recommendations for the nation.

http://iom.nationalacademies.org/Reports/2013/Educating-the-Student-Body-Taking-Physical-Activity-and-Physical-Education-to-School.aspx

Educating the Student Body is a consensus report from the Institute of Medicine addressing physical activity and physical education in the school environment.

www.letsmove.gov

Let's Move! is a national campaign to promote activity and proper nutrition to address the obesity issue of America.

www.letsmoveschools.org

Let's Move! Active Schools is a comprehensive program used by school champions (teachers, administrators, and parents) to create an active environment in the school.

www.physicalactivityplan.org

The National Physical Activity Plan is a comprehensive set of policies, programs, and initiatives that aims to increase physical activity in all segments of the American population.

www.physicalliteracy.ca

This is an excellent resource on physical literacy from Canadian Sport for Life.

www.shapeamerica.org

SHAPE America is a national organization designed to advance professional practice and promote research related to health and physical education, physical activity, dance, and sport.

Chapter 5

Before- and After-School Activities

www.shapeamerica.org/admin/loader.cfm?csModule=security/getfile&pageid=4575

The SHAPE America website is the host to numerous position statements and resources. This one is a position statement on before-school and after-school activities.

Comprehensive School Physical Activity Program

www.shapeamerica.org/advocacy/positionstatements/pa/loader.cfm?csModule=security/getfile&pageid=4726

The SHAPE America website is the host to numerous position statements and resources. This one is a position statement on comprehensive school physical activity programs.

Healthy Cooking

http://kidshealth.org/kid/recipes/index.html

KidsHealth website is sponsored by the Nemours Foundation's Center for Children's Health Media. This website is designed to communicate complex medical information and advice about a wide range of physical, emotional, and behavioral issues that affect children and teens. This link is part of the recipe section for healthy cooking.

www.eatingwell.com/healthy_cooking/kids_cooking

Eating Well is a website that contains information on healthy nutrition habits. This link is to the Kids Cooking section under Healthy Cooking.

www.cookinglight.com/food/healthy-kids-recipes

Cooking Light is a website all about food. This is a section for healthy recipes and meals for kids.

Hall of Shame

www.pecentral.org/professional/hos/index.html

PE Central is an excellent website full of resources for anyone teaching physical education. This section of the website contains information about the Hall of Shame.

Healthy Snacking

http://adph.org/NUTRITION/assets/HVMPSnackList.pdf

Alabama Department of Public Health has an excellent resource for healthy vending machine snacks.

http://cspinet.org/nutritionpolicy/healthy_school_snacks.html

The Center for Science in the Public Interest is a consumer advocacy organization that provides consumers with current, useful information about their health and well-being. This link is about healthy school snacks.

www.webmd.com/parenting/features/healthy-snacks-for-kids

The WebMD website provides health information, tools for managing health, and support to those who seek information. This link is from the Parenting section on healthy snacks for kids.

www.foodnetwork.com/recipes/articles/50-after-school-snacks.html

The Food Network website offers recipes, articles, and videos to help families to cook and eat together. This link is about healthy after-school snacks.

Healthy Vending

http://adph.org/NUTRITION/index.asp?id=4929

www.adph.org/NUTRITION/assets/HVMPFactSheet_R.pdf

Alabama Department of Public Health has these two resources for healthy vending options.

Let's Move Active Schools

www.letsmove.gov/active-schools

Initiated by First Lady Michelle Obama, the Let's Move campaign is an excellent site for information on nutrition and activity. The Active Schools section encourages schools to sign up to address the need for a comprehensive approach to providing physical activity in schools.

Proper Hygiene

www.cdc.gov/flu/protect/covercough.htm

The Centers for Disease Control and Prevention (CDC) has an excellent website with numerous resources for the classroom teacher. This link addresses proper hygiene.

www.colgate.com/en/us/oc/oral-health/basics/brushing-and-flossing/

Colgate offers information on their website on how to brush teeth properly.

http://classroom.kidshealth.org/classroom/prekto2/personal/hygiene/germs_handout2.pdf

The KidsHealth website also has excellent handouts that are ready to use for classroom teachers. This link provides an example.

Recess

www.shapeamerica.org/advocacy/positionstatements/pa/loader.cfm?csModule=security/getfile&pageid=4630

The SHAPE America website is the host to numerous position statements and resources. This one is a position statement on recess.

School Wellness Policies

www.fns.usda.gov/tn/local-school-wellness-policy

The United States Department of Agriculture's Food and Nutrition Service has an excellent site to help schools with school wellness policies.

www.actionforhealthykids.org/tools-for-schools

Action for Healthy Kids is a great website for classroom teachers. The Tools for Schools section offers useful tips and information on creating a healthier classroom and school.

Using Physical Activity as Punishment

www.shapeamerica.org/advocacy/positionstatements/pa/loader.cfm?csModule=security/getfile&pageid=4737

SHAPE America's website is the host to numerous position statements and resources. This one is a position statement on using physical activity as punishment.

Chapter 6

www.nationaleatingdisorders.org

This nonprofit organization advocates on behalf of individuals and families affected by eating disorders. The organization provides education, campaigns for prevention, and improved access to quality treatment, and develops programs and tools for those struggling with food and exercise issues.

www.cdc.gov/bam

CDC BAM! Body and Mind is an educational website funded through the CDC that provides tons of valuable health resources for teachers. Included on this website are lesson plans, educational games, and classroom activities on a variety of health topics.

www.kidshealth.org

Kids Health is an educational website with health information for parents, kids, teens, and educators. Special sections ranging from growth and development, diseases and conditions, pregnancy, nutrition and fitness, and emotions and health are offered in visually appealing formats.

www.gonoodle.com

This website is dedicated to helping teachers incorporate movement into the classroom. It provides dozens of videos that teachers can use in lesson planning to get their students up and moving.

Chapter 7

http://hopsports.com

This website is an instant resource tool that includes activity breaks to energize learning.

www.pinterest.com

Search Pinterest for "Action for Healthy Kids" and "Just Dance Kids" for brain breaks that you can use in your classroom.

Rhine-o Enterprises, LLC. (2012). Team Shake (Version 2.3.0) [Mobile application software]. Retrieved from http://itunes.apple.com.

Excellent app for dividing students into teams.

www.humankinetics.com/products/all-products/Build-It-So-They-Can-Play-eBook-3440685

Sullivan, T., Slagle, C., Hapshie, T.J., Brevard, D., & Brevard, V. (2012). *Build it so they can play: Affordable equipment for adapted physical education.* Champaign, IL: Human Kinetics. This book can help you find practical ways to build equipment for adapted physical education.

Chapter 8

www.pecentral.org/lessonideas/classroom/classroom.asp

This website includes integrated lesson plan activities that are designed by teachers for teachers.

http://lessonplanspage.com/physical-education-health

Lessons are designed for teachers by teachers.

www.atozteacherstuff.com/Lesson_Plans/Health/index.shtml

Another website that includes health lesson plans.

Chapter 9

www.activeacademics.org

Active Academics includes active lesson ideas to enhance learning in the core academic subjects.

www.pecentral.org/lessonideas/classroom/classroom.asp

This website includes integrated lesson plan activities that are designed by teachers for teachers.

www.sparkpe.org/abc/abcs-instructional-materials/classroom-activity-recess-sample-lessons

This section of the SPARK website includes sample lesson plans for the classroom teacher. The program is a product that schools purchase, but the site offers some free lessons as well.

Chapter 10

http://jfmueller.faculty.noctrl.edu/toolbox/index.htm

The Authentic Assessment Toolbox is a website that provides an overview of authentic assessment in the classroom, including rubrics for assessment, strategies for developing portfolios, and other valuable information.

www.davidkatzmd.com/abcforfitness.aspx

ABC for Fitness are activity bursts for the classroom. The program defines how to incorporate physical activity into brief, multiple episodes for classrooms without taking away instructional time. Helps students obtain a physical activity level essential for positive health and well-being.

www.cspinet.org/new/pdf/schoolfundraising.pdf

This report shows how schools can be healthy and profitable. Suggestions are made for how some school fundraisers can be improved and how some types of fundraisers should be avoided altogether. It also provides recommendations for healthy and practical fundraising alternatives.

www.healthiergeneration.org/take_action/schools/snacks_and_beverages/fundraisers

This site presents healthy fundraising options to help raise revenue without undermining healthy habits. Topics include a fundraising presentation, food service partnership, innovative ways to use school resources, and raising support.

www.ruddrootsparents.org/food-marketing-in-schools

This site is designed for parents and educators and targets food marketing in schools. It addresses advocacy, how to take action, and recent news, and it features a sign-up for the latest updates through an e-mail newsletter.

Index

Note: Page references followed by an italicized *f* or *t* indicate information contained in figures and tables, respectively.

A

academic achievement, and health 4
active classrooms
  about 98
  activity and brain breaks 98, 107
  behavior management 103-105, 112
  best practices for activity lessons 102
  classroom management and organization 99-102
  communication in 101-102
  equipment needs for 99, 100-101, 100*t*, 108
  grouping students 100
  inappropriate practices 102-103, 104*t*-105*t*, 109*t*
  integrating movement into lessons 99
  safety 103, 110*t*-111*t*
  spacing of students 100
  start and stop signals 99-100
activity breaks 98, 107
administration, school
  advocacy tips for 72
  policymaking 13, 173-174
advertising 174
advocacy
  about 68, 105*t*
  administration/policymaker tips 72-73
  in the classroom 68-69
  correspondence 72-73
  media interviews 71-72
  for more physical activity in school 68
  for parents and the community 71
  in the school 69-70, 70*t*
African Americans' health 11-13, 12*f*
air pollution 5
alcohol 10, 166*t*
Alliance for a Healthier Generation 81
American Diabetes Month 82
American Heart Month 83
American School Health Association (ASHA) 172

ancient civilizations 6-7
anorexia 87
antibiotics 9
arsenic 5
assessment
  authentic 170-171
  formative 169, 170*t*
  summative 170
auditory-musical learning style 41*f*, 42*t*, 88
authentic assessment 170-171

B

back-to-school supplies 94-95
backward design planning 164
bacteriological phase of public health 9
bathroom and water breaks 80-81
behavior change, transtheoretical model of 38-39, 40*t*
behavior management 103-105, 112
best practices
  about 164
  assessment 169-171, 170*t*
  fundraising 173, 173*t*
  learning environment 171-172
  marketing and advertising 174
  planning ahead 164
  policymaking 173-174
  professional development 172
  sample health curriculum plan 167*t*
  school vending 173-174
  school wellness policies 173
  teaching methods that work 164-168, 168*t*-169*t*
binge eating 87
biology and genetics 13
bodily-kinesthetic learning style 41*f*, 42*t*, 88
body composition 36
brain breaks 98, 107
brain development and learning 35-36
brainstorming 168*t*
bubonic plague 7
bulimia 87
bullying 29, 82, 93-94

C
cancer deaths 5
Cara Tidwell brain breaks 98
case studies 169*t*
child abuse and neglect 90-92
Child Nutrition and WIC Reauthorization Act of 2004 20
children
    obesity 14-15, 16*f*
    physical activity recommendations 14
    vulnerable to environmental dangers 6
cholera 9
chronic diseases 11
class chants or cheers 79-80
class discussion 168*t*
classroom health. *See also* active classrooms; classroom teachers
    about 78
    bathroom and water breaks 80-81
    celebrations and parties 81
    everyday routines and activities 78-80
    field trips 81-82
    incentives for healthy behavior 78-80
    intellectual dimensions of 87-88
    lunchtime 80
    mental and emotional dimensions of 85-87
    monthly health observances 82-84
    physical dimensions of 88-94
    social dimensions of 84-85
    supplies for 94-95
    unhealthy teaching practices 95
classroom rewards 78, 80, 172
classroom teachers. *See also* classroom health; health education, classroom integration of
    advocacy and 68-69
    behavior management 103-105, 112
    classroom management 30, 99-102
    as example in active classrooms 98
    as mandated reporters 90
    responsibility of 14-16
    role in WSCC model 30
    unhealthy teaching practices 95
Common Core State Standards 114
community and consumer health 165*t*
community involvement 28, 71
comprehensive school health education (CSHE)
    about 42-43

challenges facing 45-46
characteristics of health education programming 47*f*-48*f*
content areas of 43*t*-45*t*
health education facilitators 46
coordinated school health (CSH)
    about 20
    academic behaviors and healthy behaviors 21-22, 22*f*
    definitions 22
    national school policies 20-21
    Whole School, Whole Community, Whole Child (WSCC) model 22-30, 23*f*, 24*f*, 25*f*
correspondence tips 72-73
counseling, psychological, and social services 25-26
critical elements 55
cyberbullying 94
cyberstalking 94

D
dance 98
decision mapping 168*t*
denigration 94
depression 85
determinants of health 13-14
diabetes 82
diet. *See* eating habits and nutrition
digital literacy 89
diseases, contagious 7-9, 88-90
drug use 10, 82-83, 166*t*

E
Earth Day 83
eating disorders 87
eating habits and nutrition
    importance of 10, 14
    National Nutrition Month 83
    nutrition environment and services 25
    obesity and 14-15, 16*f*
    promoting healthy eating 165*t*
    school vending 173-174
Educating the Student Body 68
effort movement concepts 56-59, 59*t*
e-mail 72
emergency preparedness 29-30, 82
emotional abuse 91-92
emotional dimension of health 4, 5*f*, 85-87, 164*t*
emotional states 38

employee wellness 26, 70
Energizing Brain Breaks blog 98
English language arts, and health education 115, 116*t*-117*t*, 118*t*, 123, 124
Enlightenment, age of 7
environmental conditions 13
environmental dimension of health 5-6, 5*f*, 83, 166*t*
exclusion 94
extrinsic rewards 78

F
family engagement 27-28
family homework 172
family planning 10
FEMA National Preparedness Month 82
field trips 81-82
504 plans 171
flaming 94
fluoridation 10
foods, safer and healthier 9
formative assessment 169, 170*t*
friendly gestures 78
fundraising 173*t*

G
Gardner's theory of multiple intelligences 40, 41*f*
gifted students 88
give me five 170*t*
Gonoodle 98
graphic organizers 169*t*
Greeks, ancient 6
growth and development
    about 34-35
    brain development and learning 35-36
    as content area of education 165*t*
    movement activities and learning 35
    physical development and health 36

H
Hall of Shame 103
hand hygiene 88-90
harassment 94
health
    and academic achievement 4
    defining 4-6
    determinants of health 13-14
    emotional health 4, 5*f*, 85-87, 164*t*
    environmental health 5-6, 5*f*, 83, 166*t*
    individual behaviors and 13-14
    intellectual health 4, 5*f*, 87-88
    Internet resources 89, 98
    national health observances 70, 81
    physical health 4, 5*f*, 88-94
    promoting health and preventing disease 164*t*
    six dimensions of 4-6, 5*f*
    social health 4, 5*f*, 84-85
    spiritual health 4-5, 5*f*
health, history of
    ancient civilizations 6-7
    currently, in U.S. 10-13, 11*t*, 12*f*
    Middle Ages 7
    Renaissance and Enlightenment 7
    in United States 7-10
health behavior theory 37-39, 40*t*, 41*t*
health belief model (HBM) 39, 40, 41*t*
health disparities 11-13, 12*f*, 14
health education. *See also* best practices; National Health Education Standards (NHES)
    about 34
    Common Core State Standards 114
    comprehensive school health education 42-46, 43*t*-45*t*, 47*f*-48*f*
    growth and development 34-36
    improving health behavior 37-39, 40*t*, 41*t*
    integration ideas for classroom 115
    learning styles 40-42, 41*f*, 42*t*
    linking NHES with academic standards 115-116, 116*t*
    National Health Education Standards (NHES) 24, 24*f*, 114-115, 116*t*-117*t*, 164, 167*f*
    ten content areas of 164*t*-166*t*
health education, classroom integration of
    about 114
    Common Core State Standards 114
    grade-specific interdisciplinary activities 116-118, 118*t*, 125-140
    integrated activity plans 119-120, 141-142
    integration ideas for 115, 123
    linking NHES with academic standards 115-116, 116*t*-117*t*, 123, 124
    National Health Education Standards (NHES) 114-115
health fairs 170
health services 13, 25

Healthy, Hunger-Free Kids Act of 2010 21
Healthy People: The Surgeon General's Report on Health Promotion and Disease Prevention 10-11
heart health 9, 83
height 36
Hippocrates 7
home communication 79
homeplay work 69

I
immunizations 9
impersonation 94
impetigo 7
incentives 78
index card questions 170*t*
Industrial Revolution 8-9
infectious disease control 9
influenza 7, 82
intellectual dimension of health 4, 5*f*, 87-88
Internet resources and safety 89
interpersonal learning style 41*f*, 42*t*, 88
interviews, media 71-72
intrapersonal learning style 41*f*, 42*t*, 88
intrinsic rewards 78

J
Jenner, Edward 7

K
key informant interviews 28
KidsHealth in the Classroom 34
Know/Wonder/Learn charts 169*t*
Koch, Robert 9

L
lazy eights 98
lead exposure 5-6
learning centers 169*t*
learning environments 171-172
learning styles 40-42, 41*f*, 42*t*
leprosy 7
life expectancy 8, 9, 12-13, 12*f*
life skills 34
locomotor/transport skills 55-56, 55*t*, 56*t*, 57*t*, 58*t*
logical-mathematical learning style 41*f*, 42*t*, 88
lunchtime 80

M
mandated reporters 90
manipulative skills 55-56, 55*t*, 56*t*, 57*t*, 58*t*
marketing and advertising 174
mastery experiences 38
maternal and neonatal medicine 10
mathematics, and health education 116*t*-117*t*, 123, 124
media interviews 71-72
mental and emotional dimension of health. *See* emotional dimension of health
miasma phase of public health 9
Middle Ages 7
Minds in Bloom (website) 98
modeling 169*t*
motivation, student 68-69, 78-80
motor vehicle safety 9
movement activities and learning 35, 69, 99
movement concept skills 56-59, 59*t*
multiple intelligences, theory of 88
muscular growth and development 36
MyPlate 14, 16*f*

N
National Bullying Prevention Month 82
National Center for Missing & Exploited Children 89
National Cyber Security Alliance 89
National Drug Facts Week 82-83
National Health Education Standards (NHES)
   about 24, 24*f*, 167*f*
   classroom integration of 114-115, 116*t*-117*t*
   curriculum alignment 164
   Standard 1 177
   Standard 2 177-178
   Standard 3 178
   Standard 4 178
   Standard 5 179
   Standard 6 179
   Standard 7 179-180
   Standard 8 180
national health observances 70, 81
National Influenza Vaccination Week 82
National Nutrition Month 83
National Physical Fitness and Sports Month 83-84
National School Lunch Program (NSLP) 20
National Standards & Grade Level Outcomes for K-12 Physical Education (SHAPE America)

about 25, 25*f*
Standard 1   55-56, 55*t*, 56*t*, 57*t*, 58*t*, 144, 181-191
Standard 2   56-59, 59*t*, 144, 192-195
Standard 3   59-60, 60*t*, 144, 196-198
Standard 4   60-61, 61*t*, 144, 199-200
Standard 5   61-62, 62*t*, 144, 201-202
naturalistic learning style 41*f*, 42*t*, 88
neglect 91
nonlocomotor/nonmanipulative skills 55-56, 55*t*, 56*t*, 57*t*, 58*t*
nonsuicidal self-injury (NSSI) behavior 87
No Soda November challenge 82
nutrition. *See* eating habits and nutrition
nutrition environment and services 25

O
obesity, in children 14-15, 16*f*
1-minute essays 170*t*
online simulations and games 169*t*
outing 94

P
parents, advocacy for 71
Pasteur, Louis 9
performances or skits 170
physical abuse 91
physical activity/inactivity 10, 12, 14, 15*f*
   building into day 172
   defining 52-53
   joy of movement 60-61, 61*t*
   in physical literacy 59-60, 60*t*
   promoting physical activity 165*t*
   as punishment 69, 78, 103, 104*t*
   in WSCC model 24-25
physical development and health 36
physical dimension of health 4, 5*f*, 88-94
physical education. *See also* best practices; National Standards & Grade Level Outcomes for K-12 Physical Education (SHAPE America)
   about 52
   defining 53
   developmental appropriateness 53-54
   National Standards for K-12 physical education 55-62, 144-145
   physical literacy 54
physical education, classroom integration of
   about 144

grade-specific interdisciplinary activities 146-148, 148*t*, 155-159
integrated activity plans 149-150, 160-161
integration ideas for 145-146, 153
linking physical education with academic standards 146, 154
National Standards for K-12 Physical Education 144-145
physical environment 26
policymaking 13, 173-174
portfolios 170
preventing intentional injury and violence 166*t*
privileges 80
professional development 105*t*, 172
promoting health and preventing disease 164*t*
promoting healthy eating 165*t*
promoting physical activity 165*t*
PTA/PTO meetings 71
public announcements 79

R
rabies 9
recognition, student 78-80
relationship movement concepts 56-59, 59*t*
Renaissance, the 7
report cards 71
respiratory etiquette 90
risky health behaviors 11
role playing 168*t*
Romans, ancient 6-7
rubrics 170

S
sanitation 9
scaffolding 168
school completion 12
schools
   advocacy in 69-70, 70*t*
   sample wellness calendar 70*t*
   school violence 93-94
   school wellness policies 173
school supplies 80, 94-95
science, and health education 115, 116*t*-117*t*, 118*t*, 123, 124
self-efficacy 38
self-injury behavior 87
sexual abuse 91

sexual behaviors, risky 10
sexual development 165*t*
SHAPE America. *See also* National Standards
    & Grade Level Outcomes for K-12 Physi-
    cal Education (SHAPE America)
    advocacy resources 72
    Appropriate Instructional Practice Guide-
      lines, K-12 103
    professional developments 172
skeletal growth and development 36
smallpox 7
Smart Snacks in School regulations 173
smiling 78
social and emotional climate 26-27
social cognitive theory (SCT) 38
social dimension of health 4, 5*f*, 84-85
social factors, and health 13
social skills 60-61, 61*t*
social studies, and health education 115,
    116*t*-117*t*, 118*t*, 123, 124
space awareness 56-59, 59*t*
SPARK curriculum 59-60
spiritual dimension of health 4-5, 5*f*
spoken praise 78-79
sporting behavior 60-61, 61*t*
sports equipment, as rewards 80
standard precautions 90
standards, national. *See* National Health
    Education Standards (NHES); National
    Standards & Grade Level Outcomes for
    K-12 Physical Education (SHAPE Amer-
    ica)
stoplights 170*t*
stretching 98
strokes 9
subjective norms 39
subject-matter teachers. *See* classroom teach-
    ers
suicide 85-86
summative assessment 170
Supplemental Nutrition Program for Wom-
    en, Infants and Children (WIC) 20
syphilis 7

T
T-charts 169*t*
teachable moment 169*t*
teachers. *See* classroom teachers

testing practices 105*t*
theory of planned behavior 39
think-pair-share 168*t*
tobacco 10, 12
transtheoretical model of behavior change
    38-39, 40*t*
trickery 94
tuberculosis 7, 9

U
United States
    current health status 10-13, 11*t*, 12*f*
    determinants of health 13
    history of health in 7-10
    leading causes of death in 10, 11*t*
    life expectancy rates 8, 9, 12-13, 12*f*
universal precautions 90
U.S. Dietary Guidelines for Americans 25

V
vaccinations 8
vending, school 173
Venn diagrams 169*t*
verbal-linguistic learning style 41*f*, 42*t*, 88
verbal persuasion 38
vicarious experiences 38
violence, school 93-94, 166*t*
visual-spatial learning style 41*f*, 42*t*, 88

W
water breaks 80-81
weight 36
wellness calendars 70*t*
wellness policies 20, 173
Wellness School Assessment Tool (WellSAT)
    21
Whole School, Whole Community, Whole
    Child (WSCC) model
    about 22-23, 23*f*
    applying the model 28-29
    best practices 29-30
    community involvement 28
    counseling, psychological, and social ser-
      vices 25-26
    employee wellness 26
    family engagement 27-28
    health education 24
    health services 25

nutrition environment and services 25
physical education and physical activity 24-25
physical environment 26
social and emotional climate 26-27
teachers' roles 30
Wigglesworth, Edward 8
windshield tours 28

word webs 169*t*
workplace safety 9
written praise 79

Y
yoga 98
Youth Risk Behavior Surveillance System 10, 15, 21, 22*f*

About The Authors

Retta R. Evans is associate professor at the University of Alabama at Birmingham and a master certified health education specialist. Dr. Evans has spent more than sixteen years teaching and mentoring aspiring health educators at the undergraduate and graduate levels. During this time she has also worked to improve health curricula and develop health initiatives in schools. With the Alabama State Department of Education, she has revised the state course of study in health education and is part of a team that worked with school systems to implement comprehensive physical activity plans across Alabama. Dr. Evans received the Health Educator of the Year Award from the Alabama State Association for Health, Physical Education, Recreation and Dance as well as the College/University Health Education Professional of the Year Award from the Southern District Association for Health, Physical Education, Recreation and Dance. Dr. Evans was principal investigator on a National Institutes of Health grant investigating the effectiveness of classroom-based physical activity on cognitive performance in elementary-aged children.

Sandra K. Sims, associate professor at the University of Alabama at Birmingham, has more than two decades of experience as a public school teacher. Since 2005 she has taught physical education methods courses as well as the course for elementary classroom teachers integrating physical education and health education into the classroom. Besides being named Physical Education Teacher of the Year for Alabama and Southern District SHAPE America for two years, Sims was selected as Teacher of the Year for her school, system, state, and district.

health. moves. minds.

SHAPE America – Society of Health and Physical Educators is committed to ensuring that all children have the opportunity to lead healthy, physically active lives. As the nation's largest membership organization of health and physical education professionals, SHAPE America works with its 50 state affiliates and is a founding partner of national initiatives including the Presidential Youth Fitness Program, *Let's Move!* Active Schools and the Jump Rope For Heart/ Hoops For Heart programs.

Since its founding in 1885, the organization has defined excellence in physical education, most recently creating *National Standards & Grade-Level Outcomes for K-12 Physical Education* (2014), *National Standards & Guidelines for Physical Education Teacher Education* (2009) and *National Standards for Sport Coaches* (2006), and participating as a member of the Joint Committee on National Health Education Standards, which published *National Health Education Standards, Second Edition: Achieving Excellence* (2007). Our programs, products and services provide the leadership, professional development and advocacy that support health and physical educators at every level, from preschool through university graduate programs.

Every spring, SHAPE America hosts its National Convention & Expo, the premier national professional-development event for health and physical educators.

Advocacy is an essential element in the fulfillment of our mission. By speaking out for the school health and physical education professions, SHAPE America strives to make an impact on the national policy landscape.

Our Vision: Healthy People—Physically Educated and Physically Active!

Our Mission: To advance professional practice and promote research related to health and physical education, physical activity, dance and sport.

Our Commitment: 50 Million Strong by 2029

Approximately 50 million students are currently enrolled in America's elementary and secondary schools (grades pre-K to 12). SHAPE America is leading the effort to ensure that by the time today's preschoolers graduate from high school in 2029, all of America's students will have developed the skills, knowledge and confidence to enjoy healthy, meaningful physical activity.